D1527804

Voices from the Pastime

*Oral Histories
of Surviving Major Leaguers,
Negro Leaguers, Cuban Leaguers
and Writers, 1920–1934*

by
NICK WILSON

McFarland & Company, Inc., Publishers
Jefferson, North Carolina, and London

Cover: The Infield of Dreams 1935. *Left to right:* Charlie Gehringer, Billy Rogell, Hank Greenberg, Marv Owen. Courtesy of Transcendental Graphics, Mark Rucker.

Library of Congress Cataloguing-in-Publication Data

Wilson, Nick, 1947–
   Voices from the pastime : oral histories of surviving major leaguers, Negro leaguers, Cuban leaguers and writers, 1920–1934 / by Nick Wilson
      p.   cm.
   Includes bibliographical references and index.
   ISBN 0-7864-0824-3 (softcover : 50# alkaline paper) ∞
   1. Baseball players — Interviews.   2. Baseball — History — 20th century.   3. Sportswriters — Interviews.   I. Title.
   GV865.A1W55   2000
   796.357'092'273 — dc21   00-26695

British Library cataloguing data are available

Manufactured in the United States of America

McFarland & Company, Inc., Publishers
  Box 611, Jefferson, North Carolina 28640
  www.mcfarlandpub.com

To my father, Verle W. Wilson.

If the final scenes of *Field of Dreams* could come true,
I would build a park today

Contents

Acknowledgments

My thanks go to these individuals, without whose help the task would have been impossible: first my mother, Rose Maloof Wilson, whose constant encouragement and tutelage lit my path. To Gladis Duarte who was the marvelous inspiration and interpreter for the Cuban chapter. To my dear friend and super-secretary, Linda Esser, who believed in this project and wouldn't let me give up during the most trying periods. To my first cousin, Nancy Reed, for her encouragement and invaluable advice. And especially to all the wonderful men who gave me their time and shared their lives.

Special thanks go to the following people for the work on the major leagues: John D. Hayworth; Morris Eckhouse of SABR; Pete Weston for introducing me to Clyde Sukeforth and generously lending me his baseball book collection; the folks at the National Baseball Hall of Fame and Museum; Nathan Blackman of the International League, Kathy Gardner of the Toledo Mud Hens; Will Anderson for his photos; Thomas Gilbert for editing and direction; Peter Sgroi; Joe Culinane; and last but not least John Moore at the *Denver Post* for giving this project its first exposure.

Special thanks go to the following for help with the Negro leagues: Dick Clark for his editing and advice; Jay Sanford for introducing me to Messrs Robinson and Radcliffe; Brent Kelley for the introduction to the Reverend Tinker; Don Motley of the Negro Leagues Baseball Museum; and Terry Embke of Joy Enterprises. For the Cuban chapter special thanks go to Mark Rucker and Peter Bjarkman for editing and advice; Jose Hevia; Oscar Garmendia of the Cuban Baseball Players Association; Mimi and Raoul Duarte for their detective work. Finally, for their help with the chapter on the writers, I would like to thank Barbara Lockert at the National Sportscasters and Sportswriters Association; Jim Street at the Baseball Writers Association of America; and most of all my friend Harold Rosenthal.

Introduction

There were over 1,500 men who played major league baseball during the golden age of the 1920s. Today, fewer than 20 are still alive. There were over 850 men who played in the Negro leagues during the 1920s. Today there are only three.

These men saw the greatest players in the history of the game: Babe Ruth, Josh Gibson, Lou Gehrig, Satchel Paige, Walter Johnson, and Martin Dihigo. Now they are the last living ballplayers who can tell the story of that era. They are the last remaining members of a very elite club.

When this project began in April 1998 my intentions were to complete a short article on the oldest surviving ballplayers from the major leagues. But the enterprise soon became a Rocky Mountain avalanche, gaining mass and power as it moved forward.

By July 1998 I had completed interviews with 12 of the white major leaguers and realized I had enough material for a book. However, I felt that there was huge gap in the complete oral history of the golden age. What if there are Negro leaguers still alive from the 1920s? How about Latin American ballplayers?

While editing the Bill Rogell story, I came upon one of his anecdotes about a fight that he had with a sportswriter in Detroit. Why not contact the oldest baseball writers, I thought. All of these men together could provide a complete mosaic of the times.

I had set difficult standards by limiting the interviews only to ballplayers who began their careers in the 1920s. I found several men who had actually begun their professional or semiprofessional careers as early as 1916, and I sought out writers who had begun their careers no later than the 1920s and early 1930s.

Although the theme of this project is the golden age of the 1920s, it does include personal anecdotes that date through the 1940s. Milestones such as Clyde Sukeforth's first meeting with Jackie Robinson or Mel Harder's coaching the Indians' famous pitching staff of 1954 cannot be dismissed.

It wasn't long before I started to expand the text of this book with historical background information, other notes, and quotes from some of the best baseball historians alive today. I have consulted with seven experts nationwide on subjects such as Cuban baseball, the history of the game in the 1920s, and the Negro leagues. Over 55 books and magazines were used as reference and background support. I wanted to create the most comprehensive book on the 1920s ever written.

As my search for more interviews grew I realized that I wanted more from these men than just a narration of their careers. I asked for personal information about their childhood at the turn of the century. What were their early struggles? What inspired them and how did they get their first break?

Only one of the surviving ballplayers refused to grant an interview and another asked that his interviews not be published. In addition, a small number of the others were prevented by health and legal limitations from participation in the project.

The stories these men provided are more than autobiographies. They are entertaining but also offer a lesson in history, often revealing little known facts.

Willis Hudlin tells what it was like to pitch against the two most formidable teams of that period: the 1927 Yankees and the 1929 Philadelphia Athletics.

Several men tell first-hand accounts of their personal experiences with Babe Ruth. One remembers joining him in happy dugout conversations while another tells a stunning story of seeing Ruth alone and dejected in a grandstand seat in Yankee Stadium.

They tell of the paradoxical Ty Cobb who at once seemed amicable but then angrily turned on a Jewish sportswriter for defending a black man.

Several relate experiences with the comical but shrewd Casey Stengel, who got the attention of his minor league players by slamming a bat against their equipment lockers.

One writer reveals the newspaper's silent conspiracy that prevented the publication of Negro League box scores.

Several historians and one former player make claims that there were men of African descent who played major league baseball as early as 1911.

One Negro leaguer tells about the day in 1927 that he discovered the greatest slugger in the history of baseball: Josh Gibson.

Another man reveals that he is the last man alive who wore the uniform of the 1927 Yankees.

My hope is that each chapter is digested individually, with time allowed to consider the hope, joy, and triumph of each of these men.

Bill Veeck once said, "Baseball is a game to be savored rather than taken in gulps." So are these autobiographies. In many cases their stories read like a plot from Horatio Alger.

Baseball was, and still is, at the core of their souls. The cadences of the game, the choreography of the play, and the shared experience of the team are recalled as if this all happened yesterday. Most of these ballplayers complain about modern baseball's excesses and greed, but watch their game on TV religiously. They are centurions of their era, and they seek to maintain the aura that surrounds the golden age. Their names may now be obscure, but their sole accomplishment resonates golden with every man and boy in America, for they achieved the elusive dream of crossing that chalk line onto a major league ball field.

A common theme was the hard-edged side to life during that era. They all seemed to be tough and hungry, yet stoic and resilient. In most cases these men had no other marketable skills. So baseball was their only escape from the tedium of the mines, factories, and farms. If they were injured they would lose their livelihood. It was a raw, tough life. They were not comforted by self-esteem therapy nor did they have time to find their feminine side. There were no unions to stand beside them, and the reserve clause denied them the chance to seek better pay with another ballclub. It was a struggle to survive in a world without government safety nets.

The Negro League–era ballplayers who are featured in this book shouldered the additional burden of segregation. They tell explosive stories of discrimination and triumph. The hardships they endured eventually paved the way for the likes of Jackie Robinson, Hank Aaron, and Ken Griffey, Jr.

The oldest living ballplayer from the Cuban leagues, Rodolfo Fernandez, recalled growing up in the slums of Havana and fashioning gloves of cardboard and bats from tree limbs.

The five baseball writers interviewed shared very personal anecdotes about the heroes of the 1920s. I was struck with the casual way they related their experiences. "Well, Babe Ruth said this to me..." or "Ty Cobb and I talked for several hours in his hospital room about..."

It is as if we were sitting in their living rooms or on their front porches listening to their unique stories, and I wanted to recapture the same feelings I had when I met my first former major leaguer.

I remember, I was a ten-year-old baseball geek growing up in the small factory town of Beloit, Wisconsin. My father arranged for me to visit a man who lived only two blocks away. Our neighbor's name was Ed "Patsy" Gharrity and he was a catcher for the Washington Senators from 1916 through the 1920s. His house was small and neatly kept, but I remember being disappointed that it was not a cathedral of pictures, awards, and equipment (that was long before I realized the sacrifices of marriage). But I sat in his living room enraptured by his stories. Before I left he allowed me to slip on his old catcher's mitt. It was the same leather that caught Walter Johnson's fastball. That moment was 42 years ago and I will never forget it.

Each of these men invite you to sit down, relax, and listen to their stories and allow them to remember.

1. The Major Leagues

"A great many people ask me just how great my control really is. If anybody wanted to hang up a new straw hat over the plate and bet me fifty dollars that I couldn't hit it, if I cut loose with all I had ... I'd advise that particular spectator to get another hat. I'll venture to say I could hit a hat eight out of ten times without exerting myself very much."
Grover Cleveland Alexander,
1929 interview.

The 1920s were singularly the most important decade in the history of baseball. Changes in ground rules, the creation of a league for black Americans, dramatic changes in offensive strategy, and a strong central governing authority changed the game forever.

The legacy of the three most important figures during that decade — Babe Ruth, Kenesaw Mountain Landis, and Rube Foster — still impacts baseball today. This chapter lays the historical groundwork for the interviews that follow.

In 1931 sports journalist Paul Gallico was asked to sketch a retrospective on the 1920's for the *Saturday Evening Post*. His opinion has not been questioned in the 70 years since.

The article began: "The Golden Decade is the most amazing ten years of sport in the history of play. Never in the past has there been at one time such a brilliant collection of super athletes ... whose appearance and peak have been coincidental."

In 1999 *Sports Illustrated* reconfirmed Gallico's assertion by naming 1927 as the best single year in sports history this century.[36]

It was the era of Jack Dempsey, Bill Tilden, Bobby Jones, Johnny Weiss-muller, Helen Wills, Red Grange, and, of course, Babe Ruth.

Above all, baseball was America's game, the national pastime.

Amateur, semipro, and professional teams flourished in every meadow and park in this country.

Researchers and historians argue about the exact time frame that can be legitimately recognized as the golden age of baseball. To limit it exclusively to the 1920s could be too restrictive. For example, *Baseball Weekly Research* determined that the years between 1924 and 1934 are best representative of the golden age because no fewer than 47 future Hall of Famers were playing each year during that period. Only the year 1970 came close with 32 future inductees.

At the dawn of the golden decade the prospects for baseball were dark. The integrity of the game was threatened by rampant gambling, while attendance at major league parks had been anemic since 1914.[34] In addition, club owners were pilloried in the press as profiteers for raising the cost of a bleacher seat from 25 cents to 50 cents.[33]

As the decade 1910–19 was ending, rumors started to surface that members of the Chicago White Sox might have fixed the 1919 World Series in exchange for money. It was another example of the epidemic of big league gambling. Rumors of fixing championship games during the first two decades of the twentieth century precluded this latest episode.[8]

Stories of the 1919 scandal spread by mouth and print for almost one year before charges were leveled against eight members of the now infamous "Black Sox" team. The confirmation of this fix threatened to destroy the very foundation of the game: the trust of the fans.

Reeling from its catastrophic possibilities the 16 major league club owners voted to change their leadership structure. Since 1903 baseball had been governed by a committee of three men called the National Commission. By 1920 this commission was paralyzed by internal bickering and power plays. *Baseball Magazine* editor F. C. Lane wrote, "Many loyal friends of baseball had begun to despair of returning (to) sanity."[33]

On November 12, 1920, the panicked club owners voted to replace the three-man commission with one, all-powerful czar.

JUDGE KENESAW MOUNTAIN LANDIS

An Illinois federal district judge named Kenesaw Mountain Landis was guided into office through the insistence of Chicago Cubs owner Albert Lasker. Before he would accept the position, Landis demanded — and received — unlimited powers to arbitrate disputes and discipline players and owners.

Historian Thomas Gilbert asserts, "Landis may not have been what the baseball owners wanted, but he turned out to be what they needed." He added, "Landis set out to reshape baseball according to his own vision."[5] Incorruptible, but intolerant, Landis set out to restore the public's faith in the game. He banned the Black Sox conspirators from baseball and eventually forced out the cantankerous president and founder of the American League, Ban Johnson. Within his first few years he had banished 15 ballplayers. For the next 24 years Landis stood at the epicenter of baseball. No violation was too insignificant to escape his wrath.

He suspended Babe Ruth for participating in an unauthorized barnstorming tour in 1921. He threatened Giants owner Charles Stoneham for providing box seat accommodations for gambler Arnold Rothstein.[5] And in 1931 he fined Cubs catcher Gabby Hartnett for autographing a baseball for mobster Al Capone at Wrigley Field.[46]

Baseball writer Fred Lieb called Landis the savior of baseball.

He wrote, "Landis … lifted up the national game with his own hands and the very tone of his voice."[35] But Landis also enforced the color line and prohibited major league teams from playing Negro clubs. Even his staunchest supporters admitted that he was racist, vulgar, vain, and regularly drank bootlegged whiskey.

RULES CHANGES

Prior to Landis assuming his position in January 1921, monumental rules changes had already been agreed to. Beginning in 1921 umpires were instructed to throw out baseballs that were discolored, adulterated, and difficult to see. This action was in direct response to the tragedy on August 16, 1920, when the Cleveland Indians shortstop, Ray Chapman, was killed by a pitch from the Yankees' Carl Mays.

Spitball, shine ball, and emery ball pitches were outlawed by baseball's rules committee in December 1920. With these two rulings the balance that had favored pitchers for two decades suddenly tilted toward offense.

The effects were immediate and astounding. From 1910 to 1919 there were 76 pitchers who registered a season ERA of under 2.0 (minimum 20 games per season). From 1920 to 1929 there were two only.

As a conciliation to those pitchers who relied on spitballs for their livelihood, 17 men were allowed to continue using this pitch. One of the men who was allowed to continue throwing the spitball, Burleigh

Grimes, won more games during the 1920s than any other major league pitcher: 190.

Many fans believe that the new era of baseball also included a conspiracy to design a much livelier ball. In 1915 a *Baseball Magazine* editorial echoed a growing public sentiment for change. In an article, titled "What the Baseball Public Want," the author wrote, "The fan pays perhaps 75 cents for a seat in a major league park. He likes action. He wants hits.... Using a slightly livelier ball will remedy all this. Baseball is the people's game. Why not give them what they want."

A reply to the editor's plea came from the firm that made baseballs for both leagues, the Reach Company. President George A. Reach stated, "We are prepared to give what is wanted." He added, "We could make the ball so lively that the infielders would have difficulty in handling it."[31] But in 1922 the company publicly denied ever tampering with the ball at the beginning of the decade.[34]

Rumors of a doctored ball persisted throughout the 1920s and alternated between the sublime to the ridiculous. In 1926 a baseball writer named Arthur Mann claimed that the National League had secretly reintroduced the dead ball. He announced that, "The sluggers ... will find it very difficult to hit beyond the hands of an awaiting outfielder."[56] Mel Ott, Chuck Klein, and Hack Wilson soon proved him "dead-ball" wrong.

The strategy of offense changed in 1920 to a more power-oriented style. There was less of the dead ball style offense, which included hit-and-run and bunting.

Thomas Gilbert said, "Since balls were regularly retired after the slightest scuffing the batters gained the advantage. No more would a ball be kept in play after it was blackened by tobacco juice, ripped by belt buckles, and pounded into mush by over use."

Suddenly home runs became the vogue. The power hitters of the 1920s produced 9,890 total home runs compared to 3,975 hit during the previous decade.

During the 1920s major league batting titles were won by averages exceeding .396 in eight of the ten years. There were seven batters who hit over .400. However, since 1929 only two men, Bill Terry and Ted Williams, have hit .400 or better.

Once-disillusioned fans flocked back to the major league ballparks to see the new power style of play.

Attendance in the decade 1910–19 was a dismal 56 million. During the decade of the 1920s it shot up to 93 million.[34]

These fans wanted to see one man in particular.

GEORGE HERMAN RUTH

He changed the game forever. No one had ever seen balls hit so far and high before. Even his pop flies were in the stratosphere. The game of bunts, hit-and-runs, and stolen bases was set aside. Power was the new strategy and Ruth was its director.

Ruth was born to play baseball and live larger than life. While he was still in his prime a professor at Columbia University conducted a series of 20 physical tests on the slugger. These included tests of strength, speed, sight, and muscular and nervous reactions. The professor concluded that only one in one million men could have achieved the results that Ruth displayed.[35]

He was also the game's l'enfant terrible.

Ty Cobb remembered, "I've seen him at midnight, propped up in bed, order six huge club sandwiches ... along with a platter of pig's knuckles, and a pitcher of beer. And all the time he'd be smoking big black cigars." But then he added, "I never saw a man who could beat you so utterly — and do it every day, virtually — with his mere presence on the field."[37]

Babe Ruth's childhood years were less than idyllic, however. He was labeled incorrigible. His days were spent on the streets or in his father's tavern. "I learned early to drink beer, wine, and whiskey, and I think I was about five when I first chewed tobacco," he once said.[35] From the age of seven until he was nineteen Ruth was detained at a reform school called St. Mary's Industrial School in Baltimore.

From his earliest days at St. Mary's to his rookie years at Boston he suffered ridicule about his full lips and wide nose that, to some, resembled Negro features. Released from the institution by signing a professional baseball contract, he went out into the world at the age of 19, undisciplined and raw.

Ruth began his major league career in 1914 with the Boston Red Sox as a pitcher and soon developed into one of the greatest hurlers of that period. During the 1916 and 1918 World Series he pitched 29⅔ consecutive scoreless innings. At the age of 21 he won the American League ERA title while notching 23 wins.

But by the end of the decade his three-year relationship with the Boston Red Sox owner Harry Frazee was heading for an annulment. One of the traits that Ruth disliked most about Frazee was his stinginess. In 1919 Frazee sponsored a Babe Ruth Day celebration in Boston and presented his star player with a gift: a single cigar.[11]

But Frazee was living in his own little world. He treated the Boston

"Looking for Baseball Magnates," from the November 1922 issue of *Baseball Magazine*, illustrates the frustration of Red Sox and Braves fans with sales and trades of their star players. This cartoon refers to the Braves' trade of future star pitcher Hugh McQuillan to the Giants.

Red Sox as if it were a well of cash. His real preoccupation was producing plays on Broadway. After financing several failed productions he turned to his one asset that could finance his next stage play.

Frazee shocked the baseball world in 1919 when he sold Ruth to the Yankees for $125,000 and a $300,000 loan, using Fenway Park as collateral. Frazee, standing in the footlights of public condemnation, portrayed himself as the victim. In a 1920 magazine article entitled "Why I Sold Ruth," he revealed that he had acquiesced to Babe's demands for a pay raise and a three-year contract back in early 1919. But after having a great season his star player demanded more. Frazee said, "Ruth publicly announced to all the world that he would not live up to his contract. He further announced that he expected to receive $20,000 per year."

Frazee considered the demand for the raise and decided, "No individual player ... is worth any such sum of money."[33] But instead of concluding his shallow defense at that point, he then made a remark that would haunt him for years. "Ruth made 29 home runs last year, but no one knows what he will do next year, even if he has good health…. I believe the sale of Ruth will ultimately strengthen the team."[33]

Chicago Cubs president, Charles Webb Murphy, made baseball's greatest understatement when he remarked, "Do you suppose the fans of Boston are going to forget the sale of Ruth's services during this generation?"[33]

When offered the opportunity to stage a production called *No, No,*

Nanette, Frazee pawned off more of his players. He eventually sold or traded so many players to New York that when the Yankees won their first World Series in 1923 the *Boston Herald* proclaimed, "Red Sox Alumni Become Champions of the Baseball World."

By the time Ruth was sold to the Yankees he had already established himself as a boy out of control. With the move to clean up the sullied reputation of the sport, the Yankees wanted to present Ruth in a more favorable light. In early 1920 *Baseball Magazine* did a feature story on Ruth's early life and editor F. C. Lane attempted to mitigate the popular characterization. Up until that time many writers correctly labeled Ruth as a "bad boy who was sent to reform school." Challenging that description, Lane wrote that Ruth was never recognized as being bad. He was, Lane wrote, one of the "boys whose parents were unable to provide them with a suitable home."

Also attempting to sanitize his out-of-control private life, Ruth told an interviewer, "We all have our various forms of recreation. I would rather talk automobiles, dancing, tennis, or fishing." While not directly referring to his propensity for gluttony and whoring, he said, "I think a man becomes a better ballplayer by giving part of his time to other interests."

Years later Ruth admitted to baseball writer Fred Lieb, "If it wasn't for baseball, I'd be in either the penitentiary or the cemetery."[35] After Ruth came to the Yankees the New York sportswriters covered up his dalliances.[35] Fred Lieb saw him run for his life twice — once chased by a knife-wielding woman and once by an irate husband waving a revolver — and never printed a word of it until years later.[35]

Longtime New York sportswriter Harold Rosenthal said, "Ruth was 50 times bigger than the writers were and they wouldn't think of tearing him down. They didn't want to sully their own nest so they let this guy get away scot-free."

By protecting his reputation they would also preserve baseball's new image. But Ruth was perfect for his times. He reflected the carefree attitude of postwar America. He also brought fans back out to the ballparks.

Paul Hopkins, a pitcher with the 1927 Washington Senators, put it bluntly, "Back then pitchers were reluctant to throw at him or chase him back, because he was our bread and butter. He helped raise the salaries for all players."

By the end of 1921 Ruth had rewritten the record books. The new standards he set were light years ahead of previous recordholders in home runs, runs scored, RBIs and slugging average. His type of hitting had never been seen before.

Ruth lived a hedonistic life but he also had a heart of gold. He went out of his way to be with kids. Especially those who were sick or crippled. There are still a handful of people alive today whose lives were profoundly impacted by Babe's spontaneous generosity. During a barnstorming stop in Denver, Colorado, in 1927 Ruth and Gehrig were approached by a man in the lobby of their hotel requesting an autograph for his ten-year-old son. "Well, where is the kid?" inquired Ruth. The father explained that his son was bedridden with tuberculosis of the hips.

Ruth looked at Gehrig and said, "We don't have anything to do. Why don't we go to his home and see him at his bedside." Young Frank Haraway could hardly believe his eyes when he saw the two Yankee greats enter his bedroom on that October day. The exact conversation he had with them has been long since forgotten, but the boost it gave to his morale still lives in the memory of this now-retired Denver resident.[57]

Ray Kelly's first job came at the age of three, thanks to Babe Ruth. Kelly, who currently resides outside of New York City, remembers playing ball with his father in 1921 when Ruth pulled up in his dark-colored Packard. Kelly's life changed forever that day as Ruth first befriended them, then invited them to the ballpark as his dugout guests. Ruth then stunned the Kelly family by asking if "Little Ray" could be his personal mascot.

Kelly spent the next ten unforgettable years at Ruth's side, and his only memories of Babe today are of his countless acts of selflessness.[58]

Kelly's and Haraway's experiences were brief examples of the way that Ruth touched the lives of hundreds of children during his glory years.

The sale of Babe Ruth, the commissioning of Judge Landis, and limitations in pitching strategies were the foundations for the modern era in baseball. But there were other important events that received less notice.

The creation of the Negro leagues in 1920 by Rube Foster gave new life to the dream of a stable, professional venue for black ballplayers (Foster's achievements and contributions to baseball are outlined in chapter 2).

In 1925 a St. Louis Cardinal executive named Branch Rickey created the first farm club system. By investing in existing bush league clubs, Rickey started to develop a pool of home-grown talent. Up until that time major league clubs had to bid for promising young ballplayers from independent minor league clubs. It was the first example of a major league organization owning minor league clubs on a grand scale.

The electronic age was introduced to baseball on August 25, 1921, when the first radio broadcast of an entire major league game was aired in Pittsburgh by station KDKA.

Baseball also had its legends positioned behind the typewriters. The awesome lineup of sportswriters during the 1920s is unmatched by any generation. Damon Runyon, Grantland Rice, Heywood Broun, Fred Lieb, Ford Frick, Ed Sullivan, and Shirley Povich were just a few of the giants who covered every hit, run, and catch for a baseball-crazy public.

The baseball world was changing quickly and in most cases for the best. But there were dark and dangerous corners to the sport. The color line and the reserve clause were insidious aspects that were to be maintained for decades to come.

The stench of segregation prevented it from truly being a great game. The Ku Klux Klan had a national membership of 500,000 and, according to journalist Fred Lieb, its ranks included baseball greats Tris Speaker and Rogers Hornsby.

All rising stars, whether black, white or brown, were likened to the Bambino in the 1920s and 1930s. Promoters, scribes, and dreamers threw up the platitude of the new Babe Ruth. There was the black Babe Ruth, the Jewish Babe Ruth, the Cuban Babe Ruth, and the minor league Babe Ruth. In truth there may have been more talented and powerful men than the Yankee slugger. If the doors were open to all men we might be saying that Babe Ruth was the white Josh Gibson or the North American Cristobal Torriente. But because the great black athletes were not allowed to compete we will never know just how good the white ballplayers really were.

Before the advent of a players union, pension plans, and arbitration, the players lived in constant fear of losing their means of making a living. The reserve clause allowed ball clubs to actually own the careers of the ballplayers. If an individual held out for more money they could be barred for life from professional ball. A conspiracy of clubs prevented any player from seeking a better contract with another team. Even Commissioner Landis thought that the reserve clause would not survive in court, but in 1922 the U.S. Supreme Court voted 9–0 to uphold it. Many called it legalized slavery.[5]

THE GREATEST

The great appeal of baseball is the unceasing debate over who were the greatest players, managers, and teams during the past 150 years. The 1920s certainly rank as the decade with some of the greatest from each category.

Many hot stove league battles have been fought over the title of the greatest team.

While historian Thomas Gilbert names the 1927 Yankees, the 1929 Philadelphia A's, and the 1922–24 Giants as being the best teams from that decade,[32] his colleague, author Bob Carroll, lists the 1927 Yankees as the most overrated team of all time. They had, he argues, serious weaknesses at shortstop, third base, and catcher.

That is the beauty of baseball. It is the infinite well of debate.

Without question it was the Yankees who were consistently the front-runners during the golden age. In 1927 they had six future Hall of Famers on their team. Incredibly, they managed to field up to eight at any one time through 1933. The Yankees won the AL pennant six times in the 1920s and five times in the 1930s. And from 1926 through 1928 they accounted for nearly one-third of all the home runs hit in the entire American League.

After experiencing ten straight years of failure, the A's, led by Connie Mack, set out in 1924 to create a team made up of young, talented ballplayers. Money did not seem to be an issue when Mack purchased the rights to Max Bishop ($25,000) and Al Simmons ($50,000) in 1924; Lefty Grove ($100,600) and Jimmie Foxx in 1925; Joe Boley ($65,000) in 1926; and George Earnshaw ($70,000) in 1928. Mack attempted to sign a young catcher named Mickey Cochrane in 1924 from Portland in the Pacific Coast League. When the club demanded $100,000 for his contract, Mack bought the entire organization for $120,000.[48]

The A's climbed from a fifth-place team in 1924 to a pennant contender for the next nine years. In 1929 they dethroned the Yankees by winning 104 of their 150 regular season games.

The Cubs, led by the blistering power attack of Hack Wilson, Rogers Hornsby, Kiki Cuyler, and Gabby Hartnett, tormented their National League rivals from 1929 and throughout the 1930s. They had one of the greatest right-handed hitting lineups ever.

During a nine-year span in the 1920s and 1930s, the St. Louis Cardinals took the pennant five times. During that period they rotated their rosters with such Hall of Famers as Rogers Hornsby, Jim Bottomley, Grover Cleveland Alexander, Dizzy Dean, Joe Medwick, Johnny Mize, and Frank Frisch.

When it comes to baseball's greatest rookie class, 1925 ranks at the top. Newcomers that year included Jimmie Foxx, Mickey Cochrane, Charles Gehringer, Freddie Fitzsimmons, Red Ruffing, Lefty Grove, Mel Ott, and Lou Gehrig.

There is little contention over who were the two greatest managers from that period. The question is who was better, John McGraw or Connie Mack? Historians Thomas Gilbert and Fred Ivor Campbell agree that McGraw takes the honors.

Gilbert said, "McGraw tended to do it with mirrors. If you look at the personnel it's hard to believe they played as well as they did. I think that's one reason why McGraw gets so much credit. We know from watching baseball that a couple of great players isn't really what it's all about. It's the teams that get a little something from everybody that really are great. If you look at the '22 and '23 Giants they didn't have any sluggers. They had a very good infield, but it wasn't a team of superstars. You could make an analogy of them with the '98 Yankees."

Campbell said, "Connie Mack was good when he had great teams and when he discarded the great teams he wasn't good. The A's were not a middling team. They either finished at the top or the bottom."

Mack managed big league clubs for 53 years and set major league records for most games won (3,776), lost (4,025), and most games managed (7,878). He took the A's to the World Series eight times, but also ended up in the bottom half of his league 31 times.

Mack was the opposite of McGraw in many ways. Mack was tall and thin and very elegant. He would sit in the dugout wearing a suit and tie, signaling his players with code-like waves from his scorecard or straw hat. In 1944 President Roosevelt recognized Mack's contribution to America's game by proclaiming in a telegram, "Long may your scorecard wave."

Bill Werber, one of the few surviving men who played for Mack, remembers him as being kindly, but sharp. "He never unbraided or embarrassed any ballplayer in public," stated Werber. "His method was to summon a player to his office and explain what they had done wrong, and how it could be changed. He'd say, 'Now if that play comes up again would you mind doing it my way?' And, of course, that player had no alternative."[66]

The brawling, unrelenting John McGraw (nicknamed "Little Napoleon") comes in second behind Mack in major league wins and losses. He also established National League records for most years as manager (33), most pennants won (10), and most consecutive pennants won (4).

His success in the dugout was counterbalanced by a brutal and controversial personal life. He was mercilessly beaten by his father then ran away from home at the age of 12. He became a widower at the age of 25 and later when he started to achieve success he was accused of gambling and cavorting with gangsters. In 1908 he went into a partnership in a pool hall with a shady character named Arnold Rothstein who was later accused of conspiracy in the infamous Black Sox scandal.

Despite his setbacks, McGraw utilized the inherent instincts that would make him baseball's first superstar manager. He was also blessed with an imposing physical presence that intimidated his subordinates.

Editor F. C. Lane wrote, "He has the desire to drive straight through all obstacles. He cares for nothing but results. His piercing eye ... penetrating glance, is almost uncomfortable when he directs that searchlight gaze on your face."[47]

"McGraw was a driver and a lot of people couldn't play for him," observed one of the last surviving oldtimers who played for McGraw in the 1920s. The former ballplayer, who requested anonymity, said, "McGraw had a big heart for his older ballplayers, but he was very stern. He would look down the bench at us rookies after a particular play on the field and quiz us. 'What would you have done in a situation like that? You'd better be awake.' Everything was under his control. He demanded order."

According to this former player and several other sources, McGraw refused to allow his players to socialize with members of the press. Rogers Hornsby joked that a reporter once asked a Giant rookie whether or not he was married. The frightened young player replied, "You'd better ask Mr. McGraw."

Despite his combative nature, McGraw had that unique ability to shape his personality to handle the changing dynamics of a team. He was also one of the only major league managers of that era who openly praised the talents of Negro ballplayers.

Ruth, Landis, Foster, Mack, Gallico, Rickey, and McGraw: each one represents a vital character in the production that is the golden age of baseball.

Now it is time for the men who shared the stage with these giants to tell their stories.

BILL ROGELL
Born November 24, 1904

It must have been the tough times that made the 11-year-old orphan, William George Rogell, believe he could overcome any challenge. His feisty and competitive nature, coupled with a natural ability to play baseball, materialized into a 14-year major league career.

He left the game in 1940 with a lifetime batting average of .267, and a World Series championship ring from 1935.

Rogell is best remembered for being the shortstop on the Detroit Tigers' "Infield of Dreams" in 1934 that set a record for the most RBIs (462) of any infield in major league history. That infield included Hall of Famers Hank Greenberg at third base and Charlie Gehringer at second (see photograph next page). With his sterling credentials Rogell should be considered for induction into Cooperstown.

The Infield of Dreams, 1935. *Left to right:* Charlie Gehringer, Bill Rogell, Hank Greenberg, and Marv Owen. (Courtesy of Mark Rucker, Transcendental Graphics.)

Bill Rogell continued to make news as he spent the next 40 years in Michigan politics. His tough exterior and frank comments cannot hide the fact he has spent his entire life helping others. As a councilman he founded the Billy Rogell Baseball League that served the youth of Detroit for over 25 years. His contributions of time, money and valuable memorabilia to charitable causes have benefited thousands.

He and his wife have since left the Midwest and are now living in New Port Richey, Florida.

Because he had spent his first three years with the Red Sox, he was the oldest surviving member of the Boston franchise at the time of the interview. Rogell displayed an astonishing recollection of details. He quickly answered questions about his colleagues of 70 years ago by adding bits of information.

"Sure, I remember Willis Hudlin. In 1926 he was a sinker ball pitcher."

I was born in Springfield, Illinois, but I spent most of my time in Chicago because my father died when I was seven and my mother died four years later. I was an orphan boy at 11. After my mother died I went to live with one of my sisters and was eventually kicked from pillar to post. They tried to send me to an orphanage, but after one day there I left.

I went back to my sister and asked her for $20. I was going to take my younger brother, Peter, and we were going to bum our way to the West Coast. That never worked out so we stayed in Chicago.

I was the fifth of eight brothers and sisters so I lived any place I could find a bed to sleep in. There was a time when I had bread and water for breakfast and bread and water for dinner.

While I was in high school I played semipro baseball on Sundays and I was paid $10 per game. During that time I had to play under fictitious names so I could still play on the high school baseball and football teams.

I quit school at 14 because I had two kid brothers that I had to support. I sent them through school and I'm proud that both of them became successes.

When we were young, we used to cover the old balls with tape and we could only afford one ball and bat. In fact, we only had one glove for four or five of us. Between innings the guy on the other team used your glove.

My boyhood idol was Shoeless Joe Jackson. When I was a kid in Chicago, I used to work my butt off just to save a dollar. I used to go to the White Sox ballpark and sit in the left field bleachers, because he played left field.

Everyone said Jackson couldn't read or write and later I learned that he would wake up at dawn and just lie in bed waiting for his roommate to wake up. He did this so he could follow him down to breakfast and order whatever the roommate ordered. He couldn't read the menu.

I played on the sandlots and one day in 1921 a group of ex–big league ballplayers came along and they told me I was a good prospect. So they recommended me to a team in Buffalo which was the equivalent of AA baseball. I was an amateur, but they saw something in me.

A couple of years later I ended up with a team in the Southwestern League in Kansas.

One day in 1923 I was in the bank in Coffeyville, Kansas, and I saw the great Walter Johnson standing there. He lived in the area.

Well, we got to talking. I was puffed up like a balloon. So proud.

I finally said, "Mr. Johnson, I'll be seeing you in the major leagues. Just look for me 'cause I'll be there."

Just two years later I finally broke into the majors with the Red Sox and one day we were playing the Washington Senators. Walter Johnson was pitching and he was beating us 8 to 0. I didn't get called into the game until the fifth inning and I eventually came up to the plate to bat.

Well, I'll be damned if he didn't walk half way in off the pitching mound and he said to me, "Young man, you made it!" He remembered that! That's amazing! I was so surprised and shocked.

So he threw a fastball and I just stood there still in shock. Then he threw the second one right down the middle. These pitches were soft, like batting practice balls. I didn't realize he wanted me to hit one. He came down off the mound again and said to me, "Get over the shock and hit one!" I was just standing there with my mouth open. The next one he threw I hit off the left center field wall and when I pulled up at second base he turned around and said, "Nice hitting! Hope you stay for a long time." I was just a kid. I could have dropped dead.

So let's get back to 1924 when I went to Salina, Kansas.

In the Southeastern Class D League in 1924 we used to go from town to town in several seven-passenger cars, traveling at night. We would travel across desolate, wild country so I used to sit up at the front of the car with a .22 pistol shooting at rabbits. I don't know if I ever hit any of them, because we were always going so fast. But it kept us occupied.

I hit .317 that year and the Red Sox scouts noticed me and offered to buy me from this Kansas team. I found out when someone from the Sox called me on the telephone. My reaction was that I fell through the floor.

I had no particular batting style, but I used to move around the plate quite a bit. Depending on the pitcher's style, I'd either be up on top of the plate or I'd be way back. If he was a curveball pitcher, I'd be even with the plate.

When I first started in the big leagues in 1925, I made $300 per month, and during the off-season I'd take any job I could get. I peddled milk. I sold for a tool-and-die business. That $300 didn't go too damned far. It was chicken feed.

I was a switch hitter, which I picked up from just playing around as a kid. But the Red Sox tried to make me hit right handed all the time and it screwed me up. I learned a lot playing with the Red Sox, but I sat on the bench too much. I would watch and learn so when I later got to Detroit I thought I was ready.

Charlie "Red" Ruffing was one of our pitchers and he and I were great friends you know. Every time the Red Sox would play the Browns his family would come up from Illinois to St. Louis.

So his mother and father said to me, "Bill, why don't you come down to our home this fall and do a little hunting? We'd like to visit with you."

So I did a couple times, in 1927 and 1928. I used to go down and visit him at their home in Nokomis, Illinois.

Charlie was not a hunter, but we went out a few times and I enjoyed myself. After that '27 season was over we did some exhibition games in that area with Ray Schalk and all that gang.

It was in Nokomis where I got to be known as a fire chief. One day Charlie and I were walking down the street and there's a house on fire. Everybody's standing around watching and one guy has a hose, pouring water on it. I said, "Why don't you go up the ladder, break out the window, and go in there and put the damned fire out. You can't put it out from down here."

And this guy says, "Not me."

And I said, "Give me the hose."

I went up and stuck the hose in and put the fire out. So the next day someone called Charlie's mother's house and asked me to come down to city hall. It was there that they made me the honorary fire chief of Nokomis, Illinois.

You know Charlie worked in a coal mine when he was young. One day he was uncoupling some coal cars and he kicked at it to unhook the brakes and it caught his foot. It knocked some of his toes off. But he became a great Hall of Fame pitcher.

I met my wife in 1925 when I was with the Red Sox. She was a fan and she used to go to the stadium and watch the ball games. One day she asked me for an autograph and we started talking. I was single, she was single so we got together. We were married in 1930 so this year will be our sixty-eighth anniversary.

Back in the 1920s equipment was much different. They don't have gloves today. They have nets. Our gloves were flat with very little padding. I used to take the glove apart and then I'd soak it in water and let it dry out again. Then I would soak it thoroughly in Vaseline to make the glove soft and then it would dry.

Even the balls were different. In the 1920s the seams on the ball were higher and it was wound looser. Today's ball is too tight, that's why it travels so far.

Only one time I got in trouble with the press. I was just starting with Detroit and a certain sportswriter with the *Detroit Free Press* didn't think I was playing hard enough and so he wrote, "Rogell is afraid to step on a crack in the sidewalk for fear he would go into a slump."

Well, I was really quick-tempered back then and that comment made me so dang mad. One day I saw him on the street, I grabbed him and shook the hell out of him. That was the only way I could fight him back. After that day, not another negative word was written about me.

Maybe I'm a little hotheaded or whatever. Some of those writers thought we were a bunch of ignorant people. But you can't be a baseball player and be ignorant. Am I supposed to stand there and take it just because he's a newspaper man?

In 1930 I was traded to Detroit and I stayed there for ten years. I remember one day I was playing with the Tigers in Red Sox Stadium and they had a little incline in left field. Robert "Fatty" Fothergill was playing for us in left when a pop fly came out to him. He chased that ball and tripped and fell flat on his face on the incline and the ball hit him right in the back. I should have run out to get the ball, but I couldn't. I just stood there laughing; I couldn't help it. He was a big guy and he could drink more beer than anyone I knew.

I played ten years with Charlie Gehringer and I think he was the greatest second baseman in baseball, but very little is ever said about him. He didn't have a big mouth or show off. Charlie Gehringer and I were more than just friends, we were like brothers.

The one guy I felt sorry for was Hank Greenberg. He came up to Detroit in 1930 and boy, I never heard people call someone the names that he was called: just because he was Jewish. That hurt me as much as it did him. I know if the Tigers' players didn't hold him back he would have hurt some of those guys. Some guys on the White Sox and the Yankees, in particular, even hated us because we played with a Jew.

It just didn't make any sense at all. They were no angels in my day.

If you want to know why the 1920s and 1930s were the golden age of baseball, just look at the Hall of Fame. There are more men in there from that era than from any other time.

Take Babe Ruth. Babe was a nice guy and I liked him. In Detroit the clubhouses were right next to each other. Both teams had to go through our dugout and down a flight of stairs to get to the clubhouses. I don't know why, but every time we played the Yankees, Babe would come out early and he would sit in our dugout and start talking. He would call me "the little guy" and tell me I was the captain of the infield.

One day I asked Babe who was pitching for him today and he said Lefty Gomez. Well, I told him to watch me because I would hit a home run over the left field fence onto Cherry Street and sure enough I did. In fact, the ball landed in the back of a truck.

He wanted to be friends with everybody. He had a certain charisma, a closeness, a desire to be your friend. One thousand years from now Babe Ruth's name will still be magic.

I've played against Ted Williams, Joe DiMaggio, Cobb, Ruth, and Gehrig, but if you ask me who was the best in terms of raw, natural talent, I would have to say that left fielder for the White Sox, Joe Jackson, my boyhood hero.

Our manager on the Tigers, Mickey Cochrane, wouldn't stand for any joking or laughing on the bench. It was serious baseball and you had to watch the game. He had a reputation as a man who was hard to get along with. "Black Mike" they called him.

During most of my career I was a leadoff man and my job was to get on base. In 1934, after about 15 or 20 games we were on an eastern road trip and Cochrane says, "You're hitting fifth tomorrow."

I said, "Mike, you're crazy. I'm only 155 pounds. I'm not a home run hitter."

And he said, "Yeah, but you don't strike out very often. And you don't hit into double plays."

Well, Hank Greenberg was in a slump. The kind that everyone gets into. So he puts me in fifth and I hit in over 100 runs that year.

The next year I went back to Florida thinking I'd hit fifth or fourth, but he puts me back in leadoff.

I said, "Mike, they pay me extra for RBIs. I don't get much for being a leadoff man."

He said, "You're the best leadoff man and that's where you'll be." *[For more information on Cochrane see the postscript.]*

The smartest pitcher I ever faced in all my time in baseball was Mel Harder of the Cleveland Indians. He eventually became the pitching coach for the Indians in the 1950s.

We had our tricks to win games and get the edge. I chewed tobacco ever since I was four years old so when our pitchers got in trouble, they'd throw the ball to me and I spit tobacco in the glove and rub dirt on the ball so it would dye black. Well, that ball became so tough to see we'd get the next hitter out.

I'll never forget the day Tommy Bridges was pitching against the Yankees in New York. Tony Lazzeri was hitting and suddenly I heard their third base coach yell something. Well, I knew he was stealing our catcher's signs and telling Lazzeri what pitch was coming next. I called for time out and called Mickey Cochrane out to tell him what was happening. We came up with a plan.

On the next pitch, our catcher signaled for a curveball and sure enough the third base coach made a certain sound. Bridges wound up and threw a fast ball that missed Lazzeri's ears by four inches. When Lazzeri got up off the ground he yelled at the third base coach, "No more signs, no more signs!"

We never had helmets to protect us at the plate. I've been beaned several times, including once by Lefty Grove, and I think three times by Bob Feller. Lefty Grove had an incredible fastball that would rise, but one day I got three hits off him. I heard him say, "That little S.O.B. isn't going to hit off me again!"

So the next time I came up, he threw at my head. It's a good thing I threw my hand up first because the ball hit me in the hand and bounced up into the seats. He was lucky I couldn't get up because if I did I would have broken both of his knees.

I had to be tough and aggressive. Those were tough times. I had to stand up for myself. Once I hit an opposing catcher in the jaw for throwing a ball at me after I slid into home plate. Once I jumped on Ben Chapman of the Yankees with my spikes after he spiked Charlie Gehringer.

I believe everything in the Bible except turn the other cheek. I sure as hell never turned the other cheek.

Gehrig spiked me one time and I even have a picture of it here today. He hit a double to right center and the outfielder threw me the ball as Gehrig came into second. He could see the ball and he knew he didn't have to slide, but he did and it knocked me flat. That day I had to have seven stitches put in on my knee.

I immediately grabbed him by the hair and stuck his nose in the dirt. I was ready to fight and 40,000 people booed me. Look, I was 155 pounds and he was 210 pounds. Then I warned him that he had better watch his foot the next time I came down to first base, 'cause I'll step right on it.

But you know he was the nicest guy. I'll never understand why he slid. That was my livelihood. If they're out to get me I'm going to get them.

I remember playing with a couple broken fingers. I just taped them up because we had to play. If you didn't, somebody else got your job.

I played in the 1934 and 1935 World Series and we won in 1935 against the White Sox. In the 1934 series against the Cardinals I accidentally hit Dizzy Dean in the head on a double-play ball. He didn't duck. Just as I crossed the bag and threw the ball to first he got in the line of fire. I never did see him. I had so much time that I threw it softly. He was lucky because I could have fractured his skull.

Gehringer was standing next to him when he got up. Charlie told me that the first thing Dizzy Dean said to him was, "Did I break up the double play?" Can you believe that?

The next day I met up with him on the field. That was the only time I ever talked to Dizzy Dean. I walked over to their dugout and I presented him with a steel army helmet. Boy, was he surprised. I thought all the Cardinals were going to fall off the bench laughing.

When we won the World Series in 1935 we could barely afford to pour beer on each other. The most money I ever made in baseball was $15,000 in 1935, but I had three families to support. My own, my wife's, and my brother's. It was the Depression so I had to work at anything I could find in the off-season. I even sold cars. I was lucky though because nobody was working back then. The Lord gave us our skills. Believe me, few are chosen and given that ability to play major league baseball.

Baseball Today

To tell you the truth I watch baseball on TV today, but I enjoy watching kids play more. The ball they've got today is a rabbit. If Babe Ruth hit that ball today he'd kill an infielder.

We played in a different era and you can't compare that one against this era. People like to see home runs and they build the parks to accommodate that. The pitching is terrible and the umpiring is worse.

Now they show you that picture from center field and you can see the ball cross the plate in a replay. I watch that and I see fellows being called out on a pitch that is six inches outside. How can an umpire do it?

They call strikes if you hit the back end of the plate on a curveball. Maybe I didn't get the right education during my time in baseball. I always thought it had to cross the front of the plate. Here I go getting critical again. I'm sorry, but maybe my era was different. I don't know.

Life After the Game

I left the Cubs after my only season with them in 1940. I entered politics and stayed there for 40 years in Wayne County, Michigan.

During the 1940s people were buying war bonds and I got an idea. I thought that since I've got all these baseballs, I'd put them up for bid to increase sales of the bonds. I participated in the war bond drive and I gave away most of my mementos to raise money. I gave away a uniform, some bats, and balls. I don't have a damn thing and I don't regret it.

You know I'm 94 years old and I love to get up in the morning and see the sun. Things are more beautiful than most people realize.

During the four years Rogell played with the Red Sox they finished in last place each season. After Red Sox owner Harry Frazee had sold Babe Ruth and 14 other players to the Yankees over a five-year period, many fans believed that their team had been cursed.

From 1925 through 1928 the Sox had only one player on their roster who made it to the Hall of Fame. Unfortunately Red Ruffing was totally ineffective while he wore the Boston uniform. In fact, Ruffing did not find success until he was traded to — you guessed it — the Yankees in 1930.

The manager of Rogell's 1925 Red Sox was Lee Fohl, better known as the "Doctor of Hopeless Teams." From 1915 through 1926 Fohl was fired from three American League teams, always failing to win in the clutch for pennant races or ending up in contention for a miserable spot in the cellar. By 1939 Fohl was reported to be pumping gas at a downtown Cleveland filling station.[1]

The Red Sox most effective pitcher in 1928 was a rookie named Ed Morris, who won 19 games. As usual, the Yankees proposed a generous trade: $50,000 and two players for Morris. But in an uncharacteristic move, the Red Sox declined. This time they were going to hold fast and keep a promising young player on the payroll.

One day before spring training began in 1932 Morris attended a fish fry in his honor in Century, Florida. During the festivities he got into a brawl with a friend and was stabbed to death.[1, 8] (For more information on the Boston Red Sox see the Bob Cremins interview.)

Mickey Cochrane was Rogell's manager at Detroit from 1934 through 1938. During his 13 years as a catcher Cochrane was known as a sunny, carefree man. Despite losing a fortune in the stock market crash of 1929, teammates would occasionally find him happily strumming a ukulele in the clubhouse.[1]

Cochrane captured the imagination of baseball fans all over America in 1930 and 1931 when he successively hit .357 and .349.

On October 30, 1931, a baby was born in Commerce, Oklahoma. The father, Mutt Mantle, idolized Cochrane so much that he named his new son Mickey.[7]

Cochrane was the player-manager of the Tigers in early 1937 when he was struck in the right temple by a fastball. The attending physicians gave him a 50–50 chance of surviving the triple skull fracture.[1] He did recover, but was forced to spend the rest of his baseball career managing from the bench.

Although he led the Tigers to the World Series in 1934 and 1935, the stress of managing turned his mood sour. In 1936 he was reported to have had a nervous breakdown.[8] So the man who once entertained his teammates with jokes and music now became known as Black Mike. Cochrane was elected to the Hall of Fame in 1947. (For more information on Mickey Cochrane see the Ray Hayworth interview.)

WILLIS HUDLIN
Born on May 23, 1906

George Willis "Ace" Hudlin has known only two professions in his life: farming and baseball.

He played his first major league game at the age of 20 for the Cleveland Indians and retired as a scout for the New York Yankees at the age of 68.

In 1927, his first full year in the majors, Hudlin was considered by the national press to be a phenomenon. And he did not disappoint his supporters. He went on to be the ace of the Cleveland staff for nine years, winning fifteen games or more five times. He ended his pitching career in 1944 with a record of 158–156 and an ERA of 4.41. At the time of these interviews Hudlin was the second oldest surviving member of the Cleveland ball club and one of only three remaining from the 1920s.

Hudlin was the most informative of all the ballplayers relating to strategy and the science of pitching. His deliberate style of speaking belied a very sharp and educated mind. Consistent with most of the other men in this book he was blunt and critical about the condition of baseball today. But he also admitted that his love for the game has not diminished in over 90 years.

Today he resides in Arkansas with his wife of 51 years, Hilda.

His advice to those seeking a long life is "Take care of yourself. That's number one. Do some form of exercise to keep your strength."

I'm just a farm boy. I was born in Wagoneer, Oklahoma, and I grew up on a farm and stayed there until I was 22 years old. If I hadn't made it into the majors I suspect I would have stayed there all my life.

We raised cotton, corn, wheat, oats, and some cattle and all our work was done by hand. Since we couldn't afford machines we used mules and horses to plow. I bet I followed those mules for a million miles.

Whenever we would get a break during the day and in the evening we would throw the ball around. Really, all I wanted to do was play ball.

We had a family of nine. Five boys and four girls, and I was right in the middle. I am the last surviving member. All of them are gone except me. We were poor country people so we didn't have electricity, just kerosene lights. Back then standard plumbing equipment was an outhouse.

In high school I played basketball and football, but baseball was my true love. When I was growing up I sent, by mail order, for some training books written by Christy Mathewson and Walter Johnson. I would read them at night and just practice, practice, practice during the day. Fortunately my brother Lee was baseball-minded too and caught me in the fields and behind the barn anytime I wanted. At that time my boyhood idol was Babe Ruth, when he was pitching for Boston.

Wagoneer had its own team, which we called a "country ball club" back then. We bought our own uniforms for $2 and we played one to two games a week. We didn't get any salary and we had to pay for our own traveling expenses when we played the other towns in the area. But we just loved to do it. I started playing for them when I was about 15 years old.

Since my folks didn't own a car we got rides to our games from the other players in their cars or we rode to games on horses. If our family wanted to get to town we either took the horse-drawn wagon or we walked the six miles.

I guess it was a success story that I made it from that kind of a life all the way to the big leagues. You have to love baseball and play it as much as we did to [be] good enough to get to the major leagues. You have to play it all the time and that's what we did.

In 1925, after I finished high school, I worked on the railroad in a roundhouse in Shelby, Oklahoma, and played semipro ball on weekends for the railroad team.

I started my pro ball in Waco, Texas, in 1926 and opened the season for them in San Antonio. I pitched my last game for them on August 26 and I got word that the Indians were interested in me and some other fellows. That week I was sold to Cleveland along with six ballplayers for $40,000.

When I found out I was going to be a major league ballplayer I didn't celebrate too much, but I remember that I jumped up and down with joy. I remember that my salary for my first complete year I was paid was $1,500.

I found it difficult to go from a small town to a big city. I was unfamiliar with that. I was a small-town kid from Oklahoma. I was very much overwhelmed. Imagine this, everything I owned was in one duffel bag. I took a train to St. Louis and was met by the scout that signed me. He then escorted me on to Cleveland.

When I started the veterans didn't think much of us rookies and they didn't pay much attention to us. They did very little to help us and we didn't get much help or direction.

My best pitch was a sinking fastball and it came naturally, but when you come up to the big leagues like I did, you don't know how to develop new pitches. You go into the majors still learning.

My first big league manager was Tris Speaker. He was in the twilight of his career. He was all gray hair, but he could still get the ball. He was still a very good outfielder and still pretty fast. He was a dedicated man and a great ballplayer all of his life. He was a good hitter but, no, he didn't have the power of Gehrig and Foxx. He wasn't a power hitter, but he had such a smooth swing; such a pure hitter. [*For more information on Speaker see the postscript.*]

My first game for Cleveland was in late August and I went in as a relief pitcher and I faced Babe Ruth. I thought, "Oh, my God!" I spent all my life reading about Babe Ruth and now here I am pitching against him. I was wondering what I was going to do. I couldn't run. I've got to pitch to him. I didn't have a good curveball back then, but I threw the curve and it was a good position. I got him out on a slow ground ball to second base. I'll never forget that.

For nine years I pitched against him and he hit only five home runs against me. I have a book that tells how many home runs I gave up to him in 1927 and I think it was two. You can figure that out for yourself. I think I got the best of that matchup. [*Hudlin surrendered Ruth's 500th career home run on August 11, 1929.*]

All hitters have weaknesses; some more outstanding than others. It's just a matter of pitching to that weakness often enough. Ruth's weakness was low outside and low inside. He was the type of hitter that went for home runs all the time. With two strikes on him he'd swing as hard as if he had no strikes on him.

Babe had a quick, long swing. He had a quick bat because of his powerful wrists and forearms. Ruth stayed ready to hit at all times. That bat was still and just lying back there waiting. Some hitters have a lot of bat motion that will make them be late on the swing; not Ruth.

Jimmie Foxx was another man with quick wrists. Ruth had a powerful upper swing while Gehrig swung down. That's why Gehrig hit so many line drives for hits. Ruth loved a fastball because it didn't take him off his stride. Power hitters can time a fastball better than a change-up or curve.

They walk Mark McGwire a lot today and we would do the same with Ruth back then. Anytime Ruth could beat you or tie the game we'd walk him. We didn't get booed by the fans in New York when we did that. They rather expected it.

I pitched against Ty Cobb for three years. I never did see him do anything outrageous, but I sure heard about it. He was at the end of his career with the Philadelphia A's when I played against him, so I didn't see him during his great years. He didn't steal much on me. Not enough to bother me. I don't remember him hurting me much.

[*Records show that Hudlin was the sixth most effective pitcher against Cobb, holding him to a batting average of .238.*]

He spread his hands apart on the bat so he could control the direction of the ball and he just about always got a piece of it. He got his hits now and then off me, but he wasn't someone that I dreaded.

The guys that hurt me the most were Mickey Cochrane, Joe Cronin, and Charlie Gehringer. Those three gave me the most trouble. I pitched against Ted Williams and Joe Di Maggio a lot, but still those three gave me more trouble.

There were two ways I would pitch to a hitter. You could pitch to his weaknesses or you could pitch badly to his strengths. The good hitters are trained to lay off pitches that they are weak at hitting. But sometimes they'll go after bad balls that come close to their hitting zone, because that's their strength. So they are more apt to go after a bad pitch near their zone than they would a good pitch in their weak zone.

Willis Hudlin in 1927. Courtesy of Mark Rucker, Transcendental Graphics.

My best year was 1927. I was only 21 years old and it was only my first full year. I finished up 18–12, so they started calling me Ace, because I was their leading pitcher. This was the year the Yankees were hitting all those home runs, but I got a lot of attention from the press too.

The one game I remember the most was in May 1927. That day I beat the Yankees 6–5 in 11 innings. But the reason I remember it so well is that while I was on the mound in the eleventh inning they stopped the game. Someone came out on the field and made the announcement that Lindbergh had just landed in Paris.

Before the advent of the public address system in 1929 a player change or a public service announcement was made by a stadium employee carrying a giant megaphone. A quick turn in front of the first base stands and then the third base stands were all the fans could hope for.

The Depression hit everybody in 1929, but I didn't lose any money because I didn't have anything invested. I was fortunate, because so many people lost everything they owned.

I didn't work during the off-season, but I went back to Wagoneer to fish and hunt with my brothers and my friends. Later on I picked up golf.

Back then, when you knew which day you were going to pitch you would start studying three days ahead of time. You would take the lineup for the opposing team and go over it by yourself and figure how you would pitch to those guys. I would review their weaknesses. You've got to know this.

Back then you'd pitch on three days' rest: now you get five days' rest. You were expected to pitch all nine innings every three days. How did we do it? We had to do a lot of hard running on the middle day. Running, running, running. We'd run like the devil. You had to punish yourself to pitch in hot weather.

Today they put so much strain on the bullpen pitchers. I think most pitchers today could pitch nine innings if they'd let them. If they would run they could get themselves in good enough shape to pitch a complete game.

We used to go to Hot Springs, Arkansas, about two weeks before spring training, because they had hills and a park where we could work out. Originally they would send their older players to go there early, but I would go anyway. This early training was mainly for pitchers and catchers and since there wasn't any place for hitting we would just run and climb hills and take in the hot springs bath. [*For more information on Hot Springs see the postscript.*] After that we would go to New Orleans and later Lakeland, Florida, for regular camp.

In 1936 I developed a chipped bone in my right elbow. I believe I was throwing a slider in a game one day and all of a sudden I felt this pain. It continued to hurt when my arm motion got to a certain spot. When you favor that spot you're not going to get stuff on the ball that you normally would.

They didn't operate. But I've always wondered whether I should have had it operated on rather than wait it out like I did. I was used to winning 15 or 16 games per year, but that year I was 1–5. The team did not have it operated on and let it go. It eventually worked itself out. It healed itself. The next year I came back and won 12 games and stayed another five years.

My worst year was 1940 because I pitched for four teams that year [*Indians, Senators, Browns, and Giants*]. That's a year I would like to forget.

When you get old and you're still trying to play it's tough. You know you're through, but you want to hang on. That's what it amounts to. All I wanted to do was just play baseball. All that year I worried about being traded and released.

After I stopped pitching in 1944 I became a manager in minor league baseball until 1954. I became the pitching coach for the Tigers from 1957 through 1959 and then I scouted for the Yankees until 1974. Oh, all I've done all my life is baseball.

Comparing the Two Greatest Teams

Two of the best teams in the 1920s were the 1927 Yankees and the 1929 Philadelphia A's. I faced them both. Both clubs had good pitching, but the Yankees had a little bit more power. I think the Yankees of 1927 would win in a series. I don't think the Yankees had a pitcher as good as Lefty Grove though.

If they could have, the A's only needed Lefty Grove by himself. He was that fast. When Lefty Grove was pitching for the A's it was tough. His fastball looked like an aspirin coming down. There was always the chance of getting hit in the head by one of those pitches and you'd think about those things. It just would have been too bad if you were beaned. That's how hard he could throw. You'd try to hit all right, but we didn't dig in like you would with any other pitcher.

But I got a home run off of him one time in Boston in the late 1930s. He was with Boston [*Red Sox*] after Philadelphia and he had lost his good stuff. I hit a curveball off him and beat him 5–3. It was revenge for losses in the 1920s.

The A's had great hitters like Al Simmons, but Jimmie Foxx was the toughest for me on that team. He gave me lots of trouble. Also Mickey Cochrane.

The Yankees had Combs, sometimes leading off, and he hit about .356 that year. Then I had to face Ruth, Gehrig, Meusel, and Lazzeri. That bunch there was a murderous crew. With them you had to think ahead. Think about who was coming up next. It affected the way I pitched. How careful I pitched. If I got Ruth out I had to face Gehrig and then Meusel. I could never let down. They had some good pitching to go with it. [*Waite*] Hoyt, [*Herb*] Pennock, [*George*] Pipgras.

When I knew my turn would come up against the Yankees I tried not to be nervous. I knew I had to go out there. It was a part of the job. You can't get away from it. I couldn't run off and hide. I had to face the music. I believe the 1927 Yankees could beat the 1929 A's because they had a little bit more power.

The Washington club gave me trouble in the 1920s, because they were a hit-and-run club. Not too much power, but a lot of hit and run.

Baseball Today

I watch [*Mark*] McGwire and [*Sammy*] Sosa today on TV and they are a lot stronger than Ruth was. But, if they were up against the pitchers of the 1920s and 1930s I don't think they'd be hitting as many home runs as they are now.

Life After the Game

Today I follow the game. I watch four to five innings each night and get sleepy and go to bed. When you get old like I am it's tough to get around. Being young is something else. I look back and say how lucky I was. Those were the good old days ... I know that now.

During Hudlin's first four years with the Indians, 1926 through 1929 his team bounced from second place to sixth to seventh to third place respectively. When he first joined Cleveland he shared the roster with two future Hall of Famers: their manager-player Tris Speaker and Joe Sewell.

Speaker resigned his position as manager and requested his release as a player from the Indians on November 29, 1926, amid allegations of gambling. Speaker, Ty Cobb, and retired Indians outfielder Joe Wood were accused of conspiring to fix and bet on a regular season game seven years earlier.

On January 27, 1927, baseball commissioner Kenesaw Mountain Landis exonerated them. For the 1927 season, Speaker joined the Senators.

Hudlin was in the information spotlight on May 13, 1929, when he beat the New York Yankees 4–3 at League Park in Cleveland. That was the first game in which major league teams played with numbers sewn on the back of their uniforms. That practice became mandatory in 1931.

Hot Springs, Arkansas, had been a mecca for ballplayers since Cap Anson first brought his Chicago White Stockings there in 1886.[14] Its mountains, therapeutic springs, race track, and golf courses provided relaxation and reconditioning all year long.

Babe Ruth, who never did anything in small measure, once played 54 holes before dinner at the local country club. Popular legend contends that Ruth was so loud with his curses and obscenities that other golfers could measure his success or failure from the clubhouse bar.[1]

CLYDE SUKEFORTH
Born November 30, 1901

Clyde Leroy Sukeforth was a Maine farm boy who dreamed of becoming a professional baseball player. From his modest start as a catcher with an industrial league team in 1921 to his *final* retirement as a scout in 1975, Sukeforth has seen a lot of history. He also made history. On a humid August morning in 1945 he introduced Branch Rickey to Jackie Robinson. Sukeforth is the only living witness to that historic meeting.

Because of his contribution to the integration of our national pastime, Sukeforth was featured several times in Ken Burns' historical epic Baseball *(initially aired on PBS in September 1994).*

Although a near-fatal accident curtailed his major league playing career, he prospered in the National League as a catcher for ten years and left baseball with a .264 batting average.

For the next 42 years Sukeforth managed minor league teams, and scouted and coached for the Dodgers, Pirates, and Braves. His highlights include representing the pennant-winning Brooklyn Dodgers as their manager for one game in 1947 and watching his friend Jackie Robinson take the field for the first time in a Dodger uniform on April 15, 1947.

In 1952 Sukeforth had followed Rickey over to the Pirates and convinced his boss to sign a Latin American ballplayer by the name of Roberto Clemente.

In 1990 Sukeforth revealed a little-known piece of baseball history: he had been a part of one of Brooklyn's darkest days.

He told baseball writer Will Anderson that he was Brooklyn's bullpen coach during the final playoff game on October 3, 1951, between the Dodgers and the New York Giants. The National League pennant hung on the Brooklyn pitching staff retiring the Giants in the bottom of the ninth inning. When the Giants threatened the Dodgers' lead and secured two runners on base, the manager, Charlie Dressen, made a call to Sukeforth in the bullpen. "Who's ready?" he asked, referring to the two pitchers warming up. Sukeforth had to decide between Carl Erskine, who had chronic arm trouble all year, and Ralph Branca.

Sukeforth told Anderson that it was his "claim to fame" that he decided to go with Branca. Branca's second pitch to Giants' outfielder Bobby Thompson became the "shot heard round the world." Thompson's three-run homer clinched the pennant for the Giants and sent Brooklyn into despair. It is still considered the single most dramatic moment in baseball history.

Sukeforth and his wife of 47 years, Grethel, are happily surrounded by their large New England family, which includes 16 great-grandchildren.

At the time of these interviews he was the oldest surviving ballplayer from the Cincinnati Reds' organization.

Sukeforth was modest about his accomplishments and brushed off questions that required comparing qualities or weaknesses of his contemporaries. He displayed a wry sense of humor and an engaging laugh, but was refreshingly direct and blunt in his response to questions.

Sukeforth's advice on longevity was to lead a perfectly normal life and work hard.

I was born in Washington, Maine, and I'm still here in this area 97 years later. I grew up in a house that had an address of Route 220, so you can figure that wasn't in town. My father was a farmer and worked out carpentering and other trades. He even shoveled snow in the winter for income. But everybody did anything they could back in those days. You had to, or else.

I went to a grade school that was about three-quarters of a mile from where we lived. My sister and I walked to the grade school and one year to the high school in the bitter Maine winters. We didn't have a bus or automobile to take us to school and, besides, there weren't any roads either. You can gather from that I go back quite a ways.

Later the town decided to build a one-room high school with one teacher for all those kids. But don't hold that cheap. The boys liked to fish and hunt but the girls became very good students.

I remember I had a ball and a mitt when I was five or six years old and I slept with it at night. We played seven days a week since I could remember. We'd go out to a pasture where we played there every night after school. I didn't have any boyhood heroes in particular, but I remember that I envied all of them.

All the towns in our area were enthusiastic about baseball. Our town managed to get ten of us together and if you couldn't afford to buy your own uniforms, you'd play in your overalls. I started playing for our town's team when I was very young.

In those early days there was an awful lot of interest in baseball. All the little towns supported some sort of a baseball club. Some of them didn't have much in the way of uniforms or spike shoes, but they'd all get together and have a few games. There was a lot of spirit to it.

Right after the first war, it got real good because the industrial plants got enthused and they supported clubs and encouraged competition. There was a lot of baseball after the war.

We got to the games in other towns usually by walking and sometimes we'd go by buckboard with four or five others from the neighborhood. I caught some, but I played anywhere they needed somebody.

After high school I had put in two years with Coburn Classical Institute Prep School in Waterville, Maine, which was highly rated. Then I stayed out of school for one year and worked for United Lumber Company from one June until the next. I've only done two things in my life: baseball and chopping wood.

I had always dreamed of playing professional ball, so in 1921 I made the Millinocket (Maine) Great Northern Paper Company ball club. There were two clubs there, because East Millinocket had a club too.

During the summer the East Millinocket club was made up of the best players from Georgetown University. In 1922 I also started pastiming [*moonlighting*] for the Augusta, Maine, Millionaires semipro club.

In the 1923 season the catcher for the East Millinocket club signed with the New York Giants, so they came after me after they checked my credentials. They must have been impressed, because they asked me to attend Georgetown University and play ball for them. So in order to play baseball I started on a two-year program of general courses at Georgetown. At the end of the two years I had to decide what major courses I wanted to pursue. They wanted to know what I was going to major in, but down deep in my heart I knew, but couldn't tell them. That was baseball.

There were no secrets in baseball way back in those days. If there was a ballplayer around who might be better than average, why, the news traveled fast. Back then the major leagues scouted the lower-level leagues even closer than they do now. If the minor league scouts didn't notice us, then the industrial plants hired us and they paid us more than we could make at anything else.

In the fall of 1925 I signed a contract with the Cincinnati club [*Reds*] and I was told to report to them in 1926 in Orlando, Florida, for spring training. I was naturally happy. I mean that's what I was living for. I celebrated that day, but I stayed sober. I stayed with my folks in Maine all winter and worked until it was time for me to go to spring training.

Well, I arrived in Florida, but the team came in a little heavier than they were in the previous season. They had two extra catchers and one extra infielder. Their number one catcher was a guy who led the National League in hitting, "Bubbles" Hargrave, and their backup catcher was a veteran. I guess the only reason they still took me was that the pitchers wanted to throw a lot in spring training so there was room for an extra catcher. [*Hargrave hit .353 in 1926 and became the first catcher to ever win a major league batting title.*]

When I put on that uniform for the first time I felt proud inside and was hoping that they wouldn't rip it off me. My first year I got a very small bonus to sign and $600 per month, which was wealth in those days.

After spring training I was optioned to Manchester in the New England League. [*Sukeforth hit .367 and drove in 44 runs in only 64 games that season.*]

Later in 1926 the Reds called me back up and I had one time at bat as a pinch hitter and I struck out. That was my first time at bat in the big leagues and I don't care to remember who was pitching. I just sat on the bench most of that time and later I was optioned back to Manchester.

In 1927 I was back with the Reds and sitting on the bench. But I was proud to be there. [*He played in 38 games and hit .190.*]

My opportunity to be a starting catcher came in 1929, but it was an unfortunate thing. Our catcher was Johnny Gooch and one day he received a telegram saying that his only child, a six-year-old boy, had died very suddenly. It seems he fell on a rusty fence and he reacted to a tetanus shot.

When that telegram came in I knew I was going to have to do some catching. And I sure did. The next day I caught both games of a double-header. In 1929 I had my best year at the plate, because I hit over .300 [*.354 in 84 games*].

I improved myself by watching other catchers who had similar qualities to myself. But no one in particular influenced or helped me improve. I just watched the guys who were doing the best job at this point and age.

We'd have clubhouse meetings before the game and the manager would ask how you're going to get so and so out. But, back then, on our club only the pitcher would decide what he would throw.

Oh yes, we played exhibition games against American League clubs. In those days when you had an open date you didn't play a round of golf. The club would arrange an exhibition game with another club so they could pick up a few bucks. Ball clubs weren't wealthy back then. We used to play quite a few of those exhibition games.

When we visited Pittsburgh we played during the day and came back to watch the Negro League games at night. I have to say that the best catcher I have ever seen play baseball was Josh Gibson of the Pittsburgh Crawfords [*see Chapter 2*].

The Accident

Ballplayers constantly worry about injuries on the field that might end their beloved occupation, but a freak shotgun blast in the off-season almost ended Sukeforth's life. As he lay on an emergency room gurney, Sukeforth, at the age of 29, feared that the only profession he ever wanted would be taken from him.

A dapper group of baseball heroes in Sloppy Joe's in Havana, Cuba, October 1930. Left to right: Pie Traynor, Wally Gilbert, Heinie Manush, and Clyde Sukeforth.

I had a hunting accident in the fall of 1931. There wasn't much I could do about it. It happened in southwestern Ohio just after the baseball season ended.

We were hunting pheasants upland and we were lined up at different distances, moving forward with our dogs. Suddenly, our dog had pointed out a bird so we started to get ready. Well, the bird jumped up before one of our fellows expected it and he took a quick shot at it. He got the wrong bird.

My friends rushed me to Christ Hospital in Cincinnati and I laid there for 16 days not knowing what would happen. I didn't suffer much pain at the hospital, because they doped me up. One shot went through my right eye and they sewed that up. They took out one of the pellets from my head and another was in too far. You can still feel the shot in the middle of my forehead and I've got one inside, where my brain is supposed to be.

I wasn't very happy but I had to hang on. To try to come back. Baseball was the only thing I knew anything about and the Depression was going on. It permanently damaged my eye, although I could tell night from day. That's all. I wasn't any great hitter before and that slowed me down even more.

*Despite the dangers, Sukeforth made an attempt to return to the
big leagues. Since he was a left-hand hitter his damaged right eye
made hitting even more difficult.*

*The Reds traded him to the Brooklyn Dodgers just before spring
training in 1932 and he realized he would have to prove himself all
over again. Braving pitchers, who at that time had no rules restricting
beanball pitches, and batting with no protective helmet, he played for
three more years in limited duty for the Dodgers. At the end of the
1934 season, at the age of 32, Sukeforth retired from active play.*

Making History

The Dodger organization sent me down to Carolina to manage a
minor league club in 1935. Later I went to Iowa in the Three-I League, then
to the Eastern League, and then three years with Montreal in the International
League.

After that, in 1943, I went back to work for Branch Rickey and the
Brooklyn Dodgers, doing scouting jobs.

*Historical note: when Branch Rickey became the president and
part owner of the Brooklyn Dodgers in 1942 he was already rich and
powerful. Now he was about to launch the biggest crusade of his life:
integrated baseball.*

*Rickey's first move was to create his own all–Negro team called
the Brooklyn Brown Bombers, which would compete against other
black ball clubs. He then sent his team of scouts out to scour the
Negro leagues for talent. He wanted ballplayers, he cunningly told
other owners, that would play for his new all-black team. (For more
information on Rickey see the Ray Hayworth interview.)*

Up to that time other clubs were scouting the Negro leagues but they
didn't advertise it.

Finally, the major league clubowners had a meeting some time in 1945
and they took a vote.

"Are we going to allow in the colored players?" they asked. The vote
was 15–1 against it. The one vote for it was the Brooklyn club and that set
the ball rolling.

Mr. Rickey must have been reasonably satisfied with my work, because
he called me in the office one day in August 1945. He said, "I want you to
go to Chicago on Friday and take in a game between the Kansas City Monarchs and the Lincoln Giants [*Negro League ball clubs*], paying particular

attention to a shortstop named Robinson. Now I want you to tell him who sent you and that you want to see his arm."

Everyone knew who Robinson was. Jackie Robinson was the best-known athlete in America and for a long time everything he did was a picture of grace.

So I got to the stadium in Chicago very early. I had to find out what Robinson's number was, but the concession stand hadn't opened yet so I couldn't get a scorecard. Well, I found a scorecard laying on the ground from the previous day's game and I saw his number was eight.

When he came out of the clubhouse I was down where the players go by and I called him over. I told him, "Mr. Rickey, the president of the Brooklyn Dodgers, sent me and he is especially interested in your arm." "Now why is Mr. Rickey interested in my arm?" he asked. I couldn't get him off that subject and he wanted to know if Rickey wanted him to play for the Brooklyn Brown Bombers. "If I'm going to play in the Negro leagues I'm going to stay with the one I'm with."

That's the point he kept making: if it's the Dodgers, I'm interested, otherwise I'll stay where I am.

I told him, " I just work for Mr. Rickey, Jack. I have no authority. The only thing I can tell you is that there is a lot of interest in you in Brooklyn."

Every time I tried to encourage him a little bit he was way ahead of me. He was so quick-thinking and he'd ask me questions I couldn't answer. Then he told me, "I'd be happy to show you my arm, but I fell on my shoulder the night before last and I'm not going to be able to play for several days."

That gave me an opening. It couldn't have been better. So I said, "If you're not in the lineup, why don't we meet at my hotel about six so we can talk further." And he said, "Oh sure."

So sure enough he knocked on my hotel door soon after the game and we talked. He was a very interesting fellow.

In the meantime, I had bought a couple of Pullman tickets and I told him that he could get an answer to all of those questions if he came along with me to Brooklyn. I knew he was ambitious to go higher, but he wasn't going to settle for less. In the end I suggested that he meet me at my next stop in Toledo if he was interested.

So on the next Sunday I'm in the Toledo ballpark in the middle of a doubleheader and who should I see coming in but Jackie Robinson. We had dinner and we boarded the train and we arrived in New York in the morning. We went directly to 215 Montague Street, which was the Dodgers' office.

On August 29, 1945, Sukeforth introduced Jackie Robinson to
Branch Rickey. Their historic three-hour meeting began with Rickey's
offer to sign Robinson and evolved into a dress rehearsal for the chal-
lenges that Robinson would face. Despite his part in this historic
change, Sukeforth remains modest.

Many people have gained the impression that I was the first man to scout Jackie Robinson, but everybody in America knew what talent he had. Nobody except Branch Rickey deserves any credit. They have given me too much credit.

Life on the Road

Like we used to say, they don't pay you much in scouting, but they sure show you a lot of real estate. During my years of scouting I've seen every state in the United States and most of Canada. I've seen Mexico, Cuba, Puerto Rico, and the Dominican Republic.

I got a little break in 1945, because I caught a few games for Brooklyn when they needed a catcher badly. Everyone was in the service. [*He played in 18 games and hit .294 that year, at the age of 43.*]

Tough Duty

I remember a lot of collisions that I had at home plate, but I never got hurt. That is until 1997. I got a broken pelvis in a fall here at home. That's the only time I ever had broken bones.

The Greatest

I don't like to compare the great pitchers I've seen. What's the point? It's all in the record books.

I have batted against Grover Cleveland Alexander, though, and he was a great pitcher. Supposedly he was all washed up when I saw him but he still had marvelous control. He was on his way out at that time in about 1928 and I think he was with the Cardinals when I saw him. I had one at bat against him and I hit into a ground ball out.

I will say, however, that Rogers Hornsby was the best hitter. No question. I mean all around. He not only had the average, but there was something fascinating about him. The way he could handle that bat. He was such an outstanding hitter. When we were playing against him we would be busy warming up before the game until Hornsby would come up for batting practice. Then everybody would stop and look. We loved to see that swing, the form.

He and Ted Williams were two of the greatest. Old Mother Nature did a little bit more on some of those fellows than on others. There is something fascinating about them.

The Fans

The man puts his money down and buys his ticket. He's entitled to like you or hate you. They're out there hollering and you can't please them all. You just put some cotton in your ears.

Baseball Today

I don't think that the pitching has improved that much since back then. I don't know of any secret, fluke pitch that's been invented since that time. Pitching is good now and in some cases better.

Life After the Game

I don't have cable so I can't follow the Reds, but I read the box scores every day though.

I don't care whether the game is played in Cincinnati or Brooklyn or the Dominican Republic it's still baseball. And I still find it fascinating. I'll naturally find a Little League or high school game to watch if it's nearby.

With the generous permission of Clyde Sukeforth and his family the following text is a condensed reprint of a letter he received from Jackie Robinson on July 21, 1972. Robinson died of a heart attack in October of that year.

"Dear Clyde:
"...Whenever there were problems in the early days I could always go to you and receive the warm and friendly advice that I always did. While there has not been enough said of your significant contribution in the Rickey-Robinson experiment, I consider your role, next to Mr. Rickey's and my wife's — yes — bigger than any other person's with whom I came in contact."

During his first two seasons with the Reds in 1926 and 1927 Sukeforth shared the roster with a brilliant mix of eccentric and colorful players.

Former Yankee star Wally Pipp who, in 1925, was hit on the head during batting practice and was replaced that day by a rookie named Lou Gehrig. Gehrig went on to establish a long-standing major league record for consecutive games played. Pipp went to Cincinnati and vanished into obscurity.

Carl Mays, a devastating submarine-style pitcher who is noted for having been the only big league hurler to kill an opposing player with a pitch. Mays' nasty reputation for headhunting was not enhanced when he fatally struck Cleveland's Ray Chapman in the temple with a fastball on August 16, 1920.[8]
When he retired after 15 years of pitching, Mays compiled a career record that should have allowed him into the Hall of Fame. However, his fatal incident with Chapman and his record of 54 beanings in fewer than six seasons prevented his consideration.[8]

Dolf Luque, baseball's first Cuban superstar pitcher, had a temper that was as fearsome as his curveball. Unfortunately, his weapon-wielding, fist-swinging episodes sometimes overshadowed a fabulous career (see Chapter 3).

Eppa Rixey, a hard-throwing left-hander who was inducted into the Hall of Fame in 1963, towered at 6 feet 5 inches and was not reticent about showing his anger. Sukeforth remembered, "When he pitched you didn't have to ask who won the game…. If he'd lost, the place would look like a tornado had gone through it. Chairs would be broken up, tables knocked over, equipment thrown around."[38]

Clyde Henry "Pea Ridge" Day was a country boy from Arkansas who annoyed opposing batters by exhibiting his hog-calling talents from the mound. After four relief performances in 1926 he was sent packing.

During Sukeforth's brief first year he was a teammate of a man who could easily be called the greatest hitter the world has never known.
In 1926 Baseball Magazine *called Edd J. Roush one of the greatest players in baseball, but complained, "For where they stand on shining pedestals, Cobb and Speaker and Hornsby and the rest, Roush lurks in the shadows. Ty Cobb gets ten lines of publicity where Roush gets one."*

*Roush played 18 years in the big leagues and hit better than .320
thirteen times. He finished his illustrious career with a .323 batting
average and was inducted into the Hall of Fame in 1962.*

*Despite Roush's success in being a "place hitter" he was roundly
criticized by his peers for his unorthodox hitting style. He would ran-
domly choose different locations to stand in the batter's box, then
jump at the ball, taking a sharp half swing. Sometimes, when the
pitch was out of reach, he would throw his bat at the ball.*

*Hall of Fame pitcher Burleigh Grimes remarked in frustration,
"No slab man can ever get the slightest inkling as to what Roush will
do by his antics in the batter's box."*

*He swung a 50-ounce bat and purposely ordered his timber cut
two to three inches shorter than the average. Although he gripped the
bat at the handle and never choked up he was a masterful chop hitter.*

*After Ty Cobb spent ten minutes berating him for his peculiar
style, the taciturn Roush simply replied, "If my system was so rotten,
would I be hitting .350?"*[56]

RAY HAYWORTH
Born January 29, 1904

*Raymond Hall Hayworth is the only man alive today who
played for baseball legend Ty Cobb. It was Cobb's sixth and last season as the manager of the Tigers in 1926 when he called up Hayworth, the rookie catcher.*

*The day that Hayworth first met Cobb in the lobby of a Chicago
hotel he began a playing career which lasted 15 full seasons. Hayworth's greatest natural asset was a cannon-like arm. In 1931 he dis-
tinguished himself by going errorless in 100 consecutive games.*

*When Hayworth retired as a player he had accumulated a
respectable lifetime batting average of .265. He then logged an additional 32 years as a scout for three different clubs.*

*In 1946 Branch Rickey selected Hayworth to join a small scout-
ing crew that would make history by searching out talent in the
Negro leagues.*

*In a raspy, Southern drawl, Hayworth seemed to genuinely
enjoy recounting stories about his remarkable life. His son, John D.
Hayworth, was present at the interviews and it was magical to hear*

Ray Hayworth with manager Ty Cobb in 1926. Courtesy of the Ray Hayworth family collection.

him anxiously inspire another yarn out of his father by saying, "Dad, tell us the story about...." Some of the dialogue in the following interview was a result of conversations between Hayworth, his son, and the author.

His experiences as a teenager allow a glimpse of early twentieth-century life from tobacco road in North Carolina to the coalfields of West Virginia. As a prep school student Hayworth joined a summer professional league in the Mingo County Coalfield League in West Virginia. He recalled that the only person they could get to umpire games in that area was the local sheriff, who stood behind the pitcher with an oversized .45 caliber pistol on his hip.

At the time of these interviews Hayworth was the oldest surviving member of the Detroit Tigers. He is now living near his birthplace in central North Carolina. Hayworth's secret to longevity is to exercise, but he concedes that having a healthy bloodline is essential. "Out of the nine of us in our family," he said, "eight of us lived into our eighties."

My father was an incredible man.

He was a truck farmer and a tobacco farmer and he could carpenter. He also owned a grocery store and meat market for many years in High Point, North Carolina. He was a man of many trades and it seemed he could do everything.

There were nine of us in my family and we all worked the 30-some acres just outside of High Point. The work was very hard, but we had a lot of help because there were five of us boys. We all had to work because dollars were scarce and we didn't see many back then. I grew up on that farm and lived in the same house for 44 years.

Our family came over from England about eight generations ago as Quakers and during the Civil War they made shoes for the Confederate Army. I'm still a practicing lifetime Quaker.

We raised tobacco mainly and some cotton. But tobacco was our money crop and I did everything from setting out, priming, and curing.

We were outside all day in that heat and humidity, but it didn't bother us back then. We also raised vegetables and we kept my father's grocery store supplied from our farm. Back in those days all we had were mules and horses to cultivate.

When I was about 11, we finally got a car. It was a new 1914 Ford truck for $300. That was all the machinery we had.

We started playing baseball in grammar school in Springfield, North Carolina. We had a one-room schoolhouse and, believe it or not, my Dad, when he was a boy growing up, went to that same school.

All the boys in Springfield would get together and play baseball in Regan's pasture on Saturdays. I started as their catcher when I was 12 after their regular catcher got big enough so that he had to leave. These games would draw a crowd of 40 to 50 people. They'd come in horse and buggy and on horseback to get there and see the games. It was the only team in town.

Later, when I was 14, our Sunday School class formed a team and played the teams from the industrial leagues. The cotton mills and furniture factories would sponsor their own team, so we played them once or twice a week. At that time we bought our own uniforms for $10. I did this from 12 years old through high school. Also, in high school I pitched for the High Point team and won seven games.

When I was young I was pretty accurate in throwing, but I developed my arm throwing rocks more than throwing a baseball. Yes, I practiced my skills mainly with rocks since that was my hunting weapon for squirrels.

Some boys lived on an adjoining farm about the same age as us and we'd fight each other with rocks. We didn't get close enough to fist fight, but we could throw rocks. That's where I developed throwing at long range. Well, I also developed it throwing at tin cans.

One day, when I was 45 or 50 years old, I was walking down the hedgerow on the edge of my farm and a rabbit jumped out and I picked up a rock. The rabbit made the mistake of stopping and I hit him with the first throw.

After high school I went to a prep school, Oak Ridge Military Academy. In 1923 I started at Oak Ridge and I left in 1925. I wanted to pitch at Oak Ridge but, after I started working out in the spring, the coach called me in his office. He said, "Ray, you've got one of the best arms I ever saw, but you can also throw the straightest ball I've seen. As straight as an arrow. I want you to be our catcher." So I said, "OK, Professor Holt," and I put on the catcher's gear and I never played at another position the rest of my career.

Ray Hayworth, Coalfield Leagues, 1923. Courtesy of the Ray Hayworth family collection.

Professor Holt was the best coach I ever saw and he made the school famous. Much later my brother Red attended that school and he was the ninth player that coach Holt sent to major leagues. He put a whole team into the major leagues from that prep school.

During that summer I played for a semipro team in the West Virginia Coalfield League. I worked at the Sprig Mine commissary during the week and played on weekends. That was the part of the country where the Hatfields and the McCoys lived.

One of the teams we played against was in the town of Hurt. You can tell what kind of an area that was by the name of the town. The sheriff in that area was a Hatfield and he acted as the umpire for our games. He was a bad umpire but no one ever argued with him, because he was a known killer. No one crossed him.

At the ballpark the crowds were rough and there would be gambling and heavy drinking. Once we had a substitute umpire, because the sheriff was late. Well, he didn't last more than one inning, because after he made an unpopular call he had to grab his jacket out of the dugout and race to his car.

The ball fields were very rough and at one park there was a mountain that rose above third base at a 30-degree angle. Well, to compensate, they built a level platform so the left fielder had something to stand on.

We didn't have showers so after the game we'd just jump in the river behind the mines.

It was a completely different world back in there. As an example, people used to say, "We're going to a wedding today — let's buy some ammunition."

A baseball field used in the Coalfield League in West Virginia. A view from third base into left field. Note the steep hill and platform for the outfielder. Courtesy of the Ray Hayworth family collection.

I played in that area for two summers, but fortunately in my second year I changed to a different league that was a little bit more polished. Naturally, I returned to Oak Ridge in the fall to continue my studies.

One spring day in 1925 at Oak Ridge School, we were playing a game and we saw this nicely dressed gentleman at first base standing in the crowd and somebody whispered to me, "That's Billy Doyle, a scout with the Detroit Tigers baseball team."

Believe it or not, he followed us up on a road trip, and when we got back, our coach came up to me and said, "Billy Doyle likes you and he thinks you're going to have a good chance to play professional baseball." I was having lunch when he told me and it stunned me so, that I couldn't eat. I had to go to my room to get over the shock.

In January 1926 Doyle came to Greensboro and he signed me to the Detroit club and gave me a small bonus of $250. He left me and went on to sign four other players in one sweep in our area. One of them was Tommy Bridges and we all wound up in Detroit.

Well, three of my brothers eventually played professional baseball also. My youngest brother, Red, and I were the only ones who made it to the major leagues though. My other brothers played in the C, D, and A leagues.

I went to spring training in 1926 with their farm club, the Toronto Maple Leafs, in Augusta, Georgia. We trained together with the Tigers and that's where the Detroit manager, Ty Cobb, saw me. While I was with Toronto my roommate was Carl Hubbell.

I was only there for a couple of months, because after the season started, oh, about July 10, the regular Detroit catcher, Johnny Bassler, broke his leg. Cobb called up the Toronto manager and said, "Send that young Hayworth over here, Bassler just broke his leg. Send him over tonight."

So, they put me on a train to Chicago where the team was playing. The next morning I got off the train and went down to the Forest Park Hotel and walked in the lobby. The first fella I saw there was "Sad Sam" Gibson, who had lived in my hometown. He was a pitcher on the club. We were talking there in the lobby and he said, "Look, here comes Cobb now, getting off the elevator. Let's go speak to him." So we went over and Ty says, "Well, kid, I didn't expect you to make the major leagues so soon. Did you?"

And I said, "No sir, I didn't!"

I'd never seen a major league game until that day. "Lil" Stoner pitched for us against the White Sox and he beat them 1–0.

I thought, "Boy, having on a major league uniform is the greatest thing that ever happened to me." I looked down and saw that big "D" on the front. It was really a great thrill for me to put on that uniform. I dreamt all those years about Ty Cobb, Walter Johnson, and Tris Speaker. They were my boyhood heroes and I finally got to play against so many of them.

In that first game I was down in the bullpen and someone said, "There's Ty waving down here at the bullpen." And finally this guy said to me, "He wants you. He wants you."

He put me in the game that day as a pinch hitter and Clarence Mitchell was the first pitcher I ever hit against in the American League.

So I went down into the dugout because I didn't have a bat. I was afraid to pick up one that belonged to Harry Heilmann or [Robert] Fothergill or Heinie Manush.

Well, I finally picked up a bat and went out to hit. I hit the ball pretty darn good, but I didn't get a hit. That's how I broke into the major leagues.

Then we went over to Philadelphia and I caught my first game. The Philadelphia pitcher was John Quinn, an old spitballer, and I got a base hit and drove in a couple of runs. I got my first hit on July 19, 1926.

Then we went on down to Washington and Cobb said, "Boy, you're the catcher today!" And that about scared me to death. So I looked up to see who was warming up for the Senators and it was Walter Johnson.

I said, "Oh, my Lord, I have to hit against the great Walter Johnson!"

And I did. I caught seven innings and I hit a couple of balls pretty good off him. Ty Cobb pinch hit for me in the seventh inning and got a double and we won the ballgame, 2–1.

I sure do remember the first time I hit against Walter Johnson. That big sweeping sidearm, like a slingshot. Boy, he could really hum that ball!

When I first went up to Toronto to play they gave me a contract for $300 a month. Now, when I came back to Detroit from that road trip, Mr. Frank Navin, the owner of the Tigers, asked for me to come up and see him. I went up to his office and he said to me, "Son, how much did they pay you in Toronto?"

I said, "$300 a month."

And he said, "We don't pay anyone here less than $500 a month." So I got a $200 raise.

My dad never played baseball and he didn't know a thing about it. He used to discourage us a little bit, but the first year I played professionally, I sent him a check for $75. And for the first time in my life I got a letter from him. He was thanking me for the check and from that time on he understood that I could make a living from baseball.

My mother was always a great fan and she came up and saw me play every game of the 1934 World Series. She sat in the box near our dugout and really enjoyed it.

I'd like to talk about Ty Cobb.

Everybody wrote so many bad stories about him, but when I got there there weren't any fist fights or cussing. Ty Cobb never had a fight while I was there and I never did see him do anything bad. I never had a drink with him nor saw him take one. Ty Cobb took good care of himself and he was still a battler at that late date in his career when I got up there.

Even though he was older and just had an operation on his eyes, he could hit better than just about anybody on the team. He could say, "Why don't you do it this way?" and of course we had disagreements on how we made plays. Not that we fought, but this happened on every team I was ever with.

Cobb never cussed at us or treated us wrong, but he expected us to play as hard as he did and do the things he did. But nobody had the ability to play the way he did. He was all business: strictly baseball. No joking around.

Well, I wanted to pick out the good things I saw in Ty Cobb and so I wrote a special story on him once. Of all the stories about Ty Cobb, one of my favorites is about a meeting we had in the clubhouse one day.

He said, "Fellas, I'm not going to talk baseball today; I want to tell you something else."

He said, "You know major league players' lifetime is rather short, so whatever amount of money you make, just be sure you take a little of it and put it away for a rainy day."

And he said, "I want you to look at this bill in my pocket." And he pulled out a $10,000 treasury note and said, "I want everyone of you to take hold of it and look at it, because this came to me from Coca Cola for stock I bought."

Back then we would sit around as a group in the lobby of our hotel if there was a day off or a rain delay. Cobb would sit right in with us and would talk baseball: how to play pull hitters; how to pitch certain people in the league; who was the toughest pitcher.

Since I was only 22 years old, this was a big thing to me to listen to all of these veterans. It was like going to college.

We had some great ones like Harry Heilmann and Red Wingo, "Fats" Fothergill and Lou Blue. We didn't have much pitching, but boy, could they hit.

After my first year in Detroit I spent two years in Double A. Then in 1929 when I was at spring training, Detroit's manager, Bucky Harris, said, "Ray, I think you ought to go down to Toledo and work with a young manager named Casey Stengel. Very few people recognize his ability to teach young players how to hit."

I spent almost one year with Casey Stengel in Toledo. I think he influenced me more than anyone else. At that time I was a dead-ball hitter, hitting every ball to left field.

So I went down there and every day old Casey would stand in back of the batting cage and watch me hit curveballs. Well, pretty soon I got the knack of it and I could hit behind the runner at first base rather than pulling the ball to left.

Casey's meetings were pretty good. Back then we traveled by train and all our stuff was placed in trunks. When we would stay in a town all the trunks were on the floor in the middle of our clubhouse. So Casey would take a fungo bat and walk over to a trunk when he really wanted to make a point. He would take that fungo and rap one of those trunks and it sounded like a cannon going off. I was so thrilled listening to him.

He had a meeting one Sunday in the clubhouse and he said, "Fellas, do you all read the stock market much?"

And he said, "Well, I'll tell you, you better follow the railroad stocks because the way you guys are playing, a lot of you are going to be riding the rails."

I had to stay in the back with my head in the locker so he couldn't see me laughing. I had a high regard for him. He had a lot of strange ways of saying things, but he knew baseball.

When we were traveling, he could start in with a story that would take you from one state to another. When he got through, everyone would ask, "Well, what the heck did he say?"

This was 1929 and I hit .330 that year. In the fall I went back to Detroit and took over as first-string catcher from that point on. I was their steady catcher until 1934 when Mickey Cochrane came over. Mickey could hit those tough right-hand pitchers and I could hit the tough left-handers, so we helped each other out.

A lot of the players had superstitions back then. Some would purposely step over the chalk line because it was bad luck. You would never dare go by a hairpin without stepping on it because it meant you would get a base hit. Not long ago I was walking down the hall, here where I live, and I saw a hairpin and I said, "I've got to step on that. It might be a base hit."

We had some real characters on that ballclub. One was "Fats" Fothergill. I used to live downtown at a hotel in Detroit and would walk over to the ball field every day. Fothergill lived there too and sometimes I'd walk out with him. Every once in a while he'd just stop and say, "Hey, kid, I can really hit that ball, can't I?" And of course I'd have to reply, "Yeah, Robert, you sure can." Every once in a while it would just hit him and he'd have to ask me.

They didn't have weight-reducing belts back then, so they'd take an automobile inner tube and split it open and wrap it around him so he'd get rid of his gut. He had a beer belly, and he had a truly big one.

Earl Whitehill was another one. He was a real competitor and a fine left-handed pitcher. He was also a fiery-type fella. He married a girl who was real well known: a celebrity. She was the Sun-Maid Raisin girl [*Violet Oliver*]. Even now I'll see a Sun-Maid raisin box and think of her. She was a great friend of Babe Ruth's wife, so the two couples hit it off together real good.

I remember a guy named Rip Collins real well. When I first came up he invited me and Johnny Neun to go out and live in this furnished home that he had rented until his family came up. We just loved staying out there with him because we'd buy the groceries and he'd do the cooking. Boy, could he cook. He could make the best biscuits.

After he got through with baseball he went back to Texas and became a sheriff for many years. He was a tough, hard-rock guy for sure. I'm sure he must have been a good sheriff. He was a great character.

I played ten years with Charlie Gehringer, one of the greatest ballplayers. He deserved to be in the Hall of Fame. He didn't talk very much, but he was dead serious. He took his job very seriously. In the hotel lobby he was very friendly, but on the field he was all business. He came up in 1925 and I started the next year. [*For more information on Hayworth's teammates see the postscript.*]

Every club I ever played with had beer in the clubhouse, after Prohibition. Nobody abused it. After the game they'd be so hot and sweaty and they'd have a drink or two and go home. They did that so the players wouldn't stop at a beer joint somewhere and have half a dozen bottles.

I got to know Babe Ruth better when the Detroit club sold me to Brooklyn in 1938. He was a coach there. But, I do remember that in 1926 Babe Ruth came to Detroit and Ruth got involved with a bunch of guys who took him up to an area [*Howell, Michigan*]where he could fish. Nobody ever told him that he had to have a fishing license. Well, they arrested Mr. Ruth for not having a Michigan fishing license.

The newspaper people traveled with us on the railroad and they were almost part of the club. They stayed at the same hotel with us and sat in on our private conversations. That's right. That's how they got all their stories.

They were a great bunch of fans in Detroit and they were hell-bent on winning. Back then they actually dressed up to come out to the ballpark in their suits and they wore derbies or straw hats. There were some loud ones up there but we didn't pay much attention to them. It was more formal than today.

The big thing in Detroit was the size of the knockwurst hot dogs they served at the stadium. It was a big deal. Because of the German influence they served them with sauerkraut.

During the off-season, I spent some winters at my wife's home in Christiansburg, Virginia, and we'd hunt pheasants. Other times I stayed with my brother on his dairy farm in North Carolina.

I played for Detroit in the 1935 World Series and I'll tell you there's nothing like actually playing in a World Series. It is so unusual to be a winner and get that World Series ring. I'm still wearing my ring. I've got it on right now. We had a big blowout and a banquet at the Book-Cadillac Hotel. We tore up the town when we won that one.

I returned to North Carolina after the celebration and I was asked to speak to so many groups and organizations.

I'm a widower now, but I met my wife through her brother who went to school with me at Oak Ridge.

I went home with him once and the first time I ever saw her she was 15. Three years later we struck up a friendship and it developed. We were married in 1927 and we were together for 65 years. Her name was Virginia Jones and she loved baseball and she never missed a game in Detroit. She always went with me on scouting trips after I retired from playing and the kids were grown. She traveled right with me all the time. Every time I had a good day, she put it in a scrapbook. If you'd take those scrapbooks and read them now, you'd think I was the greatest player who ever lived.

My most memorable day in baseball happened in 1935 when we were battling the Yankees for the pennant. There were about 70,000 people in the stands in Yankee Stadium and I hit a home run off Lefty Gomez.

When I rounded first base I felt like a bird flying. When I got to second base it suddenly dawned on me how hundreds of times Ruth made that same trip around the diamond. It was a great feeling. I sure never forgot about that.

I had my share of injuries. In 1938 I had two bones on my right hand broken by an inside pitch from Buck Newsom. I was out five weeks. A couple of years later my arm was injured by a foul tip and I was immediately traded to Brooklyn.

Once in the 1930s [*George*] Selkirk of the Yankees jumped into my stomach with both knees in Detroit. I didn't drop the ball though. It didn't knock me out, but my back never has been right since. I can still feel it.

They'd always try to run over you at the plate. I'd always figured that I'd give them half the plate, but I wanted the other half to myself. Ben Chapman, when he was with New York, jumped into me at the plate and poked me in my eye. It was black and blue the next day. And once I had my head sewn up.

Tommy Bridges was one of the best pitchers I ever caught. The best pitchers I ever hit against were Walter Johnson and Bob Feller. I said many times that when Johnson was pitching batting practice he could throw harder than anybody on his staff. And that was up into the 1930s. [*Johnson was over 40 years old at that time.*]

One day in Detroit in 1930 I believe, Witlow Wyatt [*a young Detroit pitcher*] and I were talking when Walter Johnson crossed in front of our dugout.

Well, Wyatt says, "Hey, Walter, I want to ask you a couple of questions."

He said, "How hard could you really throw when you first came up to the major leagues?"

And Walter said, "Son, I'll tell you a story."

He said, "I could throw it just as hard as I needed to." And he meant it too. He had such a remarkable record.

So then Wyatt asked Walter Johnson how powerful Babe Ruth really was.

And Walter said, "I'll tell you one thing for sure, when Babe hits a ball, it disappears quicker than anyone else hits one."

Bob Feller was so fast that we used to joke about it. I remember one day we were playing in Cleveland and it was a cloudy afternoon. Feller was pitching a whale of a game and the umpire called a strike on our man who was batting. One of our players on the bench hollered at the umpire, "Hey, that one sounded low to us!"

Hanging Up the Mitt

I finished up as a player in 1945 and after that I went into scouting for the Brooklyn club for Branch Rickey. Rickey was way ahead of everybody because he knew there was tremendous talent out there in the Negro leagues. So I joined George Sisler and we were sent out to scout them. That's how Rickey got the cream of the crop. We were the first ones there.

We came up with [Don] Newcombe and several others. Also during that period I scouted Junior Gilliam and I even saw Josh Gibson catch.

We were sent up to Springfield, Massachusetts, one night and Newcombe was pitching for his club up there. Boy, did he show us something!

In a meeting the next morning Mr. Rickey asked, "Ray, what did you think of him?"

And I said, "I can sum it up in a few words, Mr. Rickey. He can throw harder than anyone you have on your staff."

Rickey jumped up and bit the end out of his cigar. So they went right out and signed him.

I scouted for the Dodgers until 1948 and then I had a chance to go to the Chicago Cubs as a special assignment scout. I eventually wound up as director of scouting. I still have a copy of the original scouting report I made on a young fellow named Ernie Banks.

Buck O'Neil was the manager of the Kansas City Monarchs: the team that Banks was playing with. Buck recommended that I spend a week with the team and I was there one night when they were playing in Davenport [Iowa]. Out in the woods behind the outfield fence there was a big water tank, and when Banks came up to bat he hit one out into the woods and clear over the water tank. I thought that if he did it once he could do it again.

After that week was over I called the general manager of the Cubs and said, "You'd better jump on this one quick. He's the real thing. Don't let him get away." The next morning they bought Ernie Banks for $22,000.

I heard that later the owner of the Cardinals, Mr. Busch, offered Mr. Wrigley $500,000 for Banks.

Mr. Wrigley said, "I don't want $500,000. I want another Ernie Banks."

After that I went to the Milwaukee Braves and stayed with them for nine years until I retired in 1973.

Back in Milwaukee there was this young kid whose folks owned a Ford dealership in town. He used to come out and sit in the box with me and visit and talk baseball all the time. He was so interested in the game that he later bought a team. He was Bud Selig. I let him come down and sit in my box at the stadium and he never forgot it. Now he's the commissioner of baseball and a great friend of mine.

Life After the Game

Today I'm pretty healthy. I haven't played golf for several years, but I'd say that the secret to longevity is exercise and family history. My great-great grandfather, Eli, lived to be 94 years old.

My brother Red was with the Browns and made it through the World Series of 1944. He was a rookie that year and that was quite a thing for a rookie to catch every game of the World Series. He still lives near me.

My grandson is J. D. Hayworth the Republican congressman from the sixth district of Arizona. This is his second term and he's on the Ways and Means Committee in Washington. We are very proud.

I watch a great many baseball games on TV today. I follow Atlanta because I worked for the Braves for so many years and I know people in that organization. I've got the best seat in the house here in my Lazy-Boy chair in front of my TV. There isn't a better box seat anywhere.

So many of us oldtimers still dream baseball every night. Very seldom does a night go by where there isn't a little baseball somewhere in my dreams. I play. I catch. I hit.

A typical nightmare we have is that we rush to the ballpark and we can't find the gate to get in. Either that or our uniform is missing. Sometimes I lose my glove or my mask and I can't find it anywhere. It's typical.

The Tigers finished in sixth place during Hayworth's first professional season in 1926. It was also Cobb's last year as a Tiger, ending a string of 22 years in the same uniform. Cobb was forced to resign by American League president Ban Johnson after charges of gambling were leveled against him and Tris Speaker by former major league pitcher, Hubert Leonard. Both Cobb and Speaker were exonerated by

Baseball Commissioner Kenesaw Mountain Landis, and Cobb went on to play his final two years with the Philadelphia A's.

Even Damon Runyon could not have conceived the characters that Ty Cobb managed during the mid–1920s. One of the most colorful players on Hayworth's original Tigers team was Robert "Fats" Fothergill. A native of Massillon, Ohio, Fothergill stood 5 feet 10 inches and weighed in at 230 pounds. He earned a reputation as a terrible defensive player, but his offensive skills kept him in professional ball for 12 years.

In the off-season Fothergill played semipro, minor league, and outlaw football, but he could not shed the poundage. Ty Cobb recalled, "Fatty's food tabs looked like we were keeping an elephant in right field."[37] His liquid diet and an early retirement from professional ball caught up with him in 1938. He died in Detroit, Michigan, at the age of 41.

One of Hayworth's battery mates, and his one-time roommate, was a man born 100 years too late. Baseball Magazine called Rip Collins the "Wild Texan Ranger on the Hurling Slab."

Collins had a long but inconsistent career in professional baseball, and he seemed to live every moment to its fullest pleasure. A native of Weatherford, Texas, Harry Collins was tagged with his nickname because of his copious consumption of a backwoods spirit called Ripy Whiskey.

"When I was six years old," he bragged, "I could drain off a goblet of beer and smack my lips."

After a brief career of shooting at border thieves as a member of the famed Texas Rangers he joined the New York Giants in 1920 and notched a 14–8 record in his rookie year.

Collins freely admitted that he was really destined to live a life "free of the irksome restraints of civilization." He pined, "I was cut out for ... a good horse, a good gun, and plenty of elbow room." During prohibition he gladly regaled reporters with stories about his forays into Mexico and his love affair with tequila. In a 1926 interview he admitted that, during his last trip there, he ran over a Mexican pedestrian with his automobile and barely made it across the Rio Grande in advance of a mob screaming, "Kill the gringo."[56]

After retiring from baseball in 1931 Collins returned to east-central Texas, where he was elected sheriff. A recent baseball biographer summed up Rip Collins' 11-year career with the phrase, "A million dollars' worth of talent and 25 cents' worth of enthusiasm."[7]

Earl Whitehill, the husband of the Sun-Maid model, was another eccentric. Although he was Detroit's long-time staff ace, Whitehill is best remembered as a flashy dresser with a combustible personality. He would fight anyone, including Ty Cobb, who once attempted to order him off the mound during a game.[27] He would berate any teammate who failed to put in a 100 percent effort.

The imperious Whitehill left the game holding the dubious title of accumulating the highest ERA of any pitcher in history who won more than 200 games.

PAUL HOPKINS
Born on September 25, 1904

Paul Henry Hopkins joined the Washington Senators in 1927 and lasted only two seasons, but his name will forever be in the record books as the man who gave up Babe Ruth's fifty-ninth home run in 1927.

He retired from big league baseball with a record of 1–1, an ERA of 2.96, and a truckload of stories about the greatest ballplayers in baseball history.

After a 30-year career in banking, Hopkins retired to a small town in Connecticut, not far from his birthplace.

Hopkins granted this interview only two weeks after the death of his wife. Jean and Paul Hopkins had been happily married for nearly 70 years. At the time of this interview he was the oldest surviving member of the original Washington Senators ball club.

His sage advice on living to a ripe old age is to have a healthy blood line. "My father lived to be 91 and my mother lived well into her eighties."

I was born in the town of Chester, Connecticut.

I was five years old when I first fell in love with baseball and by the time I was fifteen years old I was playing summer ball near Lake Placid, New York.

My father was a fairly decent ballplayer himself — not in league play — but still a pretty good left-handed pitcher. So he taught me quite a bit. Even though he loved the game, he and my mother never saw me play with the Senators. Oh, they supported me all right, but they were just homebodies.

Later I attended Colgate University and pitched for them. During the summers I played in a country league.

My boyhood idol was Christy Mathewson and in 1926 I was fortunate enough to meet him. He happened to be recuperating in Saranac Lake, New York, where I was playing ball that summer, and even though he had TB [*tuberculosis*] he would walk down and umpire for us at first base. He looked OK on the days we saw him, but when he would have an attack he couldn't come down for a day or two.

He was gassed during the First World War and he never recovered. In fact, he died that fall after I met him. I enjoyed talking to him, but you might say that he never wanted to talk about himself. He was one of those types that always wanted to help everyone else.

In 1926 George Weiss, the owner of the New Haven ball club in the Eastern League, had someone follow me around for a while watching me pitch college ball. You know Weiss because several years later he became the general manager of the Yankees.

Finally they made me an offer and signed me up. They offered me $4,000 before I got out of college. But in those days schools didn't allow students to be professional players, so you couldn't accept money for playing. No one knew that I accepted their money until I graduated.

During that time I had a chance to sign up with the Detroit Tigers, but I couldn't because I had accepted that money from Weiss and I was tied up.

While I was pitching for Weiss in 1927, Walter Johnson was sent up to New Haven to look me over. When he got back to Washington he advised Clark Griffith, the owner of the Senators, that they ought to have me. The minute that I found out that Weiss had sold me to the Senators for $25,000 I told them that I was going to stay home and not report until I got a little bit of the deal. They were only going to pay me a few hundred dollars a month and yet I was worth $25,000. That was a lot of money back then.

Eventually, Clark Griffith called me personally and said, "If you don't report tomorrow you'll be suspended from baseball." I would have been out of professional baseball forever. No one could have touched me, because Clark Griffith owned my career.

So, naturally I ended up going with the Washington Senators. My first major league game was very memorable. It was 1927. That was the game that Ruth was attempting to hit his fifty-ninth home run. That was the home run that would tie his previous record from 1921.

I remember that I was out in the bullpen and at that time the bullpen in Yankee Stadium was perched deep in left field and you couldn't even see how the game was going. Well, the call came down that they wanted me to relieve and I could see that the Yankees had three men on base. I guess I would have been nervous if I knew who the next batter was.

It was Babe Ruth. It was Babe Ruth with the bases loaded. The rest is history. I threw him a series of curveballs and he finally hit one into right field at least five rows in. He hit his fifty-ninth home run off of me and he tied the record [*see illustration next page*].

> *John Drebinger of the* New York Times *immediately wired his sports desk the following description: "The ball landed halfway up the right field bleacher, and though there were only 7,500 eye witnesses, the roar they sent up could hardly have been drowned out had the spacious stands been packed to capacity. The crowd fairly rent the air with shrieks and whistles as the bulky monarch jogged majestically around the bases, doffed his hat, and shook hands with Lou Gehrig."*

I then faced Gehrig who, in my mind, was probably the greatest line-drive hitter I ever saw. He would have hit 100 home runs if he was pulling the ball in the air like Ruth. He hit one right back at me and it would have killed me if it hadn't gone through my legs.

I followed his career a little bit because he also signed up in the Eastern League a year before I did. He was getting a pretty good salary, so I wanted the same salary he was getting when he was playing for Hartford.

The second time Ruth came up, he hit a curve ball right off the end of the bat over the shortstop's head and made a double. I turned around and said, "You were a lucky bum to hit something like that."

I do remember his exact reply. He said, "Well, you haven't been around in this league long enough to know what I can do."

At least I finished the rest of the game for four or five innings.

After the game I decided I was going to get Ruth to sign a baseball, so I picked a good one out of the bag and walked to the Yankees clubhouse. I started to go into their dressing room. I was a rookie and I guess I didn't know any better — or care. I heard someone yell at me and it was Miller Huggins, the Yankee manager.

"Hey, young fella, where are you going?" he said.

I said, "I'm going in to get Babe Ruth to sign this ball."

And he said, "No you aren't, because we don't allow anybody else in that room. The players don't want you."

Then after a moment he said, "Well, just give me the ball," and he ordered someone to take the ball in and Ruth signed it.

I've been sorry the rest of my life because I gave that autographed ball

The New York Times.

RUTH HITS 2, EQUALS 1921 HOMER RECORD

Slams 58th in First Frame, Then Gets 59th in Fifth With 3 Men on Bases.

BARELY MISSES TWO MORE

Each a Trifle Short and One Good for Triple as Fans Shriek With Joy.

YANKS CRUSH SENATORS

Win by 15-4 as Babe and His Mates Run Wild and Make 19 Safeties.

59th a Real Wallop.

Then the fifty-ninth! That, country-men, was a wallop. It came in the fifth with Paul Hopkins pitching and was an almost exact duplicate of the fifty-seventh made on Tuesday, delivered with the bases full!

Paul Hopkins –

Being in Bull Pen with no real way to find out much about progress of game until I was selected in to relieve with 2 out & the bagia loaded & not knowing who the next batter was until Ruth appeared & Threw him about 10 curver balls which he finally hit one into the right sector about 5 rows in at least & fin-ested the bust of game 4 or 5

The detailed story of Ruth's 59th home run in Hopkins' handwriting, in a note to the author.

Postcard photo of Paul Hopkins. Courtesy of Henry E. Josten, *Pictorial Gazette.*

to the 10-year-old son of the team doctor. I really wish I could have kept it.

Later the next year I met Ruth outside the clubhouse in Washington. He had just gotten married and he had his new wife with him, so I chatted with him. He remembered hitting that home run off of me. I'll never forget it either. Back then pitchers were reluctant to throw at him or chase him back because he was our bread and butter. He helped raise the salaries for all players.

I was on the pitching staff the last year Walter Johnson pitched and as an individual you couldn't beat him. He was a gentleman throughout. He had a very smooth, effortless delivery that went sidearm. He did the best he could and it wouldn't bother him if he had a bad day pitching or if he didn't do well. He was probably the most respected player in the league at that time. He made up his mind that he wasn't going to throw at anybody and he never did, because he was afraid that if he hit somebody he might kill them. Most of the players knew that and weren't afraid to crowd the plate. But he still got them out.

He did become manager for several years there and it didn't pan out for him because he expected all the pitchers to be as good as he was.

The Senators also had two comedians on the team at the same time. Nick Altrock and Al Schacht were coaches on our team and they performed an act before the game started. They'd go out on the field and pitch and catch in a funny way. They'd put on a show for about five or ten minutes. Nick was a pretty good ballplayer at one time himself, but as I recall he didn't get in to play while I was there. Altrock was quite a bit older than Schacht. [*See additional information on Altrock in the postscript.*]

While I was there I threw a lot of different pitches but I never threw a spitball. It wasn't allowed when I joined Washington. Only about four or five pitchers were allowed to use the spitball at that time because they did it before the ruling came into effect.

When I was young, the ball was a lot different than now. It wasn't wound so tight. Often times you could take the ball and put it in both hands and squeeze it and get wrinkles in it.

I went to the Senators spring training camp in Tampa, Florida, in 1928 and 1929 and I recall we did an awful lot of running. They'd bring out a giant, soft medicine ball that was six feet in diameter. You'd get in a circle and you'd pass it to each other, and because it weighed so much that ball got you in shape pretty fast. After that we had to run on the horse track on the fairgrounds, which was about a mile and a quarter long. Run, run, run.

I remember one thing that was funny when we were in spring training at the University of Tampa. That was where we were staying in 1928.

A group of the players were going to go out hunting at night and they asked Al Schacht to go along. I don't think Al Schacht was a very smart guy anyway to begin with. After it got dark they drove him out to the country. When they all arrived at their destination they sent Schacht out alone to corner something they called a snipe. They promised him that they would circle around and told him, "We'll come back after you."

Well, he got lost and wandered near a house. The owner came out and started cursing him and the guy pulled out a shotgun.

Poor Al never showed up until about noon the next day. But you know, he didn't get any snipes! I was there at camp when he showed up and we were laughing so hard. I can't remember who was behind it. It could have been Walter Johnson. It was his type of joke. He wouldn't do anything to really hurt anybody, but he liked to fool around. [*For more Senators information see the postscript.*]

I would have been a big leaguer for some time, but I got seriously hurt and I couldn't play anymore. You see, Washington had farmed me out to the Milwaukee Brewers in the American Association later in 1929 and I threw my arm out. But they continued using me as a relief pitcher. If I had been playing today they would have put me on sick leave for a month or so. I guess I was tied in with the wrong manager at the time.

That reminds me of a funny thing that happened to me that year.

There was a fellow on the Milwaukee team by the name of Charlie Robertson who had pitched a perfect game in the major leagues years earlier. One day he and I were in the centerfield in the bullpen and the manager decided he needed a right-handed relief pitcher. I had been pitching every other day and because the manager didn't like me, he kept me working without rest.

Well, Charlie didn't want to pitch and neither did I, so when the call came we both started walking in toward the mound and Charlie said, "Let's get into a fight so maybe the umpire will throw the both of us out. Then neither one of us will have to pitch." So we started rolling around in the outfield and the umpire came out and threw us out of the game.

Life After the Game

After I left baseball I used my BA degree and went into banking in Boston. That's where I stayed until I retired. Today I enjoy watching baseball, but at 93 I'm still very busy. I'm still playing golf and I have belonged to the same local golf club here since 1957. I still get mail all the time and I've got several baseballs here right now that were sent to me for signing.

On May 19, 1998, I was invited to a game in New York by the Yankees, because they were celebrating the government issuing a Babe Ruth postage stamp. It is also the fiftieth anniversary year of Babe Ruth's passing.

The Yankees picked me up in Connecticut in a great big white limousine that holds 10 people and we traveled all over the city of New York before the game. I was invited to sit on the bench and I met some of the coaches and the players.

The guy I liked the most was David Cone. I'll always watch the Yankees on TV if he is pitching, because there isn't a better guy in the world. He'll stand up for what he thinks and he'll stand up for the ballplayers if they have a problem. You can't get any better than he is.

It all was quite an experience, because later they asked me to throw out the first pitch at the game. I hadn't been on the mound in Yankee Stadium since 1927: over 70 years. It is hard to explain how I felt at that moment [*see photograph next page*].

During Hopkins' brief stay the Senators finished in third place in 1927 and fourth place in 1928.

Besides Walter Johnson, Hopkins played alongside several other Hall of Famers including manager Bucky Harris, Joe Cronin, Sam

Paul Hopkins being celebrated at Yankee Stadium in 1998. Courtesy of Paul Hopkins.

Rice, Goose Goslin, Stan Coveleski and Tris Speaker. Speaker was in his first and only year with the Senators in 1927.

One of Hopkins' coaches, Nick Altrock, is considered to be one of the most colorful individuals in the history of the game. Altrock spent 19 seasons as a pitcher and another 41 years in coaching, but it was his constant clowning that made him famous. Whether he was juggling balls on the mound, mimicking umpires from the coaches' box, or being mocked in newspaper cartoons for his excessive drinking, Altrock was constantly in the public eye.

Once, working as a coach in the late 1920s, Altrock realized that he was being heckled by a large, bald man who kept asking why he wasn't playing ball anymore. The quick-witted Altrock turned to him and responded, "For the same reason, you poor bozo, that you don't part your hair anymore."

Several Senators' veterans had a reputation for going to ridiculous lengths to play tricks on an unsuspecting rookie in spring training camp. During Hopkins' first year with the club — 1927 — the backup catcher, Bennie Tate, coach Jack Onslow, and Tris Speaker concocted an elaborate scheme. They conspired with a couple who lived near their training site in Tampa, Florida, to play a trick on an unsuspecting rookie.

Tate took the rookie, who was never identified, to their co-conspirator's residence with the promise of a romantic encounter with a local girl named Mary. The staged meeting evolved into a dramatic entrance by an armed and jealous husband and Tate was seemingly shot dead on the front porch of the house. The rookie was later found cowering in nearby police station. To add insult to injury he was retrieved by the unharmed Tate and his laughing co-conspirators, Speaker and Onslow.[1]

The day after Hopkins gave up Ruth's fifty-ninth home run, another Senator, Tom Zachary surrendered the famous sixtieth. Despite an illustrious 19-year major league career, his death in 1969 was noted in a New York Times *obituary headline that read as follows: "Tom Zachary, Pitcher, is dead: Served Ruth's 60th Home Run."*

Charlie Robertson, Hopkins' pugnacious bullpen friend, became the first major league pitcher to hurl a perfect game on the road. On April 30, 1922, making only his third major league start, Robertson led the Chicago White Sox to a victory at Nevin Field in Detroit. The next perfect game did not occur for another 34 years when Don Larson shut down the Brooklyn Dodgers in the 1956 World Series.

Bob Cremins
Born February 15, 1906

Despite all the stories he could tell about his 39 years in New York politics, Robert Anthony "Lefty" Cremins still enjoys nothing better than talking about his glorious years in baseball and boxing.

At the time of these interviews Cremins was the second oldest surviving member of the Boston Red Sox. He broke into the big leagues in 1927 in the most unorthodox way possible: he simply asked for a job.

When Boston released Cremins from his contract, he left major league baseball with no record of wins or losses and an ERA of 5.06. He spent the next 50 years of his life involved in politics and boxing. In the early 1940s he was the founder of the Pelham, New York, Boys Club, and 40 years later was elected to the Westchester (County, New York) Sports Hall of Fame.

At the age of 37 years and 7 months he entered the navy and was the skipper on an 85 foot speedboat in the Philippines during World War II.

Cremins was quick witted and extremely entertaining during the interviews that he gave. In his thick New York accent he enjoyed mixing a little bragging with a lot of self-deprecating humor. Even when he tried to stress a serious point, his wry Irish smile was almost audible.

He still resides in Pelham, New York, not far from where he was born and raised 92 years ago.

My father came from Limerick, Ireland, when he was a teenager and he became a great oarsman for the New York Athletic Club. In fact, there were five boys and two girls in the family and we were all athletes. My sister, Sheila, beat up a guy one time.

I was born just outside the city [*New York*] and I had a love for sports all my life. You'd have to say that I was involved in the two most popular sports in America during the 1920s: boxing and baseball. I fought in the New York Golden Gloves and I got third place in the middleweight division, and I'm proud to say that I'm still the same weight as I was then.

I was lucky because I learned how to box from one of the best referees in New York City, Arthur Donovan, and I learned how to pitch from the great Hall of Fame pitcher, "Iron Man" Joe McGinnity.

When I was in high school I used to pay a guy a quarter a week to catch for me in my backyard. Every morning I used to throw rocks at his window to wake him up so we could play. Then one day I hit him in the groin with a fastball and he raised his fee to 50 cents. All that practice helped because when I was a senior I pitched a no-hitter for the high school team.

Like I said, I was lucky because one of the great pitchers at the turn of the century, Iron Man Joe McGinnity, was a friend of my brother. Imagine that! Joe McGinnity taught me how to pitch. He lived in New York at the time, because he was working for our dentist in the city. He used to come up and visit us and he taught me all the different kinds of pitches. That was the beginning of a wonderful friendship.

After high school I was working for my father in his dressmaking supply business. He'd keep us busy, because he serviced all the dressmakers in New York City. At that time I used to go to the New York Athletic Club and box every day or play baseball on the Pelham Fire Department team.

Our parish priest knew the Boston Red Sox manager, Bill Carrigan, and in 1927 he told me to go see him and ask for a job. So, I took the train to Yankee Stadium where the Red Sox were playing that week, but I lost my nerve and I came home. When I confessed my fear to my brother he said, "You go back tomorrow. Don't come home until you get the tryout, or I'll beat you up!"

The next day I went back down and I met the manager Carrigan as he was going into the stadium.

I asked him for a tryout and he said, "No way."

And I said, "Look, my parish priest sent me down here to talk to you. You know him. He said you would give me a tryout."

He finally gave in and said, "Do you have your uniform? Go put it on."

Since I had my baseball uniform from the fire department team in Pelham I was ready to go.

I pitched batting practice that day and I must have impressed them because after batting practice they said that they would sign me up after they got back to Boston.

I was so excited, but I didn't drink to celebrate that night. In fact, I have never smoked and I only took five cups of coffee in my whole life.

I went to Boston and they signed me up right off the bus and I pitched batting practice every day.

Then one day we were playing the Yankees and we were behind 13–1. Carrigan asked for a volunteer to go in and pitch and I said, "I do."

He said, "Warm up because I'm going to put you in." I had been pitching batting practice that day so I went down to the bullpen and tried to get myself warmed up again.

I went in at the eighth inning and who comes up but Babe Ruth. Our catcher signaled for a fastball and my first pitch was low.

The catcher came out and said, "Damn it, Cremins, I signaled for a fast ball!"

I said, "I'm throwing it as hard as I can."

I don't remember what I threw next, but I know I was just trying to reach the plate. The second pitch Ruth grounded out to first base.

Then Gehrig came up. He hit a bullet to center field and it went between the hands of the outfielder and they gave Gehrig a two-base hit, but it was really an error.

I finally retired the side and the next day a sportswriter wrote, "The one thing you can say about Cremins is that he is the only one to get the Yankees out."

My teammates called me "Crooked Arm" because I was a left-hander, but it was not a friendly environment in the clubhouse. The veterans treated me like garbage and I was ostracized because I was trying for a job they were holding down.

Red Ruffing was one of our main pitchers and when he was young, he had the toes on his one foot cut off by a mining machine. He was very outspoken and he didn't let anyone push him around. He was so big, no one would try.

They let my contract go after the 1927 season, so I wound up opening a boxing club and teaching boxing. Eventually I got into politics in Pelham and Westchester County and on the side I designed boxing rings and was a cartoonist for the *Philadelphia Evening Bulletin*.

One time I drew the same cartoon character with my left and right hands at the same time and they printed it. I guess you can say I love to stay busy.

Baseball Today

You know, Mark McGwire is on the ball. He is working very hard to do what he does. Babe did it naturally.

When I was pitching no one ever told me what Ruth's weakness was at the plate. But I know his weakness had nothing to do with baseball. His weakness was women. He didn't know when to stop. But then Ruth hit from the left side and it's well known that all left-handers are crazy. How do I know that? I'm left-handed myself. We'd have to be crazy or we couldn't live with all of you right-handers!

Cremins' 1927 Red Sox finished dead last in the American League and repeated there in 1928, 1929, and 1930. The 1927 team mustered only 28 home runs, while Babe Ruth alone hit more than twice that number. Although they showed very little style on the field their 1927 roster was filled with players who would make good fictional characters for a novelist.

The 250-pound backup catcher, James "Shanty" Hogan, continually drove his managers crazy with his monstrous appetite for food and beer. After the Sox dropped him in 1928, Hogan was picked up by John McGraw and the Giants. McGraw tried to tame this particular obsession for fattening food by screening the restaurant receipts. McGraw's plan failed as Hogan bribed the waiters to post only fruits and vegetables on the bill.[1] Despite his culinary addiction, Hogan survived 13 years as a major leaguer.

Bob Cremins at his New York gym in 1930. Courtesy of the Baseball Hall of Fame Library, Cooperstown, N.Y.

William Jennings Bryan Harriss, better known as "Slim," stood 6 feet 6 inches and weighed in at a skinny 180 pounds. As the Red Sox staff ace in 1927 he compiled a record of 14–21 with an ERA of 4.18. He managed to strike out only 77 batters in 217 innings. The Texas country boy turned pitcher led the American League in losses in two of his nine major league seasons and managed a winning record only once.

Hal "Whitey" Wiltse was another hapless starter who was so befuddled by his bad luck that he resorted to dying his blond locks red. He finished the 1927 season with a 10–18 record and an ERA of 5.10.

When asked to comment on his team, their manager, Bill Carrigan, used the phrase, "fool[s] for punishment." He grimly added, "There's a period when you think you may get somewhere. But then the inevitable collapse comes."[29] Carrigan lost his job at the end of that season.

Although manager Carrigan had little luck with the Red Sox of that period, he did steer them to victories in the 1915 and 1916 World Series. Carrigan is best known for being Babe Ruth's first skipper when he joined the Red Sox staff as a pitcher in 1914.

For more information on the Red Sox of the 1920s see the Carl Sumner and Bill Rogell interviews.

FRANK STEWART
Born September 8, 1906

Frank Stewart is modest about his accomplishments. He grew up in the Midwest, played a little semipro ball, and then went straight into the major leagues at the age of 20.

"I still get people wanting autographs and pictures and I feel embarrassed in giving them," he says. Despite only one season in the big leagues, Stewart did achieve every American boy's dream: he did play professional and semiprofessional baseball for over seven years.

Stewart's pitching career ended in the winter of 1933 when his arm was injured in a basketball game in Minneapolis.

At the time of these interviews Stewart was the second oldest surviving member of the Chicago White Sox. He left major league baseball with a record of no wins and one loss and an ERA of 9.00.

Although he admits that he does not remember all the dates and names relating to his major league experience, his voice is as strong and clear as a man 30 years younger. Today he lives in an idyllic setting on the banks of the St. Croix River in a small northern Wisconsin town.

After I graduated from high school in Minneapolis I bounced around this area playing ball anywhere I could. After graduation in 1924 I met some friends and they wanted me to come to Wisconsin to play for a semipro team. They needed a pitcher so I volunteered to go.

In 1925 a scout came by and watched me pitch and wanted to know if I'd like to play with another Wisconsin semipro team in Richmond. So I played there for a while.

In 1927 I was playing ball in Chicago with a semipro club out of Hammond, Indiana, and somebody suggested that I go and work out with the White Sox, because they might need a batting practice pitcher. So I went down and told them what I wanted and they said, "Sure, we'd love to have you work out with us." I threw batting practice that day and nothing more was said. I felt there was no interest in me. At that time my best pitch was a sinkerball, but people told me that I had a good control and speed.

Well, after that I returned to the Indiana team and a few days later I pitched a one-hit game against the House of David. That's when the White Sox asked me to work out with them so they could look at me again.

I was very excited, but I thought that a lot of the scouts were just talking and they didn't mean anything. I was thinking that they were not interested in me because of my age [*20 years old*] and I'm not their caliber.

When I got to the stadium I saw Ted Lyons, Bib Falk, Ted Blankenship. All them were just sitting on the bench and I was amazed.

I said "My God, I can't believe it." I suited up and threw batting practice.

The veterans ignored me and they acted as though I was just taking up space. But I made the best out of the situation. No one really caused me any trouble except Bill Barrett, the starting right fielder. He gave me a bad time, because when he came to bat for batting practice, I threw the ball right at him, by accident. He almost came after me with a baseball bat.

The White Sox manager, Ray Schalk, yelled to him, "Now you leave that kid alone," and he backed off immediately. That was my first day.

I got to know Barrett after that and I liked him. He was real popular and quite a comedian. We had a lot of fun back then. We teased and played tricks on one another all the time. After that the Sox signed me and I was an official big league ballplayer.

I had to quit my full time job that I had in Indiana at the American-Bausch Magnito Company, but I didn't care. It was really a dream for me.

I had some friends from Wisconsin who were living on the south side of Chicago, so I moved into one of their spare rooms for a short time. Later I got my own apartment near them on the south side. I didn't get out on the town much, but I did have a friend, a girl friend, that I was seeing, so we did get out a little. I sure did enjoy living in Chicago in the 1920s. I enjoyed myself all the time.

One day I came out to the park and they told me I was going to be the starting pitcher that afternoon. I guess I was pretty shaky after that. So I started my first game against the St. Louis Browns and I pitched five innings and I was beaten 3–1.

The first time I walked out onto the mound in that game my feelings were very strange. I didn't know what to think of it. Our manager kept telling me, "Just get the ball over the plate."

In that game I faced the great George Sisler, who was the Browns' first baseman.

My first time at bat that day I hit one into the upper deck in Comiskey Park in left field and it was foul by six or eight inches. It was my one and only time at bat in the big leagues.

Our manager, Ray Schalk, didn't say much, but he was really nice to me and I admired him. I sat near him during the games and listened to his comments. I guess I learned a lot from him, which I was able to use later. I remember sitting next to him in the dugout, autographing cards and programs that were passed down to us.

I was with the White Sox from July through the end of the season.

When the White Sox re-
leased me they farmed
me out to Springfield, Illinois, and I had a good
year there [*Stewart re-
corded a 16–11 season in
Springfield*].

Later the Sox traded
me to the Cleveland In-
dians and they sent me
to Terre Haute, Indiana,
in the Three-I League.
[*Stewart went on to pitch
with two other Three-I
clubs: Peoria, Illinois, and
Ft. Wayne, Indiana.*]

I never did make it
back into the big leagues,
but after I left the Indians' organization after
1932 I got a job pitching
for a semipro team in
Beulah, North Dakota,
for a couple of years. I
did pretty well there, especially against the team
from Bismarck [*North

Frank Stewart in 1927. Courtesy of the Frank Stewart family collection.

Dakota*]. They were mad, because they were a larger town and they did-
n't want to be beaten by such a small-town team. To get even with us they
hired Satchel Paige to come in and they finally beat me.

Life After the Game

I met my wife, Mildred, after my big league days were over. I was playing for a semipro team in Somerset, Wisconsin, and she was from that
town. We were married for 65 years until she passed away in 1993.

My son, Frank Jr., played with the Milwaukee Braves' minor league
organization in the 1950s as a pitcher. He played ball in Denver, then went
out on the West Coast, but he got out of it to become a stockbroker.

Today I watch a lot of golf and baseball on TV and I enjoy talking about my baseball days. I saved a lot of souvenirs during my years in baseball, but the place I worked at, a nightclub, burned down and they were lost in the fire: baseballs and bats and a uniform.

I lost everything I had. Souvenirs that I was gathering and all the papers that recorded my career [*including a baseball signed by Lou Gehrig and a bat signed by Babe Ruth*].

All that time and now I don't have any proof that I was with the White Sox. Just memories.

When Stewart met Satchel Paige in North Dakota, Paige was embroiled in a salary dispute with the owner of the Pittsburgh Crawfords, a Negro league team.

In the fall of 1934 the newly married Paige broke his two year contract with the Crawfords and accepted a $250 per month salary to finish the season with the all-white Bismarck team.

Although Paige was a hero on the field, he faced problems in town. He and his wife were consigned to live in a refurbished box car on a side track in the railroad yard. For more information on Paige see the Ted Radcliffe interview, Chapter 2. For more information on the White Sox see the Karl Swanson interview below.

KARL SWANSON
Born December 17, 1900

Taking the advice of his wife to have patience, Karl Edward Swanson toiled for seven years in the minor leagues before achieving his major league ambitions.

Swanson played second base for the Chicago White Sox in 1928 and 1929. Although his major league batting average was a meager .138, he batted an impressive .302 with a fielding percentage of .972 during 13 years in the minor leagues.

He is living in Florida and still participates in local celebrity golf tournaments. At the time of these interviews he was believed to be the oldest surviving major league ballplayer. Subsequently, he is also the oldest former member of the White Sox organization.

His advice on staying young and healthy is "Don't get mad, play a little golf. Be kind and have patience. I eat peanuts and raisins every day."

I was born and raised in North Henderson, Illinois, a farm town of about 300 people near Galesburg. The 300 included a few pigs and chickens. We lived in town, but my father was a farmer and he worked for other people in the area.

At the end of the threshing season the farmers and the field workers formed two groups and they played ball against each other. I was just getting into baseball at that time and that was the start of my career. I was their pinch runner when I was just 13 years old.

We didn't have a local team, just a bunch of kids that eventually formed a pickup team. We weren't more than 15 or 16 years old. A fellow from our town would call another small town nearby and say, "Let's have a ball game Saturday."

There were about three or four towns like that. We'd get to those towns, like Rio or Alexis, Illinois, anyway we could, just to play a game. Occasionally we'd go on bicycles or in a Drury wagon if anyone had a horse we could use.

My parents approved of me playing baseball, because our town was so small there were no jobs around. So when I had a chance to make a little money I took it. We didn't have a lot of money to spend on baseball equipment when I was young so we had to use our imagination.

I had a grandfather that was a blacksmith and an uncle who worked for him. You see, our town was full of horse-drawn wagons and they would fix wagons and farm equipment and shoe horses. In the spring we would go out in the woods and find a chunk of wood, sometimes hedgewood, and we'd trim one out. They taught me how to sand down this piece of wood and that's how I made a baseball bat.

My grandmother had a pair of shoes called granny shoes, I guess. They weren't very thick soled, and one time I remember she tore one out. So I got the Sears Roebuck catalogue and I looked in there and they had some spikes for sale for 10 cents. So I said, "By golly, I'll get a pair of spikes and attach them to her shoes." I was about 12 years old then and that's the first pair of spikes I ever had.

I had to get some screws to put the plates on the soles of the shoes, but the granny shoes didn't have very thick soles. The screws were just a little too long so I had to put in a lot of cardboard and stuff in those shoes so I wouldn't cut my feet. But it worked out OK.

Well, I didn't have any baseball heroes I guess, because we didn't get the paper but once a week. I didn't have the chance to read much about the stars. I guess I liked Ty Cobb and of course I played against him when I went up, but there were very few things you could read about the stars of those days when you lived out in the country like me.

I graduated from our two-year high school when I was 16 years old and then I went to Augustana College in Rock Island, Illinois.

After one year I went to work at the Rock Island Arsenal for about six months, but it wasn't just a job. The Rock Island Arsenal had a ball team in the Factory League, along with Deere and Company and Case Company and they would give you a decent job if you would play or manage for them. So I went to work and played semipro baseball on weekends for $15 a day, with expenses if I would go out of town. Those teams were called a "clubhouse team" back then. I made a living by working five days a week and I could play Saturday and Sunday.

Later I got a job at the Meadowbrook Candy Company in Rock Island, and that's where I met my wife, Lucielle Stein. I met her at the candy factory, because she was working in the office and I was in production.

No, she was not a baseball fan and she didn't know a ball from a strike, but she was my guiding light.

When I would get frustrated she would always say, "Have patience, have patience." That was my driving force.

In 1921 I went to play for the Moline, Illinois, team that was in the famous Three-I League and they had me go on the road with them as a utility man. I was so young.

In 1922 I went to a team in Cedar Rapids, Iowa, and I stayed there until 1925. Then I went back to Moline in 1926 and 1927 where I played for Connie Mack's son, Earl. I remember in one game there I got three triples.

On the fourth of July the two teams that were playing would have contests for the fans. They would have the teams compete in things like throwing the fastest to second base or running the bases and things like that. Well, once I circled the bases in 14 seconds, which I learned later was off the record by one-fifth of a second. The man who set the record was Evar Swanson [*no relation*] who played for the White Sox after I left.

In 1928 I went to the Rock Island team. The White Sox scouts noticed me there in Rock Island. And no! I didn't know they were watching me.

That league was considered one of the very best. They got all of the raw rookies and young college kids to play because it was $125 per month to start and $175 the second year. That's how these kids got their experience and the scouts were there all the time.

It was then that Lucielle and I decided to get married. We were married at 11 o'clock in the morning on Saturday, June 16, 1928. After the ceremony we went straight out to the ballpark at 1 o'clock so I could play. That's when I heard the news.

Our manager came up to me and said, "Say Karl, the Sox have taken an option out on you. They want to buy you."

"But don't worry," he said, "they won't need you until near the end of the season."

When I told my bride she was shocked.

She said, "What? Well what are you going to do?"

"Well," I said, "I'll be here till the end of the season."

That made it better, but then they came out ten days later and said, "You're going to Chicago right away."

There I was, newly married and oh, everything all going to pieces. I mean, that was no life to leave her alone there.

Well that upset everything. I told her, "We'll have our honeymoon when the season is through." I said, "Baseball is a funny game."

When I found out I was going to the big leagues, well, I had mixed feelings. Actually it was a nice wedding present. I was older, but I played consistently good ball for everyone. I was the captain of about half of the teams I played on and I was considered to be smart.

You see I was born in 1900: that's my real birth date, December 17, 1900. But the official baseball records show I was born in 1903.

I'll tell you that story. I'm on the train going to Chicago, because I have to report the next morning at the White Sox ballpark for the first day. I was a nobody and I didn't know anyone. The newspaper in Rock Island, the *Rock Island Argus*, had said that, "the 24-year-old Karl Swanson was sold to the White Sox." Everyone thought I was 24, but I was really four years older.

So I thought, "Gosh, what am I going to do if they ask my age?"

The next day the general manager of the club was sitting across the desk from me. He asked, "Now, you're 24 years old, right?"

So the wheels in my head are going, I said, "Oh, yeah, that's right."

"What year were you born?" he asked.

"1903!" I made that up and I got through with that interview and that's what was put in the record books.

The reason I told everyone 1903 is that in the old days there were so many ballplayers that lied about their age. There weren't any big league ball clubs that wanted a rookie who was over 25 or 27 years old unless it was an emergency fill-in. A lot of the ballplayers would lie up to two to three to four years.

There was a joke floating around at that time because so many fellas were lying about their ages. One day we were getting beaten by a pitcher and one of our bench jockeys read that this guy was 24 years old. He started to laugh and shouted to him, "You can't get that ugly in 24 years!" Baseball was that way.

Charles Comiskey was the owner of the White Sox and, of course, I heard he had a reputation for being very stingy and cheap.

I don't know anything about that, but I know the ballplayers wanted to get as much as they could, too. Times were tough for everyone and even the minor leagues had to sell ballplayers to exist, because they didn't draw people except on weekends.

I had so many nicknames. Everyone had at least one back then. They called me "Swanee," "P-nuts," and some others. I wasn't big: not over 145 pounds, so "peanuts" was a good name for a smaller guy.

The veterans treated me well, but I must say now that Ted Lyons was the greatest fellow that I ever met in baseball. He was considerate and kind.

One of the pitchers we had in Chicago was Red Faber, a spitballer. He was one of the few holdovers that were allowed to throw a spitball after it was banned years earlier.

One of my first games for them Faber was pitching and I was playing second base. There was a ground ball hit down to me and I handled it. Nothing to it. And next time there was a line drive hit to me and I looked at the ball after I caught it and saw a big nick on it, so I told the umpire. Well, he took it and threw it out.

Well now, when I got to the bench Red Faber came over to me, mad as can be and said, "Say, listen young guy, *I'll* tell the umpire when the ball should be thrown out."

I found out later that he purposely ripped the ball so he could curve better. I got my "bringing uppance" real quick. That was my first week in baseball: I learned a lot, quick. [*Faber was actually the last pitcher in the American League who was allowed to legally throw a spitball.*]

Willie Kamm and "Bib" Falk and John Mostil influenced me also. They were my friends — especially Mostil. Johnny Mostil would go out in the off-season to smaller towns to join some other players and give a talk and work with kids.

My first time at bat in the majors was in Chicago. I hit a good pitch and got a hit.

The next game we went to the Yankees and here I am playing second base against Babe Ruth and Lou Gehrig. The first time up Ruth hit a ball into the right field stands and I said to myself, "Well, I'm initiated." So the third time I came to bat in that game I hit a good one into right field where Ruth was playing and he reached over the fence and caught the ball.

That was my chance to get my first home run. I said to myself, "I'll get even with you." So the next time he got up he hit a line drive right at me and it was way over my head. But I jumped as high as I could and caught the ball.

I shook the ball at him and said, "Now we're even."

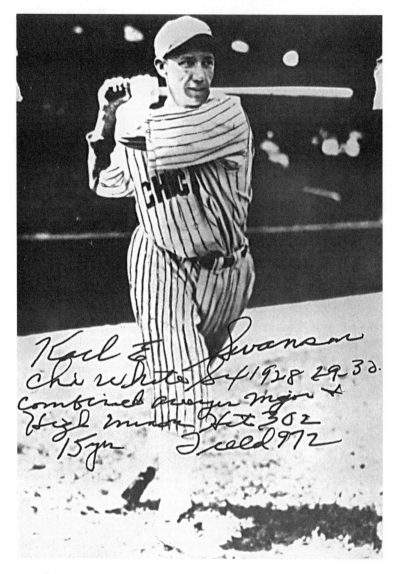

Karl Swanson in 1928. Courtesy of the Karl Swanson family collection.

By the way, I played in the City Series between the Cubs and the Sox. That was in 1928. If neither team were in the World Series, they would have a City Series. They did that in St. Louis also.

The Cubs had Hack Wilson, Gabby Hartnett, and so many great ballplayers, so we would fill the stands every day during the City Series.

The toughest pitcher I ever faced was Lefty Grove of the Philadelphia

A's because he had such a fast ball that was hard to hit. You really had to bear down to get a base hit. I didn't have any success against him.

When I first started with the White Sox, I was paid $3,000 per year. They said if you hit .300 and steal so many bases we'll give you a $500 bonus. That was my salary.

When I played we never had batting helmets of course. There's a story about a player today who gets ready to pinch hit. He puts on a shin guard, batting gloves, and a helmet, and when he gets to the plate he realizes he forgot his bat.

I came close to getting beaned several times and I was spiked a few times when I was in the minors. Some of those boys would do anything to look good and get into the big leagues. They'd throw those spikes right at you. I got a few scars on my arms and legs that still show up white when I get tanned. It was all part of the game back then and usually our pitcher would go after that guy the next time he came up.

Chicago was an exciting place back in the 1920s. I didn't get out much and so when we got through playing we just went back to our hotel. I'm sure some of the other boys got out, but I didn't.

In 1930 the Sox sent me down to a team in Toledo [*the Mud Hens*] that was managed by Casey Stengel. I liked him real well, because he ran such a loose ball club. We'd always have a meeting before the game started. He'd spend a few minutes asking the pitchers, "How are you going to pitch to this fella or that fella?" Then five minutes going over the lineup and positions. He'd finally say, "Don't worry about these guys. You know how to play. We don't need to talk about that."

Then the next ten minutes would be for stories. He'd have gag stories galore. He was a real storyteller and you know he had quite a way with the English language. And so when we finally went out on the field we'd be "loose as a goose." That is why he had very good success as a manager because he wasn't a prodder.

I always batted second so Casey used to approach the first and second hitters in the lineup and say, "I want you guys to get on base. I don't care how. Get a base hit, a walk, get hit. That is your job. The three, four and five man will drive you in."

I never saw him get angry with us and he'd always side with the ballplayers: always standing up for his boys in a dispute with the umpire. I played for him for just one year, but he sure was partial to the older ballplayers who he used to play with. He'd always try to get them to work.

He had a second baseman named Johnny Butler who he played with in Brooklyn and he kept him on the team as a favor: sort of a "right-hand man." So I was the regular second baseman, but eventually I was traded and Butler was still there. Butler was worn out, but Stengel took care of him.

I like to tell the story about Stengel when he was playing outfield for the Dodgers, years earlier. One game he chased a ball to the back part of the outfield and saw a crippled bird and he felt sorry for it, so he put the bird in his cap. No one saw him do it. So on the next play he made a nice running catch and when he came in toward the dugout the fans gave him a big hand. So he stopped and tipped his hat and the bird flew away. Everyone was so surprised. That's a true story.

Life After the Game

I stayed in baseball during most of the Depression playing with Buffalo, Des Moines in the Class A League, and Dayton and Cedar Rapids.

You know, I had a real deep love for the game of baseball, but during that time the clubs weren't making a dime.

In 1935 they tried to cut my salary, so I said, "This is enough. I'm through."

Lucielle died in 1992 after 64 years of us being married.

Today I watch baseball and golf on TV and I still root for the White Sox. I'd like to see them win, but most of the people down here like the Braves because we can get them on TV.

I play golf all the time and when my friend Ned Garver [*former American League pitching star*] comes down here to Florida during the winter we always play together.

I'm a church-going man, but I use words I shouldn't when I miss a shot. I have my own car that I still drive and I have my own golf cart for all the tournaments I'm in. I just enjoy getting around and talking to people.

I've been back to my little town of North Henderson several times, but that was quite a few years ago. You know people were so generous back there. Everyone would have big gardens with potatoes and carrots and they would share everything with their neighbors. My daughter wants me to go back and see the town. That would bring back a lot of good memories.

Although Swanson's White Sox years of 1928 and 1929 were spent with a team that finished fifth and seventh respectively, the roster included some interesting characters.

Ray Schalk, Red Faber, and Ted Lyons ended up in the Hall of Fame.

The backup catcher, Moe Berg, was baseball's first James Bond. Besides being a capable ballplayer, Berg was a Princeton grad (magna cum laude), fluent in ten languages, and quite erudite. Shortly after his career ended in 1939 he became a spy for American intelligence (OSS) in Europe and Latin America during the Second World War.[10] In 1946 Berg was awarded the Presidential Medal of Freedom, which is currently displayed at Cooperstown.

Texan Bib Falk, enjoyed a 12-year major league career, but was best known as the 1920 rookie who replaced Shoeless Joe Jackson in left field after the Black Sox scandal hearings.

Swanson's manager, Lena Blackburn, made very few headlines during his years as helmsman for the White Sox. But after retirement he started a successful business selling mud to the American League. He discovered that the fine-grained creek mud on his farm in New Jersey was the perfect cure for removing the gloss off new baseballs.

Joining Swanson on the team in 1928 was Ed Walsh, Jr., son of one of the greatest dead-ball era pitchers, Edward "Big Ed" Walsh, Sr. Junior was unable to replicate the success of his father and lasted only four years in the major leagues. His finest career performance came in the Pacific Coast League in 1933 when he stopped the 61-game hitting streak of a minor league outfielder named Joe DiMaggio.

Also joining the Sox that year was first baseman Art "the Great" Shires. The self-promoting Shires attempted to balance dual careers in boxing and baseball and failed in both.
He billed himself as "The Knockout Kid of Baseball."[4] After several professional bouts at Boston Garden he promoted a fight in 1929 between himself and the toughest football player of that era, George Trafton of the Chicago Bears. The 6 feet 2 inch, 235 pound Trafton easily disposed of the 190 pound Shires with a knockout.[2,3]
He became a lightning rod for gossip and insulting humor because of his monumental ego. One unsubstantiated story told of him attending a Broadway play in 1929. Suddenly he heard the audience break into cheers and applause just before the start of the third act. Sensing that the attention was directed at him he waved his hat, stood in the aisle, and bowed to the crowd. After taking his last bow, the embarrassed Shires looked up to find himself standing next to Douglas Fairbanks and Mary Pickford.[1]
For more information on the White Sox see the Frank Stewart interview.

Casey Stengel started his managerial career for a Boston Braves' affiliate in Worcester, Massachusetts, in 1925. He was hired by the Toledo Mud Hens, a Class AA, American Association team in 1926, and continued with them through 1931 when the Mud Hens fell into receivership. Stengel went on to coaching with the Brooklyn Dodgers, then the Yankees, and eventually became one of the most celebrated managers in baseball history.

Note: Stengel is the only man to wear the uniform of all four of the New York baseball franchises — Dodgers, Giants, Yankees, and Mets.

For more Stengel lore see the Ray Hayworth and Harold Rosenthal interviews.

MEL HARDER
Born October 15, 1909

In the 98-year history of the Cleveland baseball club there have only been seven players to have their numbers retired. Melvin Leroy "Chief" Harder was the fourth. In 1928, at the age of 18 years, Harder put on an Indians' uniform and did not take it off until the 1960s.

Harder stayed with this club his entire pitching career of 20 years. He then continued with the Indians' organization for another 16 years as a pitching coach and briefly as an interim manager in 1961. He finished his baseball career in 1969 as a pitching coach for the Kansas City Royals.

In 1990 Mel Harder's number 18 was retired into the golden shrine of Cleveland Indian history: on a plaque in right field, directly above the mezzanine level.

His resume is Hall of Fame material:

- *Retired with a 223–186 record and an ERA of 3.80.*
- *Holds the record for the most shutout innings in All-Star game history with 13.*
- *Baseball historian and writer Brent P. Kelley ranks him fortieth in his book 100 Greatest Pitchers.*
- *He was the pitching coach of the 1954 Indians, which is considered to be one of the greatest pitching staffs in history.*
- *He ranks second to Bob Feller for the most victories by a Cleveland hurler.*

Sadly, Harder is the only member of the top four all-time Indians pitchers who is not in the Hall of Fame.

Next to his longtime roommate Willis Hudlin, Harder was the third oldest surviving member of the Cleveland Indians ball club at the time of these interviews. At the age of 89 Harder was the youngest man interviewed for this project. He projected the quick response and sharp voice of a man 30 years younger. He currently resides just outside of Cleveland and his advice on aging is to keep busy and exercise.

I was born in Beemer, Nebraska, and when I was two years old my mother and dad moved to Omaha.

We were lucky back then, because my father immediately got a job with the Omaha Electric Power Company as a machinist. So I grew up in Omaha and when I was about six or seven I started to play ball with my friends. I started to play right out of kindergarten. We played anywhere we could and any time we could. For instance, when we would get out of school at noon we'd all run home, rush through our lunch, and get together so we could play baseball before we were called back to our classes. When I was in grade school we'd play every Saturday and on lunch hours. That's the beginning of my long career of playing baseball.

Lord no, back then we didn't have professional equipment and not everybody owned a glove. We used a baseball that we made ourselves by wrapping it tightly with yarn and tape.

I didn't start to pitch until I was about ten years old and that was when I joined a church league. It was there that I started throwing my sinker ball which I used throughout my career. On that team I played center field and pitched half the time.

Later, I pitched in high school and in 1926 we won the state championship. I won seven games that season and that's what really started me off.

I didn't have any boyhood idols until the World Series of 1921 and 1922. I liked Casey Stengel who played for the Giants and also Roger Peckinpaugh, the shortstop for the Yankees. Roger later became my manager in Cleveland. But I didn't have anyone I admired a lot. I just loved baseball. Period.

In 1926 the top class A amateur club in an Omaha league approached me to come and try out for the team. So I went down there to the Carter Lake team and I showed them what I could do. They asked me if I could pitch for them and I said, "Yes." I lost my first game, but then I won six straight. I was 16 years old and I was on a professional ballclub.

At first my mother and dad didn't want me to do it. They wanted me to go to work. To just get a regular job and help pay the family bills. They wanted the kids to stay home and work. They didn't know too much about professional ball, but they finally gave in because they knew I was nuts about baseball.

After the 1926 season the Omaha ball club in the Western League called me and wanted to know if I'd go to spring training with them in 1927. That year with Omaha I won four games and lost seven.

Back then the major league baseball clubs did not have a minor league farm system. They had scouts out there to search the class D leagues and the smaller leagues. That's how I was discovered, because while I was pitching in Omaha in September 1927 a scout from the Indians was following us for a week or two and saw me pitch a couple of times. They decided they wanted to buy me and that's when they started to dicker with Omaha.

When I heard they were making an offer I was absolutely excited. I was happy and so were my mother and dad. Omaha wanted $10,000 for me and Cleveland offered $5,000. So eventually they decided to split it and Cleveland bought me for $6,750.

Back then they had what was called the reserve clause and ball clubs actually owned their players. They could own you until you died if they wanted. You couldn't just quit a team and sign with someone else. The only way you could sign with another club is if they released you. If you didn't like the pay you were getting or the team you were on you could either quit the game entirely or wait for them to make a decision. You were stuck. But I was lucky because I enjoyed playing for Cleveland and they always wanted to keep me.

The one person who influenced me the most in my career was Roger Peckinpaugh, my first manager. I was only 18 when I started with the Indians and he did such a wonderful job of working with me. He treated me practically like a son and he helped me a lot. There weren't any pitching coaches in those years and you had to pick up everything by yourself.

Each team had coaches, but they were designated for different jobs you know. Like first base, third base, and the bullpen. But none of them spent time to instruct us. Before the game they spent their time organizing batting practice and things like that. Peckinpaugh helped me with the basics but nobody taught me how to throw a curveball or a slider. You had to absorb information by watching other pitchers, because the veterans didn't pay any attention to us. You had to do everything on your own.

I didn't have a curve when I first joined Cleveland, but we had a pitcher named George Uhle and I used to watch him on every pitch. He was very successful against the Yankees. He used to throw a curve and then change up on his curve and then throw a fastball. He threw four or five different pitches all the time, so I learned a lot from that.

I also learned a lot from Ted Lyons [*Chicago White Sox pitcher*] who threw a knuckleball, change-up, and curve. I really admired the way he pitched.

Of course my best pitch then was the fast sinkerball. I had pretty good luck with it and it helped me get by when I first started pitching.

My first two years in Cleveland I did mainly relief work so I didn't get a chance to face Ruth and Gehrig until 1930 when I became a regular pitcher on the Cleveland staff.

My first game I pitched in 1928 was in St. Louis. The second or third time I pitched was against Ty Cobb and Tris Speaker when they were with the Philadelphia A's. We were getting beat 7–4 so Peckinpaugh decided to put me in relief in the

Mel Harder in 1930. Courtesy of the Mel Harder collection.

fourth inning of that game. It just happened to be that in that inning I had to pitch against Cobb and Speaker. I faced both of them immediately. I got Speaker out with a fly ball to center field and then I pitched to Ty Cobb. I got two balls on him and then I came in with a ball that was pretty fat and over the plate. He hit a home run. That home run was the last of his career and the only one he got all year.

Cobb played ball like it was everything: life or death. He played to win and he played hard, but nobody seemed to like him. He was tough on the field and he had to win. I didn't have an opinion on all the stories about him one way or the other, because I didn't see him off the field.

When I first started I made $275 a month and in 1929 they gave me a $25 raise. When I became a regular pitcher they bumped me up to $450 a month, which was OK for a rookie. The club bought our uniforms and the only thing we had to buy was our own sweat shirts, our shoes, and jock straps.

My parents were behind me 100 percent. They came to Cleveland a couple of times by train and stayed for a while to watch me pitch. They enjoyed every bit of it. Back then we could get them good seats because the crowds weren't as big as they are today.

Soon after I started, people started calling me "Chief," because I was with the Indians and evidently I had a big nose as far as some people were concerned.

After the first season I had with Cleveland in 1928 I went back to Omaha and I tried to work at some small jobs, but I only worked that first winter. In fact, I didn't do anything to stay in shape during the off-season.

How did I meet my wife? She and I actually went to high school together, but we didn't know each other. When I came home in 1929 after the season, my best friend in Omaha and I double dated. So his girlfriend introduced me to my wife that night.

We dated from 1929 through 1931 and in 1932 we got married. She died in 1986. We were going to celebrate our fifty-fourth anniversary at the time she died.

One of my closest friends back then was Willis Hudlin, our best pitcher. I met him when I came in to spring training camp down in New Orleans in 1928. He had already been with the Indians for a couple of years. When I first came up I roomed with Eddie Montague, who was a short-stop. We roomed together for the full year until he was let go. Eddie's son is now a major league umpire.

Then Willis and I started rooming together. We were roommates for eight or ten years and we enjoyed each other's company very much. We had a good time together, but we behaved ourselves anyway. We still talk to each other occasionally.

Everyone asks about Babe Ruth. The first time I faced Babe Ruth it was a thrill and it was something I never forgot about. I was nervous, but after I got to pitching one or two balls I settled down and I did my best. In those years I didn't get scared about anybody. I just went out and did my job on the mound. The stars didn't bother me. And if I got beaten, well, I just took it.

I would say that very few asked for autographs in those years. You could leave a ballpark and you wouldn't see anybody waiting around out-side. About the only ones who people went after were Babe Ruth and Lou Gehrig. When they came to Cleveland it was the kids who wanted to bother them for autographs. The kids just loved Ruth so much.

I never saw Walter Johnson pitch but he came over to manage our club for about three years. His last year of pitching was in 1927 and he came over to us in about 1933. [*Johnson relieved Peckinpaugh as manager in the fifty-second game of that season and stayed on through the first half of 1935.*]

He was a very fine man and he treated me great and he worked me often. That was the beginning of my best years. I thought he was a pretty good manager, but he had some trouble with a couple of players on the club, and by the time the season was over I guess the club decided to let him go. I guess it was a difference of opinion or something.

During Johnson's time they didn't have those speed guns to tell you how fast he threw. Nobody really knew how fast Walter Johnson could really throw, but many people I've talked to think Johnson was the fastest. Of course, I worked with Bob Feller in later years, but I really can't say who was faster. [*For more information on the Cleveland Indians in the 1920's see the Willis Hudlin interview.*]

I tied for the lead in the American League in shutouts in 1934 with six I think, but that wasn't the highlight of my career. I was 20–12 that year, though, and I had quite a few complete games.

I was in four All-Star games: 1934 in the Polo Grounds [*New York*], 1935 in Cleveland, 1936 in Boston, 1937 in Washington. I pitched a total of 13 innings and didn't allow a run. I think that's still an All-Star game record for shutout innings.

In 1935 the All-Star game was played in Cleveland and Babe Ruth was invited to the game with his wife [*Claire*]. That was his last year as a player. They sat in the first aisle near home plate and after the game several of us went over and talked to him. He thoroughly surprised us. He wanted to know if we could go to dinner with him that evening. So Earl Averill and Joe Vosnick and I and our wives went out with them.

He was a lot of fun and he loved to tell stories while he was smoking those cigars. He didn't have as big of an appetite as he once had, though. He was a real good dresser and when we were with all the ladies he was a very good gentleman. When you were alone with him he was a different type of man. He was just a regular guy.

I didn't have any physical problems until 1936. I was having a real good year, because I had 13 victories and only 3 defeats going into the All-Star game break. After I pitched in the All-Star game in Boston we went to Philadelphia and I pitched after my normal three days' rest.

In the fourth inning I felt this twinge and when I went into the dugout I told our trainer, Lefty Weisman, that something happened to my shoulder. He massaged it and put some hot stuff on it and I went out and pitched the rest of the game. I won that game 6–4.

My shoulder got worse that night and the next day I could hardly lift it. They gave me ten days' rest and my next start I lasted only three innings.

So I rested it again for two weeks and the same thing happened. It was the same all through the second half of the season. The rest of the year I only won two more games and lost twelve. I had a lousy second half.

In the fall the club sent me up to Mayo Clinic, but in those years they didn't know how to treat rotator cuff or other shoulder injuries. Well, they couldn't find anything wrong with me. I had to tell *them* what was wrong. So, of all things, at the end of my three-day exam they finally told me that I should have my four wisdom teeth taken out. That's all they knew!

During that winter I rested my arm. Naturally I was concerned that I might be finished with baseball if it didn't heal. This was all I wanted to do.

When I got to spring training in 1937 I felt pretty good, but I didn't have the nerve to throw hard or cut one loose. So one day I decided to take a chance and I reached back and threw it as hard as I could. Nothing bad happened. My arm felt pretty good and I came back pretty well. That year I won 15 games and lost 12.

I believe I played against the greatest ballplayers in history. Lou Gehrig was actually the toughest hitter I ever had to pitch against, even more than Ruth. I had pretty good luck with Joe DiMaggio and fair luck with Ted Williams, but if you ask me who was the best I would have to say that there will only be one Babe Ruth. DiMaggio and Williams were great ballplayers, but I had my luck against them. Although Gehrig was tougher for me, I personally think Babe Ruth was the greatest player that baseball ever had, and that's my opinion.

Like I said, I had good luck with DiMaggio. He comes right out and says that I was one of the toughest pitchers against him. I think the [batting] average he had against me over the years was about .180 something.

Throughout my career I never studied the opposing hitters before a game. I can tell you that right now. At first, all I did was talk to the older pitchers on the club and my manager and find out what they thought of each batter. Since the older ones had pitched against them already and over the course of time they'd know what to look for. No charts or graphs; I kept everything in my head.

The Greatest Pitching Staff

The 1954 Indians' pitching staff was probably the greatest staff in the history of the game. We had Bob Lemon, Mike Garcia, Early Wynn, and Bob Feller in the rotation.

I was just finishing up my career as a pitcher in 1947 and in July of that year Bill Veeck, the president and Lou Boudreau, the manager of the club, called me in to tell me that they wanted me to be the pitching coach the next year. Since there would be a spot in the rotation open they were considering Bob Lemon to fill that spot. They wanted me to work with Bob Lemon and Steve Gromek out in the bullpen and get them ready.

You see, Bob was originally a third basemen and then he became an outfielder with a little relief pitching on the side. In 1947 the Indians decided to give him a chance as a starting pitcher. Lemon was a great pitcher, with natural stuff and a real lively fastball — sinker. He ended up winning 11 games the rest of the season in 1947. He worked on his control and also his curveball and he came up with a slider. He just started off well as a starting pitcher and in 1948 he won 20 games. Anybody that can win 20 games 7 times in 9 years, well, they're really something. He had a lot of talent.

The first time I saw Bob Feller was in 1936 when he first came up to Cleveland. But he was 16 when he pitched an exhibition game against the Cardinals. He pitched three innings and I think he struck out nine. Everyone that hit against him was amazed with what he was throwing. But, he didn't have good control at that time so the hitters had to stay loose.

I worked with him on his curveball and holding men on first base and not to be kicking so high on his delivery. We cut that down some. But as he went along he gained his control just from the new delivery, without the real high kick. He still kept a pretty good kick but that was with nobody on base. But as soon as a man got on first base he cut it down. He was very easy to work with because he was anxious to learn and to try anything. He knew what he had to do himself. As a boy his dad had him work out behind the barn on their farm in Iowa. His dad wanted him to just keep throwing: throwing to his dad or throwing against the barn.

Mike Garcia started pitching in 1948 for Cleveland and he had a terrific fastball. As the seasons went by, he improved his curveball and his control. That's what made him a good pitcher.

We got Early Wynn from Washington in 1949 and he was strictly a fastball and knuckleball pitcher. Those are the pitches he relied on. When he joined Cleveland, Early and I talked quite a bit. I told him he had to learn how to throw a curveball and a change-up and forget about the knuckleball. So he ended up being quite a pitcher because he improved so quickly.

Our fifth pitcher was Art Houtteman and we picked him up from Detroit in midseason 1953.

They all wanted to learn what they had to do and they wanted to be better. So they were anxious to improve. They were easy to work with and talk to. So, by 1954 we had one of the greatest pitching staffs ever assembled.

It wasn't luck that the team accumulated such a great staff. The Indians just found pitchers who could improve themselves. For instance, Lemon: he had the talent and he developed himself. Another thing about that pitching staff was Houtteman. You know after we got him from Detroit he became our fifth pitcher, because he couldn't get much work with the other four guys on the staff. But he was perfect for us when we had a doubleheader.

Despite the fact that he was our fifth pitcher, he won 15 games in 1954. Today he'd be the leading pitcher on most pitching staffs.

In 1954 Lemon and Wynn won 23 each, Garcia won 19, and Feller was close to the end of his career and he still won 13.

The bullpen wasn't busy. We had Don Mossi and Ray Narleski out there and they did a great job for us. They were both rookies that year and one was left-handed and one was a right-hander. Al Lopez, the manager, could choose depending on the situation.

Hal Newhauser was the third reliever and he was used around the seventh or eighth inning. But then, we didn't need him too much that year. They brought Hal over from Detroit before the start of the 1954 season. He just died a couple of weeks ago.

You can look up their records. I think they had over 70 complete games. Nowadays the whole league doesn't get that much. I'd have to say that they put together the greatest staff ever.

One Last Job

I was ready to retire in 1969, but the manager of the Kansas City club, Joe Gordon, called me up and wanted to know if I'd be his pitching coach. I had to think it over, but finally I decided to take the job. So I finished the season with him and retired. I was just getting tired and I didn't give it the effort that I used to have.

Baseball Today

I still watch the Indians all the time on TV, but it is an entirely different game today. Everything today is money. Back then we were lucky to get a check. Today rookies can make $700,000 per year and high school kids can sign for $1 million.

If you want to be a professional pitcher you have to have a loose arm and be relaxed. You have to have good control and have something on every pitch: a good curve and change of pace. Then you're on your way to the big leagues.

I have to say that I think it's ridiculous to pull pitchers after a pitch count. I hear announcers talking about pitch counts, but back in my day we never did that. Starting pitchers were gunning for complete games every time. I pitched on three days' rest so I had to concentrate. When you're pitching good ball they should leave you in there.

Today's players are stronger, but that doesn't make them good ballplayers. You can weigh 210 pounds, lift 500 but that doesn't make you a good ballplayer. If they use the treadmill for 30 minutes they think they've gotten a lot of running in. I don't think pitchers run enough today, even though they do exercise. We had to run in the outfield before every game. We did a lot of running and we didn't let up.

Note: Babe Ruth's second wife, Claire, was a cousin of future Hall of Famer Johnny Mize.

BEN SANKEY
Born September 2, 1907

If it wasn't for a change in the admission requirements at Auburn University, Benjamin Turner Sankey would have been filling teeth instead of fielding grounders for the Pittsburgh Pirates.

Although his major league career only lasted from 1929 to 1931, Sankey managed to stay in organized baseball until 1941 and earn himself a charter membership in the International League Baseball Hall of Fame. Joining him in the initial induction ceremonies in 1947 were Dixie Walker and Billy Southworth.

During his big league career with the Pittsburgh Pirates, he played shortstop, second and third base, and left the majors with a batting average of .213. Sankey was eager to tell his story and yet took a casual and indifferent attitude toward his achievements.

"It was just an everyday job," he said. "I was just trying to make a living like everyone else."

After working for Bethlehem Steel Company, Sankey retired to his home in rural Georgia. At the time of these interviews he was the only surviving member of the Pittsburgh Pirates from the 1920s.

His advice on living a long, healthy life is to not abuse your body.

I was born in a little coal mining town in Alabama, called Nauvoo. Since we didn't have football in high school and I wasn't big enough for basketball, baseball was the only thing I wanted to do. I'm sure I had a deep love for the game.

We were north of Birmingham and the towns weren't very far apart there in north Alabama. Quite a few towns in that area had teams so we always had someone to play.

Because nobody owned a car back in those days we would just load up on the back end of a truck and go to the next town and play a game. It was dirty and dusty and hot, but we enjoyed it anyway. Besides, I was only 15 when I started playing for Nauvoo. I played a couple of years for them, but we did not get paid for it.

We'd have everybody on the club — farmers, coal miners, business people — anyone who could make the team. Quite an assortment of people. The merchants in Nauvoo used to buy the uniforms for us and each merchant would put their name on the back of a uniform as an advertisement. So each player on our team would carry a different advertisement as we traveled around our area.

I graduated from high school at 16 and I enrolled at Auburn University. Of course, I played baseball there in the old Southeastern Conference. When I went to Auburn as a freshman I was fooling around in the infield during hitting practice and the first thing I know they ask me to play short and the regular shortstop moved to third. I played a little at third and second but I always liked shortstop better. Playing that position just came naturally because nobody really taught me how to play shortstop.

I was going to continue on to dental college, but in the middle of my sophomore year in 1928 they changed the admission requirements so I didn't want to go back.

My father was a doctor and he didn't like the idea me playing professional baseball. It wasn't that he disapproved, he just wanted me to be a dentist.

Rather than spend two more years in college, I had a chance to play ball and so at the age of 20 I left to play infield for Selma in the Class B League for two years. That turned out to be a good decision, because when the Depression hit in 1929 I had a steady job and I was doing something I loved.

If there were any major league scouts around then we didn't know about it. But one day the owner of the Selma club, Mr. Block, told me that Pittsburgh had bought my contract and that was it.

I don't know if I had any reaction. I'm just going along, doing the best I could. I knew it was an opportunity, but it wasn't any great thrill or anything.

I never dreamed about going to the major leagues. I wasn't overwhelmed by the idea that I was a professional ballplayer. But I knew that you had to do your best or you'd lose the job. I'm sort of phlegmatic.

I went up to Pittsburgh alone on the train, not knowing who to see or what to do. I had lived in small towns all my life. I didn't see anybody waiting for me at the train station so I just had to do the best I could, I reckon. So I registered in the Schenley Hotel because it was near the ball park.

The next morning I went up and met Barney Dreyfus [*the Pirates owner*] and he says, "Where are you staying?" And I told him I was in the Schenley and he said, "Well, you can't afford that! You better get out." He was right.

I remember the first time I walked on the field with a Pittsburgh Pirates uniform, but it wasn't auspicious. I started with Pittsburgh in the fall of 1929, and I sat on the bench most of my first season and got acquainted with the players. It was great in the major leagues, because you had good transportation and played on good fields. Not at all like the minors.

When I was there, Barney Dreyfus and his son [*Sammy*] used to travel with the team quite a few times on road trips, because he was learning the business. Barney treated us as well as any other owner but, like everyone else at that time, they were having a tough time. They had to be cheap, and they had to pinch pennies, because in those days it was pretty tough. They didn't have any money and didn't have very many people coming to the games. The fans that did come were pretty supportive but not overly enthusiastic, because when I was there we didn't win any pennants. That makes a lot of difference.

During that time I lived in the same apartment building with Lloyd Waner and Dick Bartell and Larry French and their wives. Our building was out near Schenley field so we were close to the stadium.

When I started for the Pirates I was paid $600 per month. The better players made $10,000–$15,000 per year. In those days the height of everyone's ambition was to get five figures.

I played with some of the greatest ballplayers in the National League at that time.

On our team Pie Traynor was the oldest. He came up from Birmingham in the Southern League and he was a big, raw-boned kind of a guy. He was not very graceful, but he could get the job done. It was fun to watch those hard hitters that pulled the ball down the line and see Pie play them. He'd catch the ball at third base with either hand or knock it down. He was also a good hitter, but not a home run hitter.

Ben Sankey in Pittsburgh Pirates uniform, 1929. Courtesy of the Pittsburgh Pirates.

Everybody's a home run hitter now. There were only a few people that could hit the ball out of the park in those days, I guess because the ball was not as lively as it is now.

I played golf with Paul Waner and George Grantham and two or three pitchers occasionally during the summer. Paul played a good game of golf left-handed.

The Waners were just good old country boys and they were real nice. Lloyd was the smaller one. He was not robust at all, but he was a wonderful player. He could roam the outfield as good as anybody. He was fairly fast and had a wonderful eye and if they hit it in his area, he would come up with it. Paul was a little bigger and a little stronger than Lloyd. When he was hitting he was as good as anybody. He ended up with a lifetime average of about .340.

I played against Rogers Hornsby and I played for him. He managed the Baltimore team I was on one year and I knew Rogers well. He was all business and had a great eye, and he was so good that many times if he didn't swing the umpire would call it a ball.

He was a terrific line-drive hitter and, although he was a good-size man, he had unusually small hands.

I remember I used to talk to him about the time he was the manager of the Cardinals and he put [Grover Cleveland] Alexander in as a relief pitcher in the 1926 World Series and he struck out [Tony] Lazzeri.

I liked Rogers. He was all right. He wasn't strict, but there wasn't a lot of foolishness attached to him. As a manager he was strictly business.

I didn't play against Grover Cleveland Alexander in the National League, but I hit against him in 1933 when he played for the House of David [barnstorming professional team] after his major league career was over. I was playing with Portland in the Western League and I remember he wasn't as fast as he used to be, but he still had that great control. Well, he struck me out with that screwball.

I even met Honus Wagner once. I didn't spend a lot of time with him, but I was introduced to him and shook his hand. When I reported in 1929 he was there. I'll never forget it. He had big hands and he was real stocky and bowlegged. But he was treated very respectfully.

I remember in 1930 I played against Dizzy Dean in his first game that he ever pitched. I still have a little write-up and box score that was in the St. Louis paper about that game. I got one for three and should have had another hit against him, but he knocked down a line drive and threw me out. He had a great fastball and he reared way back and let it go.

This 1922 *Baseball Weekly* cartoon depicts the average Pirate fan, enveloped by despair, in the years following Honus Wagner's retirement.

Life After the Game

I left baseball in 1941 after playing with Baltimore in the International League and I went to work for a steel company during the war.

My wife died several years ago and we were married for over 50 years. We met in college while she was studying general courses, but we didn't get married until I had been playing professional ball for a couple of years.

Well, yeah, I see the Pirates play on TV, but I don't know anybody. I can't think of one person that is still there that I knew. But they still send me schedules and rosters every year in the mail. I kind of keep up with them.

I was lucky. I played all through the Depression and we were just thankful for something to do. I finished up my career with a batting average of about .280 after 13 years of professional ball. I didn't make any money but I had a lot of fun.

During Sankey's stay with the Pirates they managed to finish in second place in 1929 and fifth place in both 1930 and 1931. The Pirates had four future Hall of Famers on their roster: Burleigh Grimes, the Waner brothers, and Pie Traynor. Although Sankey did not go into detail about Grimes, his antics on and off the field were legendary.

No one symbolized the tough, hard-fisted ballplayer of that era better than Burleigh Grimes. As a pitcher he was known as a head-hunting spitballer. On or off the field he would fight with anyone who angered him: reporters, fans, other players, and even his own teammates. During the decade of the 1920s Grimes compiled more wins than any other pitcher in the major leagues for that period.

According to baseball legend, Paul Waner gave up alcohol in the spring of 1931 and his batting average fell like a gallon of bourbon off a night stand. When manager Jewel Ens convinced him to loosen up and have a little fun Waner went back to drinking and ended the year hitting .322.[46]

During Sankey's first season as a Pirate one of their greatest pitchers was just finishing up his career. Lee Meadows won 87 games in 4.5 full seasons for Pittsburgh. His other claim to fame was that he was one of the first pitchers to wear glasses, thus earning the nickname "Specs." During one game in the late 1920s Meadows started arguing with an umpire over a bad call. At the pinnacle of his anger Meadows stormed off the mound and held the glasses in his outstretched hand.
"Here," he shouted, "You need these more than I do."[46]

CARL SUMNER
Born September 28, 1908

Every American boy's dream of playing major league baseball came true at the age of 19 for Carl Ringdahl Sumner. Directly out of high school in 1928, Sumner found himself in left field wearing the uniform of the Boston Red Sox. At the time of this interview he was the third oldest surviving member of that ball club. He finished his only major league season with a batting average of .276.
Sadly, Carl Sumner died in February 1999, only a few months after his last interview for this book.

I grew up in Arlington, in the Boston suburbs, so I was always a Red Sox fan.

And since Babe Ruth was with them when I was young I admired him the most.

I always wanted to play baseball growing up but, in fact, I was known more for football than baseball in high school. I was the quarterback.

I guess I was pretty good ballplayer in high school, though, because in 1928 the scouts came after me.

I graduated one day and went directly down to Cambridge, Maryland, a Class D league team, to play ball.

Well, Mr. Quinn, the owner of the Red Sox, brought me in for a try-out after about a month or two at Cambridge because the league broke up. He contacted me and offered to pay my way back to Boston to talk to them.

Yes, I was surprised. I was very happy and stunned. I didn't think I'd get up there that fast. I was batting about .444 when the league broke up and my batting average must have attracted them.

I was fortunate that my father approved that I wanted to play professional baseball, even though I was just a kid. He was a steam fitter and he knew this was a chance for me to make a decent living.

I joined the Red Sox in July 1928 and played in 16 games and pinch-hit some.

When I started, all the veterans were good to me and of course I thought they were all big guys. I was in awe of them and I was a little nervous. They all treated me fine, but I never had any close friends while I was there. I was just a kid out of high school. I started at $350 per month.

As I recall I don't believe I played the first day I put on a Red Sox uniform. Shortly after I got there we traveled to Chicago and Detroit and Cleveland on a road trip. I got to play finally when we got to Detroit and I know I got a base hit my first time at bat. I got a single. In fact one day I got three hits.

One of the first games I played in was in Boston against the Yankees. Babe Ruth was at bat and I was playing left field. At that time Fenway Park had a hill in the left field that had an embankment that went up to the fence. They eventually took it out. Naturally, Babe Ruth hit one to me and it went over my head. I ran back to catch it and I didn't realize the bottom of the bank was that close. So when I took a step it was the wrong step and I just fell. Down I went. I'll never forget that one. [*For more information on the 1928 Red Sox see the Bill Rogell and Bob Cremins interviews.*]

One thing that set me back on my pins happened the next year, in 1929. I spent the winter living with my parents and working to save up money to go to spring training. You didn't get paid for that. They'd pay for my room and board, but you had to have your own spending money. So I saved up and finally I had to leave for spring training. I got on the train that night and I put my money under my pillow and left it there. I think the trip took a couple of days or so.

When we got to camp in Bradenton, Florida, I got off the train and I forgot the wallet. Well, when I got back to the train, naturally, it was gone. The team manager, Bill Carrigan, gave me some spending money, about $20, against my future pay. That really set me back. I worked all winter for that money and it disappeared.

After spring training I was shipped out to a lower league to get some experience. I went to Pittsfield for a couple of months and then to Ohio and then to South Carolina.

Baseball Today

Baseball today is quite a bit different. It was more of a game then, now it's strictly business because of the money that is handed out.

It was a better game back then. They don't do the bunting as much as they used to.

Life After the Game

In 1931 I decided I didn't want to be chasing around the smaller leagues for four to five months and then try to get work the rest of the time. So I just gave up professional baseball and went to work steadily. I was able to work during the Depression and play semipro baseball and football on weekends, and twilight ball. Money was real scarce. That's for sure.

I was married in 1933 and we'll be celebrating our sixty-fifth anniversary soon.

Carl Sumner in 1998. Courtesy of the Sumner family collection.

I like to watch baseball today, well, because there isn't much else I can do. I watch the Red Sox and I'm still a Red Sox fan.

I felt good playing for that team. It was a little scary, but I enjoyed it. You know the fans in Boston always cheered a home boy and of course I was just a kid from that area. I got quite a little applause.

I'm getting letters now. Still a dozen or two a month for signing autographs. It makes me feel good. That's right. I'm surprised they're still looking me up for my signature.

I still think about baseball. I'll never lose that. I was lucky. At least I was up for a cup of coffee.

BILL WERBER
Born June 20, 1908

William Murray Werber did not officially start his 11-year major league career until 1930, but his inclusion in this book is essential. Werber is believed to be the last surviving ballplayer who wore a Yankees uniform in the 1920s. He became a Yankee in June 1927, but officially did not participate in a game until three years later.

Werber primarily played third base for the Yankees, Red Sox, A's, Red, and Giants and concluded his career in 1942 with a lifetime batting average of .271.

His career highlights include playing for the 1940 world champion Cincinnati Reds, in which he led the team in batting (.370) during the seven-game series. In addition he was Duke University's first All-American basketball player in 1929.

He is the author of numerous articles and three books and currently resides in North Carolina.

The story of how I spent one and a half months with the 1927 Yankees begins when I was a freshman at Duke University.

In the spring of 1927 we had a coach at Duke by the name of George Whitted [*National League 1913–22*]. George was a very smart ballplayer and a damned good baseball coach. When that freshman team was assembled he thought he had some good professional prospects, including me. He built a sliding pit and spent a great deal of time coaching me.

You see, I played semipro ball for the Georgetown Knickerbockers while I was a junior and senior in high school, so I learned a great deal at an early age.

He got the word out that he had a lot of good ballplayers on that freshman team, including some big league prospects. In fact, a number of us were eventually signed.

When springtime came the scouts came to see this freshman team at Duke that everyone was talking about. The group included scouts from the Pirates and the Cleveland Indians. Frank Rickey [*Branch Rickey's brother*] from the Cardinals was there, along with Larry Doyle [*National League 1907–20*] from the Detroit Tigers, and Paul Krichell from the Yankees.

They all wanted to take me to dinner to the Washington Duke Hotel and talk to me. I was happy to listen to all of them. Finally, Krichell made a proposition which was entertained by me and my father. They asked me to sign a contract with the Yankees, which obligated me to them after my four years at Duke. Although I would not become the property of the Yankees until 1930 Krichell thought it would be impressive for me to come up and work out and travel with the Yankees immediately.

He wanted me to listen to the manager, Miller Huggins, and get an education about baseball. Naturally, I accepted the invitation.

When I finished the semester in June of that year I went home to Berwyn, Maryland, for a few days. Then about June 10 I went alone by train to meet the team in New York City. I was told to go to the Colonial Hotel on 53rd Street and ask for Charley O'Leary.

O'Leary was not only a Yankees coach, he was Miller Huggins' right-hand man. O'Leary was well known because he had played a long time with the Detroit Tigers [*1904-1912*].

As it turned out, he was the only one on the team that paid any attention to me. He was very solicitous and concerned for my comforts. The next day we went out to Yankee Stadium and I was outfitted for a uniform.

When I first walked into that locker room not one of the players made any overtures to come over to say, "Hi, I'm so and so. What's your name?" These guys were pretty aloof and they had no use for a college kid.

I'd go out to shortstop and they'd run me out of there. I'd go out to the outfield and they'd run me out of there. I'd get up to the batting cage and they'd say, "Get the hell out of there, kid." I bet I didn't swing at three balls the entire time I was there.

I had a good arm and I could run faster than most any of them and I wanted to show it off. I wasn't used to that kind of environment and I wasn't impressed. I guess I was young and I had different objectives and views on life than they did. These guys were rough.

I made it my habit to get as close to Miller Huggins as possible without becoming intrusive. He was a very intelligent man and very well spoken. He was a contrast to his players because he was diminutive [*5 feet 6 inches, 140 pounds*] and didn't swear a lot. He was physically out of place.

The difference between him and Babe Ruth in size and personal values was enormous. So it was inevitable that they would clash.

The first impression that I had about Babe Ruth was a game in Chicago. I had made an entire road trip with them West sometime in late June, I believe [*Cleveland, St. Louis, and Chicago*].

In Chicago they have two rows of benches in the dugout. One in front and another in the rear. So I was up against the wall on the bench behind Huggins and O'Leary. The Yankees had finished their batting practice and then finished their infield practice, but Ruth hadn't shown up yet. Well Huggins had already turned in Ruth's name to the umpires for the batting order, so he was getting kind of upset.

Since I was sitting behind them I heard Huggins tell Charley O'Leary, "I'm going to fine him. Dammit I'm going to fine him $5,000 if it's the last thing I do." He knew Babe was not taking care of himself physically and this was against the mores of Mr. Huggins. There was a bit of unhappiness between them.

Then Ruth finally shows up and he played the entire game. He hit two home runs and two doubles and drove in seven runs. After the game I followed Huggins and O'Leary across the field to get to the visitors' dressing room.

All the way over there Huggins was shaking his head saying, "What am I going to do, Charlie? What am I going to do?"

He said, "I can't fine him $5,000 now. The newspapers would eat me alive."

So at that moment I gained my first impression of Ruth, which subsequently never changed.

But I liked Ruth. He was a very friendly fellow. He'd like you immediately if you introduced yourself to him on the street. He'd buy you a drink. He'd buy you two drinks. He'd buy you dinner. You couldn't spend any money when you were with him. He'd do anything for you and then the next day he wouldn't know who you were.

Although he was an amoral man, he was not mean or vindictive. He would stand outside of Yankee Stadium and kids would walk all over his white shoes and his cream-colored pants and he'd just stand there and sign autographs. He'd go to hospitals in the morning to see kids and he never took a newspaper man or photographer with him. He didn't seek notoriety.

The 1927 Yankees had an air of confidence that only a championship team could have. You look at the roster and see the names of Lazzeri, Combs, Meusel, Ruth, and Gehrig. All those guys were smart ballplayers and they knew they would go out and knock the hell out of anyone.

That 1927 team won 110 ball games and they were a tough ball club. But from my own experience the Yankee clubs under Joe McCarthy in the 1930s were damned good too. It's hard to compare teams because sometimes the opposition is not as good.

I was there from June through a part of July [1927] and finally it didn't seem like it was in my interest to be there anymore. I needed to be running, fielding, and hitting, and doing the things that make you a ballplayer. So I said the hell with it and I went to the Western North Carolina League to play semipro ball.

In 1930 I returned to the Yankees. I didn't have any trepidation about returning. My attitude was that whoever was playing shortstop would have to move.

That year I started to make a few good friends, including veteran Herb Pennock. After an early season ball game I was taking a shower and washing the suds off my body when I felt a stream of water in the middle of my back. It felt warmer than the water coming out of the shower so I turned around to see what it was. And there stood Ruth. He was using the middle of my back as a urinal!

Someone later asked me if I hit him, and I said no. That was his way of showing me that I was being accepted. As I said before, this was quite a bit different from the accepted behavior I was brought up with. But it wasn't uncommon there.

I liked and respected Lou Gehrig. He didn't drink and he didn't smoke and he didn't chase around with women. He was good to his mother. He would bring her down to spring training and put her up in the Don Caesar Hotel. None of the other ballplayers would do that for their mothers.

But looking at the other side of Gehrig, I have to say that he came to the park alone, he left alone, and he rarely signed autographs outside the stadium. He seemed to be closest to his roommate, Bill Dickey, but he was not real friendly with the other guys.

After I was accepted I would play bridge on all the train rides west. Ruth would say, "Get out the cards," and he and Gehrig would play bridge against Bill Dickey and myself. And we'd always beat them. That was because Ruth would sit there and sip whiskey with water for two hours.

Before long he would laugh and start to feel a little good. Then he would give Gehrig some bad bids just to irritate him. When Gehrig would complain, Ruth would raise his middle finger and then give him a raspberry sound with his lips. Ruth would continue giving Gehrig these bad bids and finally Gehrig got fed up and he would throw the cards in the middle of the table and say, "This game is over. Add it up and we'll pay you what is due."

I've got one last story to tell regarding pranks. When I was with the Red Sox in the mid–1930s we had a great pitcher named Wesley Ferrell. He was a great competitor and if a manager went out to take the ball away from him he'd turn his back on him and walk away. He was combative. Ferrell was a tall, handsome fellow, and he had a brief adventure with the movies in Hollywood.

Since he was single he always rented a car during spring training so he could get around. He would park that car in front of the Sarasota Terrace Hotel and one day a ballplayer went around behind the hotel and got a handful of fish guts and crab leavings and rolled them up in a newspaper. He opened the back door of Ferrell's Chevrolet and stuck the garbage behind the seat.

I'm not going to say who did that. Who knows? It might have been me. Well it sat there all day long. You can imagine what the heat could do after 24 hours or so.

One of our outfielders, Roy Johnson, wanted to borrow the car for a date and he asked Wesley if could borrow it. So Wesley said sure and gave him the keys. Well, when Johnson went out and opened the door the stench likely knocked him down. But he wasn't going to cancel the date so he opened all the windows and picked up his date. We saw them driving by the hotel later. He had his head out one window and she had hers out the other.

The next day at the morning team meeting Wesley pulled a stool out of the locker and got up on it and proclaimed that if the no-good lousy bum who put the fish guts in the back of his car acknowledged it, he would get off the stool and "Whup him." As his anger

Bill Werber in 1939. Courtesy of Bill Werber family collection.

increased he yelled, "And if it was two guys who did it, I'll whup both of you." All the ballplayers were just encouraging him and yelling, "Give 'em hell Wesley, give 'em hell. You can do it, Wesley." That agitated him even more and he yelled, "If there is three of you, I'll whup all three."

I quit baseball after the 1942 season to sell insurance, but I'll never forget those days. I had a rough start but I sure had a good time.

Miller Huggins played second base in the major leagues from 1904 through 1916. Given the responsibility of managing the St. Louis Cardinals in 1913, Huggins found his true niche in the game. He managed the Yankees from 1918 through 1929 and was posthumously elected to the Hall of Fame for his leadership [and babysitting] skills. His many achievements include guiding the Yanks to their first World Series and forging the tradition of Yankee Pride.

BOB POSER
Born March 16, 1910

Imagine being a young boy during baseball's golden age and dreaming, like all boys do, of meeting and befriending your favorite players. This daydream came true for one young man in a rural Wisconsin town through an incredible series of experiences.

Bob Poser, now nearly 90 years old, was introduced to the author only one week before the final submission of this book. His short stories were compelling enough to include them in this project at the last minute. His experiences not only give us a personal glimpse of several Hall of Fame ballplayers, but also invite us to ask the question, "What responsibilities do players today have to their young, impressionable fans?"

John Falk "Bob" Poser was born in the central Wisconsin community of Columbus on March 16, 1910. As the son of a respected doctor, Poser always wanted to follow in his father's footsteps, but first he wanted to become a baseball player.

Before finishing his medical training as a surgeon in the 1930s, Poser had realized his life ambition by pitching for the White Sox (1932) and the Browns (1935). He finished his major league career with a record of 1–1.

When I was a kid I would write to every ballplayer I liked. And surprisingly, they would reply. Just the other day I was looking through the letters that I received in the 1920s and they included Eddie Collins, Al Simmons, and Gabby Hartnett.

For a couple of years I corresponded with Gabby Hartnett and he would not only write back to me, but he also signed baseballs and a catcher's mitt.

Well, one night, when I was about 14 [1924] I received a phone call and this fellow introduced himself as Gabby Hartnett. At first I thought it was my brother in Chicago playing a trick. Finally, I realized it was Gabby!

He asked, "Bob, would you like me to come out and visit you and your family?"

I said, "Are you kidding?" I couldn't believe it.

Sure enough, he came out the next evening on the night train from Chicago. He stayed with us from Thursday through Sunday and then he was scheduled to return to Chicago for an exhibition game. I was quite excited and I remember that I'd wake up and think, "What are we going to do the next day?"

I remember one day we went to a football game and then another day he batted fly balls to the kids in the neighborhood. But nobody could catch them of course. The whole town knew he was staying with us, and everyone was excited because we were all Cubs fans.

That year his arm was not good because of a sore shoulder. He had seen doctors in Chicago, but it didn't seem to help. So he asked my father for some advice. My father checked him out and said, "Gabby, you need your tonsils out!" And sure enough he had his tonsils out and his arm improved.

While he was staying with us he told us a very interesting story. He said that he had broken his elbow when he was 12 years old and

Bob Poser in 1935. Courtesy of Bob Poser, personal collection.

although the doctor set it he couldn't get it to straighten out all the way. So he told Gabby that he would have to carry a pail of sand around the house four times, every night. He did that for quite a while and his arm straightened out. But not all the way. If you saw Gabby in a swimming suit he'd be holding his arm at a little angle. It never healed completely.

In fact, he told us a lot of stories, but I can't remember all of them.

I stayed in contact with him from 1925 until his death in 1972.

When he was managing and catching for the Cubs in 1938 I was interning at St. Luke's Hospital in Chicago.

I would get an afternoon off every three or four days, so I would go out to Wrigley Field and pitch batting practice for him. They had a locker for me and I parked my car with the players. I guess I did well because that was the year the Cubs won the pennant [*he said jokingly*]. My feelings for him were so great when I was a kid. To me he was greater than Babe Ruth.

Later in life he had liver problems and his blood did not clot up. He took 18 bottles of blood before he died in Lutheran Hospital in 1972. I volunteered to give blood and I called several times to talk to his son. I've always considered him one of my best friends.

About the time I was 15 years old basketball and baseball were the most popular sports at the University of Wisconsin. Their physical education and baseball coach, Guy Lowman, needed help for their spring training schedule so he contacted Ray Schalk in Chicago to come out and coach for two weeks' salary.

At that time players weren't making enough money, so after the season they would go from town to town playing local teams, or take coaching jobs with colleges. Well, Ray Schalk took the job in Madison and that leads up to the story I want to tell you.

Our local baseball team in Columbus was having a difficult time with the team from Arlington. Arlington was a smaller town than ours, but they had a bunch of tough Norwegians and they always beat us badly.

So my older brother decided to ask Ernie Nevers, the great football and baseball star, to come up and play on the team for one game against Arlington. Then someone else contacted Ray Schalk.

Since Columbus was only 30 miles from Madison, Schalk agreed to come over too. Well, Columbus played Arlington at our high school field and of course Columbus beat them.

Since our house was on the corner, across the street from the high school, everyone on the team came over after the game. My mother was so tickled with baseball that she made pies and ice cream for our guests. I just stood there and looked at these guys. Here was Ernie Nevers, the best fullback in the world and he was in my living room. Ray Schalk took me out and taught me how to throw a knuckleball. He told me to put my fingernails on the ball and push out. He explained that this neutralizes the back spin on the ball. I was a forward kid back then and I believed I could do anything. I did things that I didn't know I could do.

So when I was 15 [1925] I asked my father to drive me to Milwaukee to the stadium where the Milwaukee Brewers of the American Association played. I went down there and tapped on the back door and introduced myself to the manager Jack Lelivelt [former American League outfielder 1909–14]. I told him that I wanted to be a ballplayer.

I guess he figured that he should help any kid who had guts enough to do that. He said, "Sure, put on a uniform." They needed a batting practice pitcher that day so that's what I did. I just went out there and pitched to professional ballplayers.

The Brewers were popular and they used to draw 10,000–15,000 fans, which was good for those times. I went up there for a weekend or two in

A 1921 advertisement for D&M Sporting Goods making use of headshots that imply the endorsement of the game's top stars.

1925 and 1926, but the experience was invaluable. That's what taught me baseball.

Some of the players were young, but most of them came down to the Brewers from the majors. A lot of them were just ending their careers. That team had Ivy Griffin [*Philadelphia A's, 1919–21*], George Young [*Cleveland Indians, 1913*], Charlie Bates [*A's 1927*], Oscar Melillo [*American*

League 1926–37], and Bubber Jonnard [*six-year major league veteran catcher*].

Since some of these players were older, they were afraid they might lose their jobs because of their age. So you had to be careful. When you are pitching batting practice you can't try to strike them out by throwing too hard. All of the players were nice to me, but it was all serious business and I had to get the ball in there.

My experiences with Ray Schalk and Gabby and the players on the Brewers inspired me, because they were the best. It was all just such a thrill.

> *Schalk spent the majority of his 18-year career (1912–29) as a catcher with the White Sox. He was inducted into the Hall of Fame in 1955.*

> *Charles Gabby Hartnett spent all but one year of his 20-year career with the Cubs. He retired with a lifetime batting average of .297 and is considered to be one of the best catchers in baseball history. Hartnett was inducted into Cooperstown in 1955.*

> *Ernie Nevers became a major league pitcher with the St. Louis Browns the year after Bob Poser met him in Wisconsin. Although he had promise of a great career, he lasted only two years in the big leagues. After 1928 he found his success on the gridiron, and became one of the greatest football players of that era. Nevers was inducted into the Football Hall of Fame with another former baseball player, Jim Thorpe, on September 7, 1963.*

2. The Negro Leagues

*"I got real hotheaded every time someone told me it was too
bad I couldn't play in the major leagues because of my color.
But there were some folks who wanted me to pitch against
the whites. One of them was Stran Niglin who ran the Chattanooga Lookouts in the white Southern Association. One
day he even came up to me and offered me five hundred
dollars to pitch against the Atlanta Crackers. I just had to
let him paint me white."*

Satchel Paige, recalling an incident in 1926[30]

NEGRO LEAGUE BASEBALL

On February 13, 1920, a group of successful black baseball team owners met at the YMCA in Kansas City to make history. Lost among the headlines about Babe Ruth and Judge Landis was the story of Andrew "Rube"
Foster and his dream to create a league for Negro ballplayers. When the
meeting adjourned the disparate group of owners, led by Foster, united to
form the Negro National League. Modeled after their white counterparts,
the owners created a governable, competitive league and elected Foster as
their president.

In an era when solutions were limited, Foster founded the first organized venue for the talent that was limited primarily to barnstorming
tours. This agreement, although rarely recognized, was one of the most
profound events in the history of baseball.

During his playing days at the turn of the century, Foster was a well-
respected pitcher for the Cuban X Giants and the Philadelphia Giants. At
the end of the 1902 season, John McGraw was rumored to have secretly

hired Foster to teach his 23-year-old pitcher, Christy Mathewson, the art of the screwball.[15] After mastering this pitch, Mathewson went on to enjoy three straight 30-game win seasons.

Sensing that his future success depended on his organizational skills, Foster went into promotion and ownership. He became an entrepreneur of such pioneering capabilities that by 1919 he was the king of Negro baseball in Chicago.

Although Foster's reign in the Negro National League ended sadly after six years, his brainchild endured until the Depression took its toll in 1932.

Using Foster's new league as an inspiration, several other associations were formed, including the Texas-Oklahoma-Louisiana League (1929–31), the Negro Southern League (1920–50s), the Eastern Colored League (1923–28), and the second Negro National League (1933–48). This period was the first opportunity for talented black players to earn a steady income while playing in an organized environment.

Foster imagined an outcome far beyond a stable league. He had envisioned a league of black ballplayers who were so talented that Judge Landis would have no other option than to allow an all-black expansion club into the majors.[25]

Foster's son, Earl, told a writer that his father's dream of recognition started to gain momentum in 1926. According to Earl, his father had a meeting with John McGraw and American League president, Ban Johnson, to organize a schedule of games against big league clubs in Chicago.[17] Foster had advanced the notion that the American Giants could play sanctioned games against any white major league club that was idled by an off day.

The idea had merit, because it represented windfall income to the ball club owners. But it was never implemented. Soon after he began work on the project Foster may have succumbed to the enormous workload he had created. He was committed to a mental institution and died there four years later at the age of 51. (Foster's connections to the white major leagues were numerous. He reportedly was engaged in a business partnership in 1911 with the son-in-law of Chicago White Sox owner, Charles Comiskey.)[8]

Negro League historian John B. Holway wrote that it would be an understatement to call Foster the "Father of Black Baseball." "He was," said Holway, "Christy Mathewson, John McGraw, Connie Mack, Al Spalding, and Kenesaw Mountain Landis — great pitcher, manager, owner, league organizer, czar — all rolled into one."

Foster was selfless in his pursuit of his dream, often putting in 16- to 18-hour days. He created teams, moved franchises, and at times supported the league with his own capital.

Soon after engineering the creation of the Negro National League, the total expenditures for players' salaries jumped from $30,000 per year to $275,000.[48] After his death in the state asylum at Kankakee, Illinois, he was honored by a steady stream of mourners at a three-day open casket service.

Lester Rodney, a black sportswriter in New York during the 1930s, remembers that the Negro leagues had a life force of their own.

"The Negro leaguers seemed to move past the discrimination and had fun," he said. "Even though they had no prospect of getting to the top in what they did best, they created a thriving life for themselves. It became a good source for black business in this country."

When Rodney and others were pushing for integration in the majors in the late 1930s he discovered that some black club owners did not want the change. He recalled, "One owner said, 'your motives are good, but what you are going to do is knock out one of the few real thriving black businesses in this country.'"[68]

An obscure and short-lived attempt at integration occurred in early 1921 when an entrepreneur named Andy Lawson sought funding to create the Continental League. His strategy was unique because it called for eight ballclubs, four white and four Negro, to play against each other in a full summer schedule.

Although baseball officials and pundits knew the idea was doomed, *Baseball Magazine* courageously stated, "At every turn, in every industry, the Negro is at a disadvantage. We cannot but sympathize, however, with the attempt of the Continental League to give the colored ballplayer a show. He has never had a decent chance before."[59]

The first great black team owner was Cumberland Willis "Cum" Posey, a former Penn State student. Although he excelled at college sports, his skin color precluded a major league career. Like Foster, he saw opportunities in ownership. In 1916 he became the manager and owner of a semipro team called the Homestead Grays in Homestead, Pennsylvania.[15] Posey eventually established the team as one of the preeminent black ball clubs in the United States.

He hesitated in joining Foster's group, but when the Negro National League folded he created the East-West League.[15] As a result, Posey enjoyed 30 years as a powerful leader in black baseball until his death in 1946.

Only his crosstown rival, Gus Greenlee, could match Posey's success in Negro baseball. Greenlee lacked the education and the class that Posey possessed, but he created a small empire for himself, having started with nothing.

Born in a log cabin in 1897 in North Carolina, Greenlee accumulated his wealth during Prohibition in Pittsburgh. Nightclubs, gambling, and girls formed the foundation of his fortune.[13]

Negro League star Ted Radcliffe recalled Greenlee's personal lifestyle during the 1930s. "He had [money] buried in his yard in buckets. He had a 20-foot high fence covered with barbed wire around his house and Doberman pinschers."[24]

Greenlee started investing in black baseball in 1930 with a semipro team named the Pittsburgh Crawfords. His decision to take control of the Crawfords is considered to be one of the most important events in Negro League history. (For more details see the Harold Tinker interview.)

By 1933 Greenlee had pirated Cum Posey's best players for his Crawfords with promises of more money.[13]

As reflected in the Ted Radcliffe interview, black ballplayers frequently jumped from team to team. The financial instability of many "shoestring" ball clubs and the promise of more security forced many players to put themselves up for bidding. But Greenlee offered stability for eight years during the Great Depression. In addition, he built the only black-owned ballpark in the East in 1932 for $75,000.[2] And one of his greatest promotional achievements was to create the annual East-West All-Star contest.

He died in 1952 after suffering losses in his numbers racket by encroaching white racketeers and demands by the IRS for payment of income tax debts.[13]

During the 1920s a unique migration gained momentum when Cuban ballplayers joined the Negro leagues during the summer and American black players played in winter leagues in the Caribbean. Exhibition games and winter league ball in Latin America finally provided the black players with an opportunity to play regularly against white major leaguers.

Ken Burns' epic research project and documentary, *Baseball*, revealed a stunning statistic concerning the matchup between white and black professional teams.

They reported, "Over the years, black baseball stars played their white rivals at least 438 times in off-season exhibition games. The whites won 129 of those games. Blacks won 309."

Although major and minor league owners held tight to the color line agreement, the segregation of spectators in the grandstand area was strangely inconsistent. The boyhood stories of Harold Tinker and Byron Johnson in the following sections of this book indicate that "Negro Only" seating arrangements in stadiums in the South were strictly enforced.

However, sportswriter Lester Rodney had a much different experience. Rodney was born in 1911 and started attending major league games in New

York in 1920. "I saw games in Ebbets Field, Polo Grounds and Yankee Stadium throughout the twenties and they definitely never had segregated stands in those parks," he recalled.

Occasionally, the white major leaguers would attend Negro League games because of the aggressive style of play that was promised. Former semipro and Negro League infielder Bobby Robinson (1916–44) told the author that on one occasion he was surprised by a visit from Ty Cobb.

He remembered that Cobb came to watch a game played by the Negro League Detroit Stars in the 1920s. Before the game was over Cobb had migrated down in to the Stars' dugout and sat next to Robinson, talking baseball the entire time. Robinson recalled that there wasn't a hint of prejudice in Cobb's attitude that day. They were just two ballplayers sharing stories.

Robinson's other memorable experience with white major leaguers attending ball games occurred in 1930 in St. Louis. Robinson was playing third base for the Stars in a crucial game that would determine the Negro League pennant winner. After completing an incredible eighth inning, unassisted triple play Robinson was summoned to the first-base box seat area where nearly 30 well-dressed white men were seated. When Robinson arrived he was greeted by John McGraw and the entire New York Giants baseball team. After receiving congratulatory handshakes from each of the Giants' players, McGraw told Robinson, "If things were different you would be my starting third baseman."

The Roaring Twenties established the careers of some of the most fabled black American ballplayers in history. There is much argument as to who were the best of the best, but in the following interviews the names of Gibson, Bell, Charleston, and Paige are mentioned most often.

One of the greatest of the Negro League teams ever assembled was Gus Greenlee's Pittsburgh Crawfords from 1933 through 1935.[13]

Hall of Fame pitcher Satchel Paige called the Crawfords, "the best team ever put together in any country — the best team Negro or white."[30]

That club fielded more than half of the 14 men selected to play on the East team in the Negro League All-Star games for 1933 and 1934.[17]

Greenlee's team included the following:

1. Josh Gibson, who is the undisputed home run champion of the Negro leagues and possibly the greatest home run hitter in baseball history (see the interview with his son, Josh, Jr., below). He was inducted into Cooperstown in 1972.
2. James "Cool Papa" Bell, who may have been the fastest man ever to play professional ball.[17] According to legend he would often

score from first base on a single.[24] When he was 45 years old he played in an exhibition game against the St. Louis Cardinals and scored from first base on a sacrifice bunt by Satchel Paige.[51]

Ted Radcliffe remembers once seeing Bell make an impossible catch of a Heinie Manush line drive. "Cool Papa caught the ball — you think I'm lying!— he caught it going away backhanded."

Satchel Paige joked, "He hit a line drive past my ear. I turned around and saw the ball hit his ass sliding into second base."[67] He was inducted into Cooperstown in 1974.

3. Oscar Charleston, the Crawfords' manager, who became the uncontested champion in both offense and defense. He was compared to Cobb for his slashing, take-no-prisoners style of base running and yet was also known for his long ball hitting.[15] Updated statistics show his lifetime batting average at .353, and he hit over .400 five times.[15]

His remarkable career in baseball spanned 35 years, from 1915 to 1950.[17] He was inducted into Cooperstown in 1976.

4. Judy (William) Johnson was a slightly built third baseman who hit consistently over .300. John B. Holway calls him one of the slickest fielding third basemen in the history of black baseball: or any other baseball. He was inducted into Cooperstown in 1975.

5. Satchel Paige was a flamboyant fastball pitcher who played professionally from 1924 until his last full season in 1953. Paige knew he had phenomenal talents and he was eager to prove it to white club owners.

Sportswriter Lester Rodney remembers Paige from an interview they had in 1937. He said, "Paige challenged big league baseball that day by stating he would get a black team to play the winners of the upcoming World Series to a winner-take-all match, or contribution to charity, from the gate receipts. He knew he could beat them because he had led black teams in postseason exhibition games on the Pacific Coast and beaten white teams." Major league owners would not reply.

Finally, 11 years later at the age of 42, Paige became the first black man to pitch in the American League when he took the mound for the Cleveland Indians. He was inducted into Cooperstown in 1971.

6. Sam Bankhead was a superb infielder and outfielder during his 20-year career. He was selected to the All-Star team seven times and accumulated a lifetime .342 batting average against white major league teams.

Bankhead died tragically at the age of 70 after being shot by a friend during an argument.[13]

7. Jimmie Crutchfield was an outfielder who played 15 years in Negro League baseball and appeared in at least four All-Star games.[17] Known primarily for his great defensive skills, he occasionally challenged himself by making catches behind his back.[13]

When members of the Pittsburgh press called him the black Lloyd Waner, Crutchfield quietly observed, "(Waner) was making $12,000 a year and I didn't have enough money to go home on."[67]

The Crawfords were gutted in late 1936 after the dictator of the Dominican Republic, Rafael Trujillo, offered large bonuses to Paige, Gibson, and Bell to play for his Caribbean national team. Oscar Charleston, in a moment of frustration, throttled one Dominican agent by the neck when he flashed a wad of money in front of his players.[15] Greenlee protested in vain to the State Department in Washington.[30]

Unfortunately, during the early days of league play, accurate records were not kept. The proof of their achievements on the ball field are remembered in deeds not numbers.

Don Motley, executive director of the Negro Leagues Baseball Museum, explained, "The white newspapers did not cover the Negro leagues back then so it is very, very hard to key in on any individual's batting average." He continued, "Most of the research work that was done has been through the old small-town newspapers and talking to some of the players. It is only recent research that has dug up what we know now."

(For more information on the exclusion practices of newspapers see the Harold Rosenthal interview.)

The Negro League Museum has recently established the Buck O'Neil Research Center in cooperation with Kansas State University. Among other responsibilities, the center's task will be to compile accurate statistics on black ballplayers. (For more information on Buck O'Neil refer to the series of interviews in this chapter.)

The following pages reflect interviews with two men who played Negro League baseball during the 1920s. The last section in this chapter briefly chronicles the lives of three men who were inspired by the great Negro League players of the 1920s and 1930s.

At the time of these interviews, the oldest Negro League player was Bill Owens (1923–33). Unfortunately, he was unable to speak to the author and after a long struggle with diabetes died in May 1999.

Owens is often quoted for a powerful remark he made to a sportswriter in 1995. When the journalist asked if he would have liked to have played in the major leagues, Owens responded, "Well, we played in the major leagues! We were just as good as anybody."

TED "DOUBLE DUTY" RADCLIFFE
Born July 7, 1902

Gregarious, voluble, and enthusiastic. Theodore Roosevelt Radcliffe had barely finished one story when he started the next. But after 97 years of experiencing victory, rejection, and living on the road there are a lot of stories that need to be told.

When Radcliffe retired from a 58-year career of professional baseball, he had no idea of what he had really achieved.

"One day I was told that my lifetime batting average was .343, but you know I pitched as much as I caught," he said. Based on his career records, Radcliffe was one of the top pitchers in the Negro leagues. In fact, he was the only man ever elected to the Negro League All-Star team for both positions.

Given his accomplishments, there should be little doubt that he deserves to join his teammates Josh Gibson and Satchel Paige in the Hall of Fame.

At the time of these interviews Radcliffe was the oldest surviving ballplayer from the Negro leagues. His career may have been the stuff of dreams, but his later years were a nightmare.

Like many retired ballplayers from that era, "Double Duty" was not financially secure. In 1962 Radcliffe and his Canadian-born wife Alberta moved into a now infamous Chicago public housing area called the Ida B. Wells Projects. Crime, drugs, and gang violence grew dramatically as the years passed. Radcliffe was mugged five times.

No one seemed to care that at one time he was one of the great ballplayers in history. A hero, lost in the belly of hell. No one cared except for a local freelance writer, Claire Hellstern, and Chicago's legendary columnist Mike Royko.

Based on Royko's revealing article in 1989, the Radcliffes were moved into a church-affiliated, high-security apartment building. Through Hellstern's insistence, several local television stations took notice. Documentaries, highlighting Radcliffe's plight, were produced by two Chicago area television stations. One production garnered an Emmy.

Suddenly, almost on cue, a groundswell of interest in Negro League baseball gained momentum. By 1990 Radcliffe was earning money from autograph signings at card shows. He wrote an autobiography, appeared on several national television programs, and was summoned to the White House.

In 1997 Alberta, his wife of 58 years, died. He continues to travel the national autograph circuit regularly with his best friend and closest companion Claire Hellstern. Look for him at any tour stop: Cigar firmly planted in his gnarled fingers, leaning on his cane, flirting with all the beautiful young girls that magnetically cross his path.

I was the seventh of ten children in a family that was already integrated. My great-grandfather and my grandfather were white men. My grandmother was half Indian and half black. Man, they had some beautiful children.

My daddy was a Creole and he went to Tuskeegee Institute. You know he was a contractor and built homes for the shipyard workers. When my daddy built our house in Mobile, Alabama, my white grandfather moved in with us.

I believe I've always loved baseball. I remember we could look out my window and see the kids play on a big sandlot that was right next to my home. We'd be out there all day, every day, doing something. But we didn't let the darkness stop us. We'd make cotton balls and soak them in oil and play night ball. We'd light them and run like hell.

The first time I ever caught Satchel Paige, I was 15. [*Paige's real birth year is up for debate, although baseball records reflect 1906 as the official date. In his autobiography Radcliffe claimed that Paige and he were born on the same day in 1902.*]

Yeah, that's right I was catching Satchel Paige when I was 15 years old. At that time he was as wild as a marsh hen. He could pitch all right but he didn't develop a good curveball until 1934 in North Dakota. I'd take him on the sidelines and warm him up. It was there that he became himself. He and I grew up together in Mobile, Alabama, and when I became a professional he and I and Billy Williams' father and Hank Aaron's father all came up together.

My brother Alec and I decided to leave Mobile one day, when I was about 17 years old [*1919*]. So we went on an excursion to Newark, Ohio, to work in a manufacturing plant. They were paying $10 a day and that was a lot of money then.

When we got there we only worked the first day. I was a pretty good dice shooter so we had a game that night and I won $36. The next day we started hoboing to Chicago on a freight train.

When we got just outside of Newark the engineer of the train found me. They took my brother and put him in the back of the train in a little office. They put me up in the engine with the fireman and had me fire the engines all the way to Chicago. My brother was older than me, but I was larger, so I did the work. And when we got to a small town in Ohio the police wanted to take us off the train and put us in jail for hoboing. But the engineer told them that we were working for him. He went in the restaurant at the train station and got us both a hamburger sandwich and some pop and brought us all the way into Chicago.

They put us off at One Hundred and Fifth Street and Vincennes Avenue in the rail yards and we ran all the way to Forty-First Street where my brother lived. My oldest brother came here first in 1911 and he's still living here. He's 103 years old. He was a bellhop and since he had money he bought us both a new suit and got us cleaned up. And I've been here ever since.

The first professional team I played for was the Illinois Giants in 1920 and for every 15 games we got $50. My big break came one day when we went down to Peoria and played against the Caterpillar Tractor Company semipro team. I just turned 18, but I could throw so hard. I didn't have much of a curveball, but I shut them out 3–0 and I've never looked back since.

In 1921 I developed a pitch called the scratch ball. Some people called it the emery ball. But I would scratch it with a knife or sandpaper to make it hop. [*Radcliffe credited "A white boy named Murphy in ... Traverse City, Michigan" for teaching him that pitch.*]

One time in 1924 time we were playing way up in a beautiful resort city in Wisconsin [*Bear Creek*], and one of the head policemen was the manager of the local team. He said, "If you n____ beat us we are going to run you out of town."

So I told the white owner of our team to go down the street, two blocks, to the state police office. I told him to get us two state policemen and put one on each side of the stadium. I was so mad I hit two home runs and I pitched six innings and I struck out 14. We beat them 20–0. They couldn't hit a bull on the ass with a paddle.

So the fans threw eggs and everything else at us. The state police squad came in and took us ten miles out of town on the highway and they stayed there until we were out of sight. We had to go 90 miles, because we couldn't get any rooms.

In 1927 I was signed to play with Gilkerson's Union Giants. Their headquarters were in Spring Valley, Illinois, and they had a nice park and a place for us to stay. Oh, it was so nice. That's the first time I got $150 a month.

They gave us $1 a day to eat on when I first started, but you could eat [well]. You could get ham and eggs for a quarter. And you could get roast chicken, roast beef, or oxtail for a quarter. You could get a dozen fried oysters for 35 cents.

When we went to Wisconsin, North Dakota, Montana, and California we'd stay in the white hotels, but you couldn't do it in a place like Cincinnati or St. Louis. You had to go in the colored neighborhood and go to different people's houses. Or if you had to, you'd sleep in the bus sometimes. You couldn't bathe for three days and they thought we were kin to a muskrat.

I stayed down there with Gilkerson, on and off, until 1929.

> Gilkerson's Union Giants were not part of the newly formed Negro leagues, but were hailed as one of the best barnstorming teams in the Midwest. Their territory covered six Midwestern states and Canada. They became an attraction wherever they stopped, not only because of their baseball talents, but also they entertained the crowds with their comic antics.
> Baseball writer Kyle P. McNary credits the clowning to the fact that the players wanted to mitigate any chance of racial incidents by keeping the mostly white crowds smiling.

During the off-season I worked in Chicago. Chicago's always been a good city. In the 1920s they had some great jazz places like the Dreamland and the Coco Inn, but I've never been too much of a man for running around at night. I never enjoyed drinking. Usually me and my three brothers and some friends would play pinochle or bridge and we'd buy a case of beer and a case of pop and play cards and enjoy ourselves.

I used to work at a hotel where Al Capone lived. I used to be the bellboy at the Michigan Hotel, at Twenty-Seventh and Michigan. I've seen all of his guys and they were good tippers. They were the only people I ever had that gave me a $1 tip. Capone was a nice man to me, but he had an iron hand and I didn't have sense enough to know it.

I've had a lot of experiences in my days.

In 1928 I was asked to play with the Detroit Stars in the Negro League and that's the most I ever made up until then. They gave me $250 a month and that was good money in the 1920s.

A couple of years later the owner of the St. Louis Stars offered three men in trade to Detroit for me. So I went to St. Louis in 1930 and we won the championship. That was the Negro League championship. [*The St. Louis Stars posted a 65–22 record and defeated Radcliffe's previous team, the Detroit Stars, for the pennant.*]

Then I jumped over to the Homestead Grays.

I'll tell you how successful I was in 1931. I was on big time. I was getting $500 a month with the Homestead Grays and we won the championship. The best record I ever had was that season with Homestead in 1931. I was 19–3 and I caught 140 games and I was batting right behind Josh Gibson.

Then in the early 1930s Gus Greenlee organized the [*Pittsburgh*] Crawfords. He took me and Satchel and Josh away from the Grays and gave me $750 a month and we won the championship that year.

I'll tell you how I got the nickname "Double Duty." In 1932 at Yankee Stadium, Satchel Paige and I went back to the Homestead Grays to help them out against the Lincoln Giants of New York. They had two great pitchers, Smoky Joe Williams and Dick Redding. So me and Satchel went in and beat them. Satchel shut them out in the first game 4–0. I was the catcher in that game and I hit a home run in the seventh inning with bases loaded.

In the second game I was out in the parking lot trying to get me a gal for that night and they told me that if I pitched they'd take care of me. I shut them out 6–0. Damon Runyon reported on the game and named me "Double Duty" because I caught and pitched.

> Radcliffe told his biographer, Kyle P. McNary, that he was sitting in the lobby of his New York hotel with Sugar Ray Robinson and a group of ballplayers when he was shown Runyon's article. Radcliffe told McNary that the article read, "It's worth the admission price of two to see 'Double Duty' Radcliffe in action."

One spring in the 1930s we all were down in Hot Springs, Arkansas, at the racetrack and we were sitting upstairs with a bookie. Satchel, Josh Gibson, Buck Leonard, and I went down to the dollar window. Well, at the same time Dizzy Dean and Rogers Hornsby came up there. The man who sold them their tickets asked Dean if he knew "Double Duty" and Satchel, and he said, "Hell yes. Where are they?"

When he saw us he jumped across that line. The ticket man said, "You can't go in there!" Dean said, "The hell I can't. That's my friend." And they came over that line and sat on the side with us. The racetrack people didn't move them either. But they wouldn't let us go over there, where they were.

Ted Radcliffe attempting a tag on Josh Gibson in the 1930s. Courtesy of the Ted Radcliffe collection.

The two best white ballplayer friends I had back then were Bob Feller and Dizzy Dean.

In 1933 Satchel and I left the Negro League and went to Bismarck, North Dakota. We played up there for three years and neither of us lost a game.

Like I said, Satchel could throw hard and he had overbearing speed. But when we went up to North Dakota he became a master because he developed control. It was there that he developed his hesitation pitch. We worked on that on the sidelines until he perfected it. When he went up to the major leagues he struck out Joe DiMaggio with that pitch twice in one game. Boy, was Casey Stengel angry.

Satchel got there before me and they put him up in a caboose down in the rail yards. When I saw that, I arranged for him and me to move into the basement of the hotel. We built an apartment down there. Satchel was so happy and he said to me, "I'm going to call President Roosevelt 'cause they need you in Washington."

In 1936 he and I went to a tournament down in Wichita, Kansas, for the semipro championship. We went down there and that was the most

Ted Radcliffe in 1999 (photograph by Nick Wilson). "This is what happens when you catch Satchel Paige's fastball," Radcliffe said.

money I ever made in baseball. Every game our team won we made $1,000. [*Note: The commissioner of the National Semipro Baseball Congress that year was Honus Wagner.*]

When I was playing in the 1920s I weighed 210–220 pounds. When I pitched I'd lose ten pounds, because I'd lose more weight pitching than catching. Some days I used to pitch five days in a row relieving but I never had a sore arm. They can't pitch every three days now.

I was a nice size man for a pitcher and catcher. I could throw 100 miles an hour, and I had a nice curveball and I had good control.

I remember when I was with the Homestead Grays in St. Louis. They put me in, in relief, to pitch one strike to a batter when the count was three and two.

I never will forget in Yankee Stadium we [*the Homestead Grays*] were playing the Black Yankees. They had a good hitter up at bat and Josh was catching. I called him to come halfway to the mound where the batter could hear me.

I said, "Listen, we're leading 3–2. I ain't going to throw that SOB no fastball because he'll hit it. I'll throw him a curve or walk him."

Ted Radcliffe, 1942 East-West Negro League All-Star game. Radcliffe tags out "Cool Papa" Bell at home plate. Courtesy of the Ted Radcliffe collection.

Well, I rared up and threw him an aspirin tablet down the middle and he just looked at it. And the umpire said, "You should have swung." He had a fit. I had as good a control as anybody. I'd only walk a batter if I wanted to.

I played in Cuba for four years and I played in Mexico for six years. [*see chapter 3*]. Then I was managing a white team in Winnipeg, Canada, for eight years in the Canadian Baseball League. I was lucky enough to win three championships.

During all those years I saw the best. The best power hitter I ever saw was Josh Gibson. The fastest man I ever saw was "Cool Papa" Bell. The best pitcher was Satchel, and the smartest baseball man I've ever seen was "Cum" Posey.

Abe Saperstein was the greatest man that I played ball for. I was with him on and off for 20 some years. He gave me my first car and I've never forgotten him. We were the same age, and he was just like a brother to me.

Saperstein was the sports promoter who launched the Harlem Globetrotters. He also owned an interest in two Negro leagues in the mid–1940s.

    Saperstein is credited with convincing Cleveland Indian owner
    Bill Veeck to sign Satchel Paige to his first major league contract in
    1948.

I've got some traveling stories for you. We took a tough beating in those days.

In 1944 I was managing the Birmingham Black Barons and we were playing for the championship against the Chicago American Giants. We beat them for the pennant.

Saperstein wanted to come down to meet us in Montgomery, Alabama, that Sunday night. Abe told me, "Go tell the owner of a restaurant to fix all of you a steak for dinner. I want to let the boys know I appreciate what they did."

Well, he came down there that night to meet me. He was sitting at the table with us and they made him get up. The owner said no white man can sit with the n____ in here. So he and I had to go out and sit in my car and eat. That's the way it was.

Another time I was managing Birmingham and we were going from Birmingham to Jacksonville to play the Red Caps, because they were in our league. We stopped along the way in Georgia to get some gas and the boys jumped out of the bus to get a drink of water. So they grabbed a hose that was used for washing cars. The white owner of the station yelled, "N____, put that hose down and drink out of a coca cola bottle." So I pulled out and didn't buy any gas. We got out onto the road and we drove five miles and ran out of gas. We had to push it another five miles, but the boys enjoyed it, because they were just sick over him.

But what if we just gave up because of things like that? If we didn't try to play back then, baseball would be nothing today. Because without the colored men it would be nothing today. We broke every record in the book.

After I quit playing I started to scout for Cleveland, because Abe Saperstein was connected. I scouted for Cleveland from 1962 to 1966. Then I scouted for the White Sox and a little for the Cubs, but I didn't like to travel any more. I think I stopped scouting in 1969 or 1970. That's when Leo Durocher was managing the Cubs.

I played against him all the way back in 1932 when he was playing with the Cincinnati Reds. During my last year as a scout he sent for me to have lunch with him and the players. He told them all about me.

He said, "I wish we had him to play now. But I'd have to pay him for pitching and I'd have to pay him for catching and I'd have to pay him for pinch hitting."

Life After the Game

You know I've been to the White House three times. And you know what? Clinton is something else. I told him he was like me and he asked how? And I said, "I don't like pork chops. I want some nice tenderloin veal."

He said, "Don't talk so loud. Hillary might be listening." But he's a good man.

I know how to take care of "Duty." I don't drink and I take it easy with the women. I feel pretty good and I started to lose some weight last year. But I would like to get down to 230 pounds. But its OK. God will take care of me. I go to bed and sleep ten hours without getting up. I'm in pretty fair shape. I'm still driving my car. I like to go to the restaurant at White Sox park, which is only eight blocks from me. Every day when I'm in town I try to go to the ballpark. I go upstairs and I stand around with the big shots.

I still go on the road to do autograph shows too. I'm going to Cleveland and Terre Haute over the weekend. Tomorrow I go to Washington and next week I'm going to New York. Then to Dallas. Then I'm going to Hot Springs to get me some rest.

Right now I've got T-shirts that were printed up just for me. They say, "Thou shalt not steal — Not on my arm — The great Double Duty."

Radcliffe's seemingly disjointed and rootless playing career was typical of the black ballplayer in the days of segregated leagues. In order to survive and prosper a good ballplayer had to constantly move from team to team in search of a steady paycheck and a better life.

REVEREND HAROLD TINKER
Born March 23, 1905

Harold Chester Tinker's name may be an obscure notation in the record books of black baseball, but he was a major character in two of the most important events in Negro League history:

1. As the team captain of the semipro Pittsburgh Crawfords, Tinker was one of the men who helped encourage Gus Greenlee to invest in black baseball. Within several years the Crawfords became one of the greatest baseball teams ever assembled.

2. *In 1927 Tinker discovered and mentored a raw, young ballplayer
   named Josh Gibson. He continued as Gibson's manager until
   1930.*

   *During his semipro playing days in 1920, Tinker secured a job
   at Pathé Pictures (renamed RKO Pictures) and retired from that
   company as head of shipping in 1969.*

   *He was ordained in 1956 and continues to preach at the Central
   Baptist Church in Pittsburgh, where he has been a member since 1917.
   Tinker currently resides there with his wife of nearly 70 years, Pearl.*

   *He credits his longevity to the manner in which he has lived.
   "I've never stopped walking," he asserted.*

I was born in Birmingham, Alabama, the same town as Satchel Paige
and Ted Radcliffe. I didn't know either of them, because when I was almost
12 years old in 1917 we moved north to Pittsburgh. I've been here ever
since.

I played baseball since I was seven years old when we first made a diamond on a dirt side-street by my father's home in Birmingham. In front
of our house was a gravel street so we always played on the dirt side. I was
nuts over the game.

I used to see the white minor league ball club, the Birmingham Barons,
play at that time. The famous Birmingham Black Barons club wasn't organized then.

My sister had a boyfriend and I guess he wanted to impress her so he
took me to see the Barons play when I was eight years old in 1913. That
was the first professional club I'd ever seen. We sat in a very small section
that was reserved for black people in that old wooden baseball park. [*The
stadium, Rickwood Field, is the oldest professional ballpark still standing. It
was built in 1910.*]

I started to play organized sandlot baseball when I was 15 years old
in Pittsburgh with the Westinghouse Manufacturing Company–sponsored
team. Those sandlot leagues were like the minor leagues for the professional black teams in the area at that time.

In 1927 I was playing with the Edgar Thompson Steel Company [*Sponsored*] team and we played every evening. We didn't go home from our
jobs. We just went directly to the ball field, eight miles from the city.

There were five of us who were invited to quit the steel company team
and play for a semipro, sandlot team called the Crawfords. They were
named after the Crawford Bath House which sponsored them.

The history of the Pittsburgh Crawfords "kids'" sandlot team goes
back to 1926 when two men, Teeney Harris and Bill Harris, formed a team

for black kids. So as soon as I joined that team I was made captain and played center field.

Our first game was played in Washington Park, which looks down on the Pennsylvania Railroad Station. We had at least 1,500 people attending that game and do you know how much we collected? Eighteen dollars! It was a disgrace. After we paid the umpires we didn't have anything to take for ourselves.

A black man named Campbell who lived on the north side of Pittsburgh decided to organize a special game during the sandlot season. He would gather the best black players from the sandlot teams to play a white team in an All-Star game. He would do that a couple of times each year.

Harold Tinker in 1928. Courtesy of the Reverend Harold Tinker.

So in 1927 I was picked as the left fielder to play on that sandlot All-Star team. It was quite an honor. We didn't know who our teammates would be until the day of the game, but I soon got to know one player in particular. There was this very young boy playing third base for our All-Star team. His name was Josh Gibson.

It's amazing because the thing that attracted me was that he was only 15 years old and he was playing like a veteran that day. It was an awful playing surface with pebbles and gullies, but he was fielding like he was on Forbes Field. His arm strength was amazing. He would field the ball and purposely allow the batter to run a little bit and then shoot the ball to first base. He was something. He hit a home run in that game, which was one of the longest I'd ever seen. It went out of the park and into this mountain behind the field. He was five years younger than the rest of us so none of us knew anything about this Josh Gibson until that day.

Before we left the field at the end of that game I approached him and introduced myself. I asked him, "How would you like to play for a real baseball team?" I told him that we would like to have him on the Crawfords.

And he said, "Yes sir." That All Star game was on a Saturday and about three days later he joined us.

He was shy when I first met him. He wasn't worldly wise, but he wasn't shy on the baseball field. He played like he had been playing for a long time.

He was a good kid and he did what you asked him to do without any quarrels.

We knew he was good, but we had no idea that this was the beginning of the greatest long ball hitter ever.

As I went through life back then, my sole purpose was to develop a baseball team that would compete with, and defeat, the Homestead Grays [*at that time the Grays were an independent professional team*]. Now you must understand that for us, the Grays were the highest level that black boys could reach. If you played for the Grays you didn't have any farther to reach because we couldn't play in the white major or minor leagues.

When I first saw them play at Forbes Field I was 14 years old. My idea was that I didn't want to play for them. I wanted to develop a team that would defeat them. That was my life's ambition.

By 1930 the Crawfords were the tops in the sandlots and we wanted to keep advancing up. Although we were not playing for a regular salary, every once in a while we would get two or three dollars from a game. I'm not bragging, but we had a great semipro team. The best white team in our district never did beat us when I was managing.

At that time Gus Greenlee was a big businessman in Pittsburgh and he was one of the biggest contributors to the sandlot leagues. Bill Harris was familiar with Gus because Gus had helped the Crawfords buy uniforms when they first started. It was Bill who suggested to us that we approach Gus and have him take the team over. He knew Greenlee could take us to the next level.

Harris was the first one who went to him and I met Geenlee shortly after that time. I really think that this was a very important moment because he had never invested in black baseball before that. Eventually, Greenlee helped save Negro League baseball because he invested a lot of money in the Negro leagues. That's right. That was the first time he ever invested in black baseball.

He took over the Crawfords at Bill Harris' request, but he did not pay any money. Greenlee said that he was willing to take the team and support us, and make us a professional baseball team. But the idea of making us professional was that we had to quit our jobs and play baseball only. Gus Greenlee told us that he was going to make us all professionals and that we would go to the top of the heap among the blacks.

He gave us two weeks to decide if we wanted to quit our jobs or quit the team. And that's a decision I had to make. I'll never forget that one because it broke my heart to quit baseball and it broke my heart because I had to quit. I had four kids at that time and I had been working steadily for Pathé Pictures since my dad sent me down to apply for a janitor's job in 1920.

I played for Greenlee for several months, but he only offered us $80 a month. That's when he gave us a final alternative. He said, "Now I'll give you a contract and either you quit your jobs and play for me or you quit this team and keep your jobs."

That's about the time they brought in Satchel Paige to play for us. No one knew Satchel from this area. The first thing that I noticed about him was that he had the biggest feet in baseball. He had the biggest feet. He had a style like no one I'd ever seen. He pitched from a stretch position at that time. No windup. He was doing nothing but fastballs. Fast and faster. His change-up was a fastball.

As a matter of fact, he was with us for two weeks before he pitched. The first game he appeared in was against the Homestead Grays and that was the night I realized my life's ambition. We defeated the Grays 5–3. Satchel didn't start the game, but the starter got hit for three runs in the first two innings and Satchel came in and pitched shutout ball.

I won't forget that night because I had another day to decide on the contract and that was the night I quit. Isn't that something? I quit the night that I realized my dream.

We played two games that day. After we beat the Grays we played a white team on our home field. During the game Gus Greenlee came down to sit on the bench and I told him I was quitting and he couldn't believe it. He said, "Now you don't mean it." I told him that I couldn't live on the salary he gave me. During that time with Greenlee I had a batting average of .295. I was no long-ball hitter, but I was best known for my fielding.

I didn't play again for four years until a guy asked me to manage a semipro team team called the Hazlewood Giants. It broke my heart to give up baseball. But looking back on that time I realize that we had no future so far as financial gains. But I knew we blacks had the potential to play as good as anybody. After all, we used the same balls, the same bats.

THE DREAM MAKERS

The barnstorming Negro League teams of the 1920s and 1930s provided more than just entertainment. When the Negro leagues were created in 1920 it provided a source of inspiration and hope for thousands of black children in America.

Three men who grew up during that period explain the impact that the pioneers of black baseball had on their lives.

"BUCK" O'NEIL
Born November 13, 1911
Carrabelle, Florida

John Jordan "Buck" O'Neil, saw his first professional black club in 1923. That experience set the foundation for O'Neil's 60-year career as player, manager, and scout. During his playing career he played on nine championship teams, played in three East-West All-Star games and won a Negro National League batting title. In 1962 he became the first black coach in major league baseball.

Although retired, O'Neil is actively involved with the Negro Leagues Baseball Museum in Kansas City.

I was very young when I got to see the New York Giants in Sarasota, Florida. Those major league ball clubs were playing in spring training near my home, but at that time the only people I'd seen playing baseball for a living were white. But then I saw my first Negro League team when I was 12 years old [*1923*].

I remember I saw the Chicago American Giants and the Indianapolis ABCs, and I was very excited to see them play. These guys were making a living doing this! And they were some of the greatest ballplayers I've ever seen.

That day I saw Oscar Charleston, William Dismukes, and Bobby Robinson. That was very thrilling. I didn't get to meet any of them up close that day, but seeing them play sure did inspire me.

Oscar Charleston was the one who inspired me the most. He could do everything. Hit, run, field, throw, and hit for power. In all my years in baseball Oscar Charleston was the best ballplayer I've ever seen.

The best pitcher I've ever seen was Satchel Paige, without a doubt.

After I started playing professionally the man who influenced me the most was Bullet Joe Rogan with the Kansas City Monarchs.

Buck O'Neil, Kansas City Monarchs, in 1938. Courtesy of Mark Rucker, Transcendental Graphics.

BYRON JOHNSON
Born September 16, 1911
Little Rock, Arkansas

Byron "Mex" Johnson's professional career spanned four years during the late 1930s. As a shortstop with the Kansas City Monarchs he was selected to play in the East-West All-Star game in 1938.

He left professional ball in 1940 and pursued a career in teaching. During the Second World War Johnson saw action in the Normandy Invasion, landing five days after the initial assault.

A long-time resident of Denver, Colorado, Johnson is retired, but not inactive. He celebrated his eighty-first birthday by sinking a hole in one at a local golf course.

He and his daughter Jackie are currently working on an autobiographical account of his amazing life.

The first experience I had watching professional ballplayers was with a white team called the Little Rock Travelers of the Southern League. I went with a friend of my brother's who worked at the stadium as kind of a caretaker. We had to sit way in the back near the right-field line because that was the section reserved for blacks. It wasn't much of nothing. We had broken-down bleachers and we stood most of the time.

Later on I heard the older men talking about something called the Negro League. I was told by different people that these guys played baseball for a living! Before that I didn't know it was possible.

At that time some of the Negro League players came to Hot Springs, Arkansas, which was a resort. The whites and the blacks used to come there for those hot springs, and take in the baths. Well, a black team came from Hot Springs to play a game in Little Rock, Arkansas. I did not see a black man play professionally until that day [*around 1929*]. That's very true.

It was an All-Star team with Oscar Charleston. I was so proud of them, because I had been seeing only the white fellas playing over there in the old Southern League. Somebody told me that the Negro League players were higher than the Southern League. I didn't know that.

When I saw the All-Star team play I knew they weren't telling me anything false. They were real ballplayers. That Oscar Charleston was really something. I remember him quite well.

I guess you might say, that made me feel that I could play professionally too. I was in junior college then and I formed a semipro team. We were not in a league, but we just barnstormed. We had a man that sponsored us and he used the Missouri Pacific railroad to transport the team. We were in high style. That's when I found out all about "Bullet" Rogan and Satchel Paige and the other players. It was a good time for baseball.

We played in Shreveport and Monroe, Louisiana; Texarkana, Texas; and all over Arkansas. I got to be known around Little Rock as a pretty good athlete so people knew abut me. Then one day I got a letter from the Kansas City Monarchs wanting me to come to spring training with them. That's how my professional career started.

The first time I played with Satchel Paige was in 1939 and we toured all over the West playing exhibition games. I'd ride with him in that big, long Chrysler he owned and we had such a good time. He'd race down the road with tires screeching and I thought "Oh Lord, I'm going to die!"

One time a deer ran out in front of us and he ran off the road chasing it. He liked to have fun, and he was such a wonderful person. He used to love to collect shotguns and cameras, and everywhere we went he would look for another camera to add to his collection.

One time in front of our hotel in Bismarck he set up a camera and a tripod in the middle of the sidewalk and I said to myself, "What is he going to do now?"

So when he would see a pretty woman coming down the street he would set the automatic timer on the camera and run over to the girl and start walking next to her, like he was her date. The camera would go off and he'd have a picture of the two of them.

One of the greatest pitchers I've ever seen was Bullet Rogan. He was also one of the best hitting pitchers in baseball. When I came up he was a coach for the Monarchs. By that time he had retired from active play, but he could still hit the ball well.

Well you know I could hit any fastball, but I had some trouble with hitting a curve. So Bullet Rogan took me out to the park after everybody had left and taught me how to hit a curve. You know that open stance like Andres Galarraga has? Well that's what he taught me. He told me to stop watching the pitcher's arm and just keep my eye on the ball. Suddenly, I started to see the stitching on the ball. Yeah, Bullet Rogan taught me how to hit a curve.

In 1969 I went to Kansas City to visit a friend and I found out Bullet was still living there. He was in one of those retirement

Byron Johnson in a Kansas City Monarchs uniform, 1937. Courtesy of the Byron Johnson collection.

apartment buildings. I was with my minister and the first day we couldn't get in. But an old guy out front told me, "If you come back tomorrow I'll get you in, because I help Mr. Rogan every morning. He told me that Rogan was confined to bed.

So the minister did take me back the next day and we all went upstairs to the third floor. When I stepped in the door Bullet was in the bed across the room and he was lying there. I walked in and he turned over and looked toward me.

And I said, "Hello, Bullet Joe." He beckoned for me to come closer. "I don't see too well," he said.

When I got up there I said, "You don't remember me, but you really helped me out in 1937 with the Monarchs."

And he said, "Little Rock!"

"That's right."

He said, "I thought I recognized that voice."

It was wonderful. We talked for a little while. I was so glad to see him. After I got back home it seems like Bullet didn't live but a couple of months after that. I was always thankful about seeing him one last time.

Wilbur "Bullet" Rogan was an infantryman with the U.S. Army on the Arizona-Mexican border in 1919 when his troop played an exhibition game against the barnstorming Pittsburgh Pirates. His performance so impressed the Pirates' outfielder Casey Stengel, that he recommended Rogan to a friend who owned the Kansas City Monarchs. Bullet Rogan spent 30 years in Negro League baseball and is remembered as one of the game's best pitchers.

JOSH GIBSON, JR.
Born August 11, 1930
Pittsburgh, Pennsylvania

The son of the most powerful baseball player in Negro League history wants everyone to know about his Hall of Fame father. Conducting exhibitions and speaking at public events, Gibson, Jr., gladly tells the story of the man who, many believe, could have outslugged Babe Ruth.

Josh Gibson, Sr., started playing semipro ball in 1929 and averaged over 60 home runs a season during his 16-year professional career. He holds the unofficial record for having hit 75 home runs in 1931 and 69 in 1934.

His career home run total may have exceeded 900 and he is credited with having regularly launched balls well over 500 feet. Gibson, Sr., who was also considered to be a great defensive catcher, was inducted into Cooperstown in 1972.

With his father as his inspiration, Joshua Gibson, Jr., became an accomplished infielder and played with his father's former team, the Homestead Grays, in the late 1940s and early 1950s.

Today the younger Gibson lives in Pittsburgh and is active in supporting work for kidney disease research and heads up the Josh Gibson Foundation.

My father was born in 1911 and he came from Buena Vista, Georgia, when he was 12. My mother died in childbirth, so I and my twin sister were raised by my mother's mother in Pittsburgh.

As a kid, eight or nine years old, I would always be a batboy when my father's team played in Pittsburgh. Since my father never remarried and traveled a lot, he was actually visiting me and my sister when he came to Pittsburgh.

Some of the players on the team came up with him to visit us so I saw

Sammy Bankhead and "Cool Papa" Bell. They hung with my dad and I visited with them a lot. Definitely. My father wasn't a real outgoing guy, but he had a humorous personality when he was with his buddies.

I was about 12 years old and I started traveling with my father two weeks out in the summer. He normally sat up front on the team bus, because he was big. But when I was there I used to sit in his seat. When I traveled with my father, he would go in the back of the bus and ride the hump so I would be comfortable.

He was always working hard, trying to earn a good living for me and my sister. I know that for a fact. In the three years that I traveled with my father I used to count the states we were in. I counted 24 states in three years.

When I do my exhibits there is a picture of my father and another ballplayer that I don't recognize, down in Santo Domingo at the beach. They had these full-torso swimming suits on.

I inscribe under the picture, "No steroids, no iron — just milk." See, when he was growing up that's what they said: drink a lot of milk. That will make you big. That was the protein back then. There were no outstanding weightlifters so all they did were pushups.

His whole body was big. He stood 6'1" or 6'2" and weighed 230. He had big arms, big forearms, and biceps. I inherited his deep baritone voice.

Their spring training was to go up to the high school gym at Homestead and do jumping jacks. That's all. There was no system. Actually, the stars of the league stayed in shape because they played all year round.

My father is in Cooperstown and the hall of fame in Mexico [1974]. He was the most valuable player in Puerto Rico in 1941 and 1942. He played in Cuba and he'll be recognized for what he did in there as soon as Castro gets out.

I'll never forget his advice to me. He used to repeat, "Only the strong survive."

The one thing I didn't like about the 1930s was that they called him the black Babe Ruth. That's like calling Michael Jordan the black Bob Cousy. See, you lose credibility there. Josh Gibson was Josh Gibson. Babe Ruth was Babe Ruth.

My dad sure could hit the home runs. I have a diagram of one he hit in New York [1934] which was around 700 feet. Believe it or not. The diagram was done by Rick Roberts of the *Pittsburgh Courier*, years ago. The *Courier* was a black paper that kept all the facts and information about the game.

Some of the funniest experiences I ever had were with Satchel Paige. Sometimes Satchel used to bring the outfielders in and sit them down when

Josh Gibson, Jr., in 1951 as a ballplayer in the Provincial League, Quebec, Canada. Courtesy of the Josh Gibson, Jr., family collection.

my father came up to the plate. Sometimes he would strike my father out and sometimes my father would knock the ball into the night.

My father died in January 1947 when I was still in high school. After he died, Sam Bankhead, the shortstop on the Homestead Grays, took over as my father. He took me over and also he became the manager of the Homestead Grays.

Sammy and my high school coach, Mr. Kortner, inspired me go into professional ball. When I got my first break I went to the Youngstown Colts in the Class C Mid-Atlantic League. When I was playing professional ball I always thought about my father. Being Josh Gibson, Jr., I was always reminded about him.

My father had high blood pressure and he died of a brain hemorrhage. It was passed on to me and my sister. She died at the age of 39. I got sick and I had my first kidney transplant in 1971.

About eight years ago I had a second kidney transplant. But through it all I kept remembering what my father told me, "Only the strong survive." God has kept me here for some reason. Maybe it's to talk to writers like you to keep retelling the stories of Josh Gibson.

3. Cuban Baseball

"When they first come here they don't like it. Some boys cry and want to go home. But after they stay and make big money they accept things as they are. They can't change the laws."

Alex Pompez, owner of the Cuban Stars, commenting on Cuban ballplayers facing prejudice for the first time in America.[20]

CUBA: WINTER BALL AND THE GOLDEN AGE

A complete oral history of the golden age of baseball would not be possible without including a chapter on Cuba. There are several compelling reasons why this Caribbean island nation had such an impact on the history of baseball during this period.

1. Cuba was the first country outside of the United States to embrace the game so passionately. Baseball was introduced there in 1866 and within 14 years there were 70 organized teams playing there.[18]

   Cuban baseball clubs eventually joined two North American–based leagues. From 1946 to 1953 the Havana Cubans entered the Class C Florida International League and from 1954 to 1963 the Havana Sugar Kings joined the prestigious International League.[64]

2. Cuban ballplayers were accepted into the major leagues and the Negro leagues during the 1920s and 1930s. A cultural exchange of sorts was taking root by that time. Dark-skinned Cubans migrated to the United States in the summer to play ball in the Negro leagues. When they returned

home they were followed by black and white American ballplayers for a season of winter ball.

3. Professional baseball in Cuba was integrated. Black Americans were allowed to freely exhibit their talents on the island against barnstorming white ball clubs.

    Cuba was the country where white and black professional players could intermingle and openly share techniques. They could also get to know each other as human beings.

4. It became the mecca for major leaguers to play organized winter ball.

Baseball had been the number one sport in Cuba since 1880, but it wasn't until the last decade of the nineteenth century that professional ballplayers from America came there to barnstorm.

One of the first teams to play in Cuba was Al Lawson's American All-Stars, and it featured a skinny 17-year-old shortstop named John McGraw. When he landed in Havana in January 1891 McGraw was stunned by the beauty of the then Spanish colony.[19] His influence, both on and off the field, would be felt in Cuba for the next 30 years.

From the late nineteenth century until the early twentieth century, American teams like McGraw's were exclusively made up of stars from various professional clubs. The first time that a full-roster major league team played a game in Cuba was in 1908.

The matchup was the brainchild of José Massaguer of the Havana daily, *El Mundo*. He arranged for the Cincinnati Reds to play a series of exhibition games with a team of Cuban All-Stars in the winter of that year.[18] The Reds prevailed in only four of the eleven games.

During that tour a muscular, dark-skinned 20-year-old pitcher named José Mendez was introduced to the Americans.[15] Mendez, known in Cuba as the Black Diamond, built a strong upper body and large forearms through years of chopping sugarcane.[18] His long arms and extraordinarily long digits gave him great spin on an exploding fastball.[17]

As the years progressed he beat the Tigers, Philadelphia A's, Philadelphia Phillies, and New York Giants during winter exhibition contests. After a poor showing in Cuba by the Detroit Tigers in 1909 and 1910, Ty Cobb swore that he would never play ball against black men again.[18]

Mendez may have been the greatest pitcher ever to come out of Cuba, but his very dark complexion prevented him from displaying his talents. After he defeated Christy Mathewson and the Giants in a 1911 exhibition game the Americans nicknamed him "the black Mathewson"[15] and McGraw remarked that Mendez would be worth $50,000 if he were allowed to pitch in the major leagues.[16]

He immigrated to the United States in the summer of 1908 and played with all black teams until his retirement after the 1926 season. In 1909 he is credited with an amazing 44–2 record with his first U.S.–based team, the Cuban Stars.[16] During the Cuban Winter League season of 1921 and 1922 Mendez struck out Babe Ruth three times.[16]

His fabulous career was nearly ended in 1913 when a Cuban military patrol had mistaken him for a rebel during a civil uprising. Luckily, one of the soldiers recognized him just as he was about to be executed. He received a military escort back to Havana to ensure that he would not miss an exhibition game against the Philadelphia Athletics.[62]

In 1911 the manager of the Cincinnati Reds, Clark Griffith, broke ranks and signed two Cubans to play in the major leagues. Both Rafael Almeida and Armando Marsans had relatively short careers with the Reds, but they set a precedent. Since Marsans and Almeida had played with the All-Cubans barnstorming team, they were the first players in this century to jump from an all-black team to the major leagues.[17]

Before a Cuban could be signed, the major league owners had to prove the whiteness of the prospect by providing documents and sworn affidavits to league officials and local newspapers.[18]

By 1920 Cuba was the Paris of the Caribbean. Far away from the restraints of the recently enacted Prohibition, Americans flocked to Cuba by boat. They luxuriated on the gleaming beaches and in the exciting casinos. The race tracks attracted thousands each day and influential Americans like John McGraw frequented the Cuban American Jockey Cub.[19] Some Americans insensitively referred to Havana as "America's Tavern."[21]

Investments skyrocketed and by 1928 American companies owned 75 percent of Cuba's sugar plantations.[18] Prior to 1920 John McGraw and the New York Giants owner, Charles Stoneham, purchased an interest in a casino-racetrack complex called Oriental Park, located on the outskirts of Havana. After the uproar over the 1919 "Black Sox" fiasco, Commissioner Landis forced McGraw and Stoneham to divest themselves of the famous gambling resort in 1921.[18]

It wasn't until the 1920s that Cuban baseball players made their mark in the major leagues. Miguel Gonzalez was the first Cuban to enjoy a long career in the white leagues. Gonzalez started playing professional ball in Cuba as the catcher of José Mendez. In 1911 John McGraw reluctantly passed on him when he thought Gonzalez would not pass the color test. Although Gonzalez was even-tempered, he wasn't going to let anyone of any stature intimidate him. In 1911 he and McGraw had a scuffle during a winter league game in Havana. Forced to display an uncharacteristic humility, McGraw apologized in an open letter published in the *Havana Post*.[19]

After establishing his reputation in Cuba, Gonzalez played with an American black team, the Cuban Stars, for a short while before he was accepted to the majors.[13] He made his major league debut in 1912 with the Boston Braves and spent the next 17 years flourishing as a catcher in the National League.

Because Gonzalez was considered to be a natural leader and a gifted student of the game, the St. Louis Cardinals signed him as a coach and interim manager for the next 14 years. He was the first Latino to coach in the major leagues, and is credited with coining the common scouting phrase "Good field, no hit," when he was sent out to scout a catcher named Moe Berg.

He returned to Cuba in 1946 and purchased sole ownership of the Havana Reds ball club.

The most productive and unpredictable Cuban ballplayer of the golden age was the Cincinnati Reds' pitcher, Adolfo "Dolf" Luque (pronounced Loo-Kay). Luque blended an unhittable curveball with a hair-trigger temper. Despite his wiry 160-pound frame, he would stand up to any aggressor when he felt his machismo challenged.

He felt the sting of prejudice during his rookie season in 1914 when the fans in St. Louis greeted the light-skinned, blue-eyed Cuban with racial epithets.[18]

Unbowed, Luque went on to pitch for 20 years. He retired in 1935 with a record of 194–179 and a lifetime ERA of 3.24. He now ranks fourth among all Latin American pitchers in big league victories.[39]

During the 1920s Luque was the Reds' premiere pitcher, reaching his zenith in 1923 with league leading records in wins (27) winning percentage (.771) and ERA (1.93). He was the first Latin American to pitch a shutout in the major leagues and the first to pitch in a World Series.

Luque spent the winter months in Havana as both a player and manager of the Almendares team.[18] After 20 seasons in the big leagues and 34 seasons in Cuban winter league ball, Luque established a Latin American record of 297 victories.[39] Virtually unknown today, Luque still remains one of the greatest Latin American pitchers to ever play in the major leagues.

His controversial moments serve us today as colorful reminders of the rough-and-tumble days of the golden age.

In a game against New York Giants in 1923 Luque was not pitching effectively, and the taunts coming from the Giants' bench were intolerable. Finally, after a stinging remark from bench jockey Bill Cunningham, Luque slowly removed his glove, turned toward his antagonists, and charged the entire bench by himself. An errant punch missed Cunningham and landed on the jaw of Casey Stengel, the Giants outfielder. Both Luque and Stengel were removed from the game.

Luque was not finished. He was brooding and the challenge to his manhood had not been satisfied. He stormed out of the locker room and raced back out on the field with a baseball bat in hand. It took four Cincinnati policemen to finally escort him from the stadium.[18]

Sometime in the mid–1920s Luque's teammate, third baseman Ralph "Babe" Pinelli, hit a raw nerve by suggesting that Luque try a different pitching strategy. Luque exploded in anger and chased Pinelli around the clubhouse with a pair of scissors. As he was being restrained by his teammates, Luque challenged Pinelli to meet him at another location for a gun duel. After the dust had settled he and Pinelli made up and became close friends.[18]

There was a tender and modest side to Luque as well. After his fabulous 1923 season Luque returned to a hero's welcome. At a ceremony in Havana's Grand Stadium, Luque was presented with a new car as a tribute for his achievements.

Luque turned to José Mendez sitting nearby and said, "You should have gotten this car. You're a better pitcher than I am. This parade should have been for you."[15] Luque was humbled by the fact that a darker skin prevented Cuba's greatest pitcher from the same recognition.

The first Latin ballplayer from the 1920s to be inducted into the Hall of Fame in Cooperstown was Martin Dihigo (pronounced Dee-Go), a dark-skinned Cuban. Dihigo was more than a "five-tool man." He displayed awesome power at the plate, he could hit for average, run, and field. He was also an accomplished pitcher. In fact, Dihigo played all nine positions.[18]

He stood 6'3" and weighed 225 pounds, and when Negro League owners first saw him in 1923 a bidding war erupted. Through his 11 years in Negro League ball he recorded a 256–136 record and batted .304. He won five home run and batting titles and took the earned run average crown at least twice.[15]

Although he continued to return to Cuba to play ball each winter, he eventually left the United States in 1932 and played summer ball in other Latin American countries. He is the only ballplayer to be inducted into the Hall of Fame in four countries: the United States, Mexico, Venezuela, and Cuba.[16]

One of the greatest Cuban sluggers of the late 1910s and 1920s was Cristobal Torriente. Torriente had everything a major league team could ask for. When scouts started to scour the island for prospects he was in his early twenties and was solidly built at 5'10" and close to 200 pounds. He had established himself as a long-ball hitter even during the dead-ball era.

Legend has it that in one game in Indianapolis he hit a line drive so hard that when it shot off the right field wall the outfielder had time to throw him out at first base.[16] What he could have achieved in a major league uniform during the 1920s is left only to speculation. Sadly, the New York Giants passed on the olive-skinned outfielder because of his kinky hair.[16]

Torriente was eagerly picked up by the all-black American ball club, the Cuban Stars, in 1914. He stayed in the United States barnstorming and playing summer ball in semipro and the Negro leagues until 1934.

He batted .396 in his first season in the Negro leagues with Chicago, missing the batting title by three points. In successive years he hit .350, .389 and .331. During winter league play he consistently hit over .300.[15]

In his famous November 4, 1920, matchup with Babe Ruth in Havana, Torriente outslugged the Bambino with three home runs.

Babe, who was playing for an American All-Star team, went 0 for 3, reaching base only on two walks and an error. When the frustrated Ruth took over the mound to stop Torriente in the fifth inning, his Cuban host belted a double.[15]

No one is quite sure of his full birth date or exactly where in Cuba he was born, but his last days are sadly remembered. While playing in the Negro leagues, Torriente developed a fatal attraction to alcohol and nightlife. By 1935 Martin Dihigo found him living in desperate conditions in Chicago.[15] Cuban Hall of Fame pitcher Rodolfo Fernandez told the author that he also saw Torriente later that year coaching for Dihigo's team in New York.[54] He realized that Dihigo had given Torriente a chance to turn his life around. But his addiction to alcohol was overwhelming. Dihigo finally brought Torriente to New York, where he died destitute in 1938.[15]

One of the most powerful Cuban promoters in baseball was Alejandro "Alex" Pompez. Although little has been written about his achievements, he helped launch the professional careers of many young black Cuban and black American ballplayers.

Pompez, a black Cuban himself, was born and raised in America after his parents immigrated to the Florida Keys.[18] In the early 1920s he moved to New York to seek his fortune as a sports promoter. He acquired a baseball stadium and amusement park in Harlem and took control of the Cuban Stars baseball club.[18]

In 1923 Pompez brought Cuban superstar Martin Dihigo to the United States and folded his ball club into Rube Foster's Negro National League.[18] Rumors circulated that he was involved with the numbers racket in Harlem and was a target of New York prosecutor Thomas Dewey.[13]

There is little written today about Pompez that does not include references to his association with gangster Dutch Schultz. Some Cubans dismiss those accusations and refer to the tremendous achievements that Pompez enjoyed during his lifetime in baseball.

Fausto Miranda, a longtime writer for the *Miami Herald*, remembers Pompez with pride, "Alex Pompez was a big guy. He was the one who made it possible to put colored Cuban men in the Hall of Fame. For black people who did not play in the big leagues, Pompez got them noticed. Like Dihigo and others." Miranda discounts the charges that Pompez was involved with gangsters, "You know that if he was on the wrong side he couldn't have worked with the Giants in New York."

Pompez's relationship with the Giants and owner Horace Stoneham began when the promoter leased the Polo Grounds to hold Negro League games.[16] Their friendship eventually led to a business opportunity after Jackie Robinson broke the color line in 1947. Pompez soon became a respected source of talented black American and Cuban ballplayers for Stoneham's team. He is credited with introducing Felipe Alou, Orlando Cepeda, Willie Mays, and José Pagan to the Giants.[16] He once told a reporter that he had conspired with a Cuban witch doctor to lure Minnie Minoso into signing a professional contract.[20]

Stoneham eventually put Pompez on the payroll to scout black and Latin players and supervise them during spring training.[20] Toward the end of his career Pompez was actively involved in the Baseball Hall of Fame's special committee for the Negro Leagues.[13]

Another scout who operated out of Cuba starting in the 1930s was a Greek-American, Joe Cambria. Working for the Washington Senators' owner, Clark Griffith, Cambria is credited with signing over 400 Latin American ball players in 30 years of work.[16] Fausto Miranda said, "Cambria is still known as the Father of Cuban Ballplayers."

Cambria, according to legend, is at the heart of the oft-told story of Fidel Castro's attempt to play professional baseball. One story portrays Cambria as offering a $5,000 minor league contract to Castro, who turned it down to pursue his education. The other story suggests that Cambria passed on Castro because he was not talented enough.[23]

Perhaps the most intriguing story about the relationship between the major leagues and the integrated Cuban League is the one concerning the actual lineage of some of the players. Peter Bjarkman, a senior ranking baseball historian and respected author of 25 books, recently broached the idea of Cubans with black ancestry playing in the major leagues as early as 1911. He said, "I would go on record saying that some men with African blood clearly did play at that time. There is no question about it."

The first two Cubans to play major league ball, Marsans and Almeida, are now considered to be of black African ancestry. Baseball's ultimate biographical reference, *The Ballplayers*, flatly asserts that Armando Marsans, was half black. (See the Adrian Zabala interview.)

Felipe Alou recalls his experiences with black Latin ballplayers in his autobiography, *Felipe Alou ... My Life and Baseball*. He states that besides Almeida and Marsans, there were "A flock of other Latins who came to the big leagues before 1947 who were decidedly nonwhites." Bjarkman notes that Almeida and Marsans "clearly had some Afro-Cuban blood. They were hassled by the fans as being black and taunted around the league."

This engaging possibility does not challenge the fact that Jackie Robinson holds the respected and heroic position as the first black to break the color barrier in the twentieth century. Rather, it reveals that some degree of justice, although muted, may have been exacted against the segregationists.

It is a contentious subject to many because of its speculative and sensitive nature. Certainly no one from the 1910s and 1920s would have boasted about concealing their bloodlines after slipping in under the color barrier. Fausto Miranda believes it would have been impossible for a known player of mixed race to enter the major leagues, but concedes that there was speculation about a Cuban pitcher for the Cincinnati Reds named Pedro Dibut (1924–1925). "He had a very dark complexion," said Miranda. "But there was no proof he was a mulatto." Bjarkman also notes that Dibut was "Absolutely, very dark."

Mixed marriages in Cuba among middle- and lower-income families were not unusual. Rodolfo Fernandez remarked that during his 40 years of playing baseball in Latin America and the United States he knew several players who were definitely of mixed race, including fellow Cuban, Bobby Estalella (1935–1949).[53]

In his book *Viva Baseball*, author Samuel O. Regalado stated that the Negro League star Willie Wells had been told by a Cuban ballplayer that Miguel Gonzalez's mother was black.[16] This rumor has been dismissed by many authorities, but it adds more fuel to a subject that may have embers of truth.

Perhaps these players successfully concealed their mixed-race ancestry in collusion with scouts or major league owners. Also, one could speculate that the major league owners found it less objectionable to bring in a dark-complexioned Latin ballplayer than an American of color.

Bjarkman noted, "Since they were not African American they were passed off as being foreigners, which did not tip the racial scales among hardliners." (Washington pitcher Alejandro Carrasquel, 1939–1949[42]; Cincinnati pitcher Tomas de la Cruz, 1944[44]; and veteran Cubs pitcher Hi Bithorn, 1942–47[35] were among the other major league ballplayers who were considered possibly to be of black African ancestry.)

RODOLFO FERNANDEZ
Born June 27, 1911

---

*Growing up poor on the outskirts of Havana, Rodolfo Fernandez
found solace in the game of baseball. As a teenager in the late 1920s
he pitched in the neighboring towns trying to earn money.*

*After a short stint in the Cuban League he joined the Negro
leagues from 1935 until 1939, pitching for the New York Cubans and
the Cuban Stars. He was elected to the Cuban Hall of Fame in 1966.*

*Fernandez's heroics on the diamond are seldom observed by
baseball historians in America, but he is revered by fans in the Latin
community. One Cuban sports editor eloquently summed up his
career with this statement, "His name is etched in golden letters in
the history of our national pastime. Rodolfo Fernandez is an immor-
tal figure in Cuban baseball."*[55]

*When he retired from baseball in 1973 he was at the age when
most people start preparing themselves for retirement. But a lifetime
of hard work in the segregated leagues offered little in compensation.
Because of economics, Fernandez was forced to take a job at New York
City's St. Luke's Hospital. He labored there until he turned 73 years
old.*

*When these interviews were conducted, Rodolfo Fernandez was
believed to be one of the oldest living Cuban ballplayers from the professional ranks. Research at that time concluded that there may have
been one or two former Cuban ballplayers living in Latin America
who were older, but attempts to locate them had failed.*

I was born in Guanabacoa, on the outskirts of Havana. My father was
a laborer and we were very poor. I was the youngest of 11 children.

We didn't have any appropriate fields to play baseball so we would just
play in any field we could find. At first we would use rocks for bases, but
as time went by we found better places to play. My brother, José, was very
talented and he eventually played professional baseball also. He was a
pretty good catcher.

There was no money for bats so during my childhood we would make
a bat out of any tree limb. We had nobody to teach us the fine points of the
game, but we only had the natural instinct of Cuban boys. We couldn't have
real gloves like the kind that were sold in stores, so each of my friends had
gloves that we made ourselves. We put together a glove any way we could,
using cardboard or cloth.

We went through a lot to learn how to play, but the big percentage of the boys just loved the game so we just endured. We would make the ball out of anything we could find: like some old socks we would make into a round shape with something heavy on the inside. It was the kind of ball that was only good for the street. It was very rustic.

But, just like baseball itself, our equipment evolved. As the years went by I began to play in other clubs, first as an amateur and as time progressed I made it to play professional.

As it happens here in the USA the great players begin in elementary school and then go to high school. They learn not only to play ball by instinct, but they also have coaches and people who teach them how to play. Then it becomes a career. But for me it was purely by instinct. I didn't have anyone to teach me how to play and improve. However, I liked it so much that I worked hard and eventually I became a ballplayer.

In Cuba baseball was played a lot and it was quite the craze. As a child I didn't have money to go to the games and of course most of the professional games were played in Havana. Even though it only cost five cents to go from my town to Havana I couldn't afford it. Not even to see the episodes of the American western movies which were shown in the cinemas. They would show part of a episode one day, only to have it continued the next day. But the next day maybe I didn't have the five cents. It seems impossible, but it did happen all through Cuba.

I always was a pitcher, because I liked it very much. I am a right-hander. I pitched mostly what is called a straight fastball. This is the first pitch that I learned when I started throwing a rock to hit a target. So later one learns different pitches, such as a curveball and others, by playing every day.

I played every day in the 1920s against whoever we could find to play. When I was 16 and 17 years old I tried to make a living with the other boys playing ball in the other towns. Sometimes we would take one dollar a week. It was a difficult time.

Then one day in 1929 my brother took me to a ball game in Havana and I met Martin Dihigo. He was, what one could say, the biggest baseball figure in Cuba. I was not playing at that time for any team in Havana, but later I did play with him. Not only that, I did play against him.

I played in Mexico once and he was the manager and I played here in the United States and he was the manager. He was an extraordinary figure. His was the greatest name that existed at that time.

But you can say a lot about Martin. He had extraordinary qualities, because he could play any position, which is something that not anybody can do. A pitcher usually knows only how to pitch and a third baseman can only play his position. Martin was the greatest player of all times. He was a hero and inspiration to the black ballplayers in Cuba, because he was so good.

The younger generation in Cuba today doesn't know that we existed, because that information is being kept silenced.

In professional ball discrimination did not exist in Cuba. But in amateur ball there was some. Maybe you don't believe it, but in Cuba there were things that were wrong. The amateurs did not like the colored ballplayer in their amateur leagues. Since I had trouble playing in the amateur leagues, we played around the small towns hoping to make a little money.

Everybody — blacks and whites — got together in the winter league professional ball, though. But the amateur league was tough for the colored ballplayers. This was class and economic discrimination, not color.

As time evolved and one became better known one could move up to professional status. In 1930 I was hired by a scout to play for the Almendares team in Havana. We were scouted by guys who were also looking for boxing prospects.

The two rival teams in Cuba then were Almendares and Havana. Also there was Marianao and Cienfuegos. There were people within the same family who were for one or the other teams. At dinner time family members wouldn't even sit at the same table because of the rivalry.

When I started with Almendares you would not believe it. The situation politically in Cuba was very bad. So we played for nothing at first. Somebody asked me one time why I would play if I didn't make any money. I told them that I play because I love baseball. There! Sometimes I made about one dollar a game. It seems impossible. Later the situation improved and we were paid a salary. Believe it or not, one year I pitched for Almendares I won the championship. I was the best and I played for only $125 a month.

Then the trips came, which were many, and I enjoyed them very much. We were very lucky because we had a chance to play in Mexico, Puerto Rico, Venezuela, and Canada. We got to see and meet some great ballplayers wherever we went. After I started to play in these different countries I made $200 a month.

In the 1920s and 1930s there were many of us Cuban players who were recommended to certain black clubs in America. So, many Cuban black players, like myself, played in the black leagues in the summer. We also had a chance to play in Puerto Rico, so we could play all year long.

When I played in the United States in the black leagues in 1935 I found that it was really high quality baseball. Very extraordinary. We would actually make enough to pay for our meals and then earn a salary too!

Rodolfo Fernandez in an Almendares
uniform in the 1930s. Courtesy of the
Rodolfo Fernandez collection.

When I played for the New York Cubans we would make long, long trips by bus when we were playing in the South. On the road sometimes we would drive 200 miles after finishing a game, because we would play again the next day. Sometimes we did not have a chance to stop and eat. It was a lot of tough work and sacrifice, but we loved the game so much.

I found that I couldn't play in the major leagues because of my color. This was very important to bring up and I think we need to talk about what happened. That was such a primitive thing. Sometimes we wouldn't find a place to sleep, so we would sleep on the bus. There were many places we could not enter to eat, but oftentimes there was a white Cuban ballplayer around and he would fetch food for us. All of this is enough to make a movie.

I was proud though, because when we would play in the United States, people would point us out as Cubans. This was because the Cubans had something that other people thought was special. Cubans have what they have because we were born with natural ability and intelligence for this game.

In 1936 the Brooklyn Dodger club went to Cuba to play exhibition games and we, the Cuban All-Star team, played against them. Leo Durocher was the manager for that team. I had a high point in my career pitching one day against them. This is very important because I pitched what they called the Nine Zeros — a shutout.

I also pitched against the New York Giants in 1937 when Bill Terry was the manager. They came down to Cuba and we played six games against them. I pitched one game and I beat the Giants 4–0.

I beat the Cincinnati Reds in Puerto Rico 2–1. You know how much I made for that game? Just $15.

But I'm very proud of those games. Although I didn't play in the big leagues I played against big league teams in which I won.

There was another important figure in Cuban baseball. His name was

Pompez. You know everybody called him Alex Pompez, but his name is Alejandro. He did work for the New York Giants when they started to sign the colored ballplayers. He took all the best colored ballplayers and tried to get them into the Giants. He was a very tough guy. But by the time Pompez was helping black ballplayers I was too old.

One year I played in three different countries. I remember in 1937 I played in the Dominican Republic for one summer season. When I finished there I went to play in Venezuela, which was the first time I played in South America. After two months in Venezuela I went to Cuba, because they had started the winter league.

Life After the Game

I was in baseball over 40 years. I quit pitching because I had trouble with my arm, so I coached and managed up until about 1973 in the Dominican Republic and other places.

After I quit baseball I had to find a job, because I needed the money. So I went to work for a hospital that was four blocks from my house. I retired from the hospital about 14 years ago, in 1984.

All my family in Cuba has died. My brother José, who played baseball with me when we were young, died in Cuba about 15 years ago. I didn't go back to Cuba since 40 years ago. You know how bad the situation has been for the Cuban people. Because of their government I didn't have a chance to go back and see my family before they died.

I lost everything that I had left behind in Cuba before the revolution in the 1960s. Everything. Somebody took it, broke it, threw it out.

Baseball Today

I look at the Cuban players of today. They are not pampered in Cuba. They had a tough life there. That's why they are so exciting to see now. Some of them risked everything coming over here on a boat. Look at "El Duque" Hernandez [*New York Yankees pitcher*]. He always dreamed of playing for the Yankees. And now he risked his life to see the dream come true. He could have disappeared.

We, the ballplayers who played for the black leagues, have been the object of a lot of interest and activity in the last few years. For example, with the Yankees and Mr. George Steinbrenner. There was a celebration at Yankee Stadium five years ago. A group of us from the Negro leagues came together and Mr. Steinbrenner gave us a special seating area with all sorts of attributes and gifts.

Last year they had a celebration in Atlanta and in June 1998 they had one in Milwaukee. All of this happened when we least expected it. We had the opportunity to live those moments that we were not able to have. We were not able to demonstrate who we were, or what talents we had, in a big league ballpark when we were young.

Now after all these years we have been recognized. Now Martin Dihigo is in the Hall of Fame, even though he didn't play in the big leagues. But, according to all the statistics and because of all the writers and baseball experts, he has been recognized.

You know when we played we did not have a record of our achievements. No one kept records so we did not have any propaganda about ourselves. I played all over South America and the Caribbean and America, but I don't have a book or a record of my accomplishments. Everything I say to you is in my memory, believe it or not.

I still get people requesting pictures and autographs. When these people ask me what I want for my autograph I just laugh and tell them to send me something for my arthritis.

After the world champion Giants lost five out of six games to the Cubans in 1937 (including Fernandez' shutout), a frustrated Bill Terry tersely summed up his feelings to a New York Times writer.

"This thing has long ceased to be a joke," he said.[15]

Fernandez's comments regarding an economic segregation in Cuban amateur leagues certainly challenges the notion that Cuban baseball was completely integrated. Baseball writer Peter Bjarkman claims the main reason for this discrimination was that amateur teams were sponsored by all-white social clubs like the elite Havana Tennis Club.

Rodolfo's brother, José, began his professional career as a catcher in the Negro leagues in 1916. Although he was light-skinned, he never had the opportunity to play in the major leagues. He was good enough to spend 35 seasons in professional ball, including a long stint with Alex Pompez's Cuban Stars.

His son, Pepe, played in the Negro leagues for two years. José died in 1971 at the age of 75.

MEMORIES OF CUBA

The following interviews reflect experiences of ballplayers who came to Cuba for the first time during the golden age. The author extracted these anecdotes from the original interviews in an effort to present the entire Cuban experience in one chapter.

There is also a brief interview with Adrian Zabala, a light-skinned Cuban, who went on to sign with the Giants' organization in the late 1930s. Zabala, who grew up during the 1920s, was inspired by the great Cuban players of that era.

TED RADCLIFFE
Negro Leagues 1927–46

A lot of us Negro League players went down to Cuba and Mexico and Puerto Rico to play. I played in Cuba for four years and believe me the people in Cuba were great and the women were beautiful. It was so nice and wonderful down there. I loved it.

The first Cuban players I remember seeing were Cando Lopez, Yo Yo Diaz, and Martin Dihigo in 1928 [*Cuban Stars*]. Martin Dihigo was one of the best all-around players that ever lived.

Later I caught Dihigo in two no-hitters in Mexico and I pitched against him and beat him 1–0. But we were good friends. He and his wife and kids used to come with me to the racetrack.

When I was going to Cuba in 1937 and 1938 Rodolfo Fernandez was on the same team with me. We still talk and I see him all the time when I go to New York. He's another one who I was good friends with.

The stadium in Cuba was one of the best I have ever been to in my whole life: Tropical Stadium. Left-field line was 399 feet, right-field line was 399 feet, and center field went on forever. No home runs hit out there, but you could hit them between the outfielders and get an inside-the-park home run. I just loved that place because I could throw what I wanted up there and let them catch it in the outfield.

Of course I knew Mike Gonzalez and Dolf Luque. Gonzalez was a friend of mine. But I'll have to tell you about Luque.

I was the leading pitcher in Cuba for four years in a row and I had been pitching with Mike Gonzalez's team. One year I didn't go back so Dolf Luque sent for me to play on his team. He kept calling me so I finally went back to play for him.

We were leading the league by ten games and I had won eleven straight games that year until this one game. We had this boy named Rodolfo, a Cuban-born player at short. He threw the ball away on a play to first.

Martin Dihigo pitched against me in that game and he beat me 2–1 in 12 innings. That was the first game I lost.

So in the clubhouse Luque and I got into an argument over the loss, and he called me a son of a bitch and I called him a son of a bitch. Then he pulled out a gun and shot at me. The owner of the Cuban Stars, Mr. [*Alex*] Pompez, was in the room and he hit his [*Luque's*] arm. If he hadn't hit him he would have shot me in the head.

Mr. [*Jorge*] Pasquel, a Mexican baseball promoter, was there in Cuba and he gave me a two-year contract for a $1,000 a month to go to Mexico to play. He also gave me $2,500 in advance and so I left with him.

Well, Luque came after me and wanted me to come back to his team, but I wouldn't talk to him. He shot at me, I'll tell you.

Everyone loved to come down there to gamble. Leo Durocher spent a lot of time down there. Him and George Raft were doing the poker games. The guys who owned the casino were good friends of mine.

My wife was lucky once down there. I never will forget they had a horse down there in 1939 called Charlie Chaplin. They wouldn't let him race in the United States because he was 14 years old. I didn't pay no mind because he was 75 to 1. My wife bet on him anyway and he won the race. They paid $222. I just loved Cuba.

[*The actor, George Raft loved baseball as much as he loved gambling in Cuba. During his youth he was a batboy for the New York Highlanders, later named the Yankees.*[4]]

CLYDE SUKEFORTH
National League 1926–34

We trained down in Cuba several times in the 1920s and early 1930s and we just loved it. Their government came up and recruited us. I went down there with some of the greatest players in baseball. We had Bill Terry at first base. "Rabbit" Maranville at second; Glenn Wright at shortstop; Paul Waner at third; and Carl Hubbell pitching. I caught every inning of the tour, which was 4 to 6 weeks long.

I was honored that I was asked to go, because all of the players were famous except me. I guess I was along just to make them look good.

The people were baseball crazy and they were very nice to us. At that time the Cuban leader wanted to get his people's minds off politics so he arranged for two barnstorming All-Star teams from the United States.

The first year we went we encountered storms off North Carolina and the ride over on a boat called the *Morro Castle* was rough. The next year it burned and sank.

I was already playing on the Reds with the greatest Cuban pitcher, Dolf Luque, and of course I saw him pitch in Cuba. He was a short, little right-hander: kind of stocky with one of the greatest curveballs you ever looked at.

BOB CREMINS
American League 1927

I was 15 when I first went to Cuba on the SS *Siboney* out of Pier 13 in New York [*1921*]. One of the guests on our boat was Thomas Edison and I was a deckhand. That's how I paid for my trip. Everyone wanted to go to Cuba back then. The kids were running around half naked because it was so hot. You know, just a pair of skivvies on. Baseball was everywhere. They were baseball crazy.

When I went back to New York I was playing for the Pelham Fire Department and we used to play some of the Negro League teams on Sundays. So once we played the Cuban Giants and some of those great players I saw from Cuba were on the team. They were very good.

ADRIAN ZABALA
Born August 26, 1915

Adrian Zabala's experience as a young man in Cuba in the 1920s is very similar to that of many young men who grew up in rural areas of America. Unable to see professional players in Havana until he was a teenager, Zabala was suddenly inspired to lift himself from the amateur ranks. His professional career lasted from 1935 until 1957 with a short stint with the New York Giants.

He currently lives in Florida with his family.

I was born about 20 miles from Havana in eastern Cuba, in a small town called San Antonio de los Baños.

When I was 13 years old I was on an amateur team and our manager that one year was the famous Rafael Almeida. His family was from the Canary Islands or were Portuguese. He was definitely dark-skinned but that didn't stop him from getting into the big leagues though. He played third base for Cincinnati way back before I was born.

He was called "El Principe" [*the Prince*] because he was dressed really nice all the time. He dressed like he had a million dollars. He had a cigar in his mouth and always dressed in white. He wore a white Panama hat and had a big ring.

He was a very nice man, but I was young and he didn't pay much attention to me. I remember one thing about him. He always tried to teach us to pull the ball to right field. He said, "When you get a man on first base try to hit the ball to right field because the first baseman has to hold the runner. You've got a big hole out there."

The first time I saw professional Cuban ballplayers I think was around the late 1920s. That day I was playing on our town's amateur team in Havana. After the game I didn't go back to my town to be with my family, but instead I went to the ball game. And there I saw the Almendares team play. Besides Cubans they had guys there from Puerto Rico and black ballplayers from the United States.

Yes, watching my fellow Cubans play professional ball made me want to try to play. I saw Bob Estalella and Dolf Luque and Mike Gonzalez down there on the field. There were a lot of people watching them play in the ballpark and it was very exciting.

I said to myself, "Gee I can do this. I've got to try this. Try to play ball professionally." After I became a professional I played with all those Cuban guys that I saw that day.

Of course, in Cuba black players and the white players all played together. We were just like family and we had to protect one another. We just wanted to win, because if we won we made more money. We would fight for each other.

Back then the fans used to play music during the game. There was one guy with a siren that would drive you crazy. Every time there was a home run or a strikeout he would sound the siren. There was one guy with a trumpet and a group that would play the bongos. Yelling and singing. They weren't paid for that. They just did it because they wanted to.

The first time I pitched professionally was in 1935 for the Marianao team. When I started there, they called me "Country Boy" because I came from a small town.

I played for several Cuban greats including Dolph Luque. He had a hot temper. He wanted you to do it just like he'd say or he'd get mad at you. I had a fuss with him a couple of times, but the next day we'd forget about it. I guess he liked the way I pitched.

But in the beginning I was a little wild and I didn't have good control, you know. So I'd make a mistake and gave up a home run and he'd get on me. He'd say, "Hey, I told you this or that." Luque would fuss and fight with everybody.

One time one of our players was on second base and Luque was coaching at third. This guy tried to steal third base and they threw him out. We didn't know how Luque would react, but we knew he was mad. Luque didn't want him to try to steal.

Suddenly he started to play like he had a machine gun in his hand and he pretended to point it at the player on the ground and went "Tat-tat-tat-tat." Everybody started laughing, including Luque.

One time we were playing against Almandares in Tropical Stadium and Luque was our manager. I was pitching and the game was 3–2 in our favor. In the ninth inning Almandares got two men on base with two outs. So the batter was Hector Rodriguez, who eventually played with the White Sox. He hit a fly ball to right field, which was an easy play. So we all started running to the clubhouse because we thought the game was over. Our right fielder, Pedro, came in on the ball and it hit him right on top of the head. The ball was hopping all over the outfield. I was walking across the infield to the clubhouse and people started yelling. Well, Pedro was looking for the ball and the two runners scored and we lost the game. Oh boy, Luque was mad. But I'll never forget, we were all laughing so hard. We had a saying, "The ball is round but sometimes it acts like it's square."

Martin Dihigo was my manager once in Cuba. If you did something wrong he'd just say, "You know you did this wrong. Next time do this and this." He tried to teach you. He was much different from Luque.

One day he said to me, "I know you had only one day rest, but today is the last day of the season and we have to win. You've got to pitch today. I don't want to finish in last place."

Even though I had no rest I agreed with him. We respected him because he knew a lot about baseball. I always listened to him because he was a very good teacher. Actually, he was good at everything. A great pitcher, a good hitter, and fielder.

One time we had a poor guy on our team playing shortstop who was also from my town. He was married and had two or three kids and he wanted to play baseball real bad so he could make a living. One day he made an error on a play and we ended up losing the game. Of course, Dihigo wanted to let him go, but I told him he was poor and he had three kids. If he didn't have a job playing ball he would have a very hard time.

Adrian Zabala in 1945. Courtesy of the Zabala family collection.

So Dihigo went over to the guy in the locker room and told him he could keep his job. He didn't let him go because Dihigo wanted him to support his family. The guy wanted to cry. Dihigo knew how to treat people. He was nice to everybody.

It was 1936 when I first met Joe Cambria and my life changed. A friend of mine asked me to go to Tropical Stadium, because Cambria had heard of me and he wanted to see how I threw the ball. So I got out there and started warming up. I threw the ball about six or seven times and I was throwing pretty good. I had good speed.

Cambria said, "You don't have to throw anymore. You can go." That's what he said to me. Then he said, "Do you want to go to the United States?" And I said, "But, I don't speak English! Besides that I have to speak to my daddy."

"You know," he said, "they pay you money to play." He explained the situation to me. He wanted me to call him Papa Joe.

When Cambria asked me to play I was glad. I wanted to get away from Havana and go someplace new. So I went to my dad and he said, "If you go play ball how are you going to make a living?"

I said, "Daddy, they'll pay me to play baseball!" He couldn't believe it.

So he said, "Oh, Oh." And he changed his mind and he let me go.

I went to the United States in 1936 to spring training with Joe Cambria in Daytona Beach and then Palatka, Florida. But I was unhappy. I couldn't speak English and I couldn't get to know anybody. In 1937 I went up to play in Panama City, Florida, and I made $65 per month. But you know, I would come back to Cuba every year to play in the winter league.

The New York Giants bought my contract in 1939 and I played in Jersey City. Bill Terry was my manager.

My professional career lasted all the way up to 1957. But through all that time I'll never forget when I was young and I first saw all those Cuban ballplayers. I said to myself, "Gee, I can do this." And I did it.

4. Baseball Writers

"The sport writer joins hands with the player as the creator of baseball. Without his keen eye, shrewd judgment, and graphic pen the game would never have advanced beyond the embryo stage. To him, baseball owes a staggering debt. Some writer introduced each coming baseball star to the waiting audience of the great American public, some group of writers gave to each player the reputation he carries."

John J. Ward, 1915[26]

THIS CHAPTER IS DEDICATED TO THE MEMORY OF HAROLD ROSENTHAL.

The 1920s was an era when, for the vast majority of Americans, images of Babe Ruth's swing and Walter Johnson's fastball could only be captured in the mind's eye. The average baseball fan could only rely on the swift and eloquent pen of the sportswriter to describe history unfolding. Metaphors were the fuel that transported the images to the most rural fan.

Jack Lang, the prizewinning New York journalist, described the golden age of sportswriting best.

As far as history's sake, the giants of this industry were working in the twenties. Back then the writer had a chance to elaborate. Writers waxed poetic for five or six paragraphs before they even told you who was playing. Sometimes you didn't get the scores until the fifteenth or sixteenth paragraph.

They described the weather, the stadium, the crowd — which you couldn't get by with today.

Back then the only way people got their sports was through the newspaper.

"Broadcasting the Score," a light-hearted depiction of the knothole clubs that abounded during the first decades of the century, before brick and concrete park walls became standard.

There are precious few sportswriters still alive today who were active in the late 1920s or early 1930s. The gentlemen who relate their stories in the following segments are important to the theme of this book because they are the last scribes of that era.

They invite you to sit down and listen to their wonderful stories about the near-mythical gods they knew. These five men can tell us what Ruth, Cobb, Hornsby and Alexander were like as a gifted young players. They can also paint a sobering picture of their final years.

Each of these journalists were young baseball fans during the late 1910s and early 1920s. Blessed with the unique gift of translating their experiences into an articulate phrase, they offer a rare look at what baseball was like from the perspective of a young fan in the early years of the decade.

They can also evoke scenes of the early newsroom that we have been conditioned to from movies from the 1930s, like *Platinum Blond* and *Front Page*, which solidified our stereotypes of the frantic, exciting world of journalism. The eclectic mix of diverse personalities that powered the authors to eloquence were as sensational as any fictional Hollywood characters.

The golden age supported the greatest collection of baseball writers ever, and Grantland Rice was their king. *Baseball Magazine* hailed Rice as "The Ty Cobb of Sports Writers."[26] He wrote sport's most recognizable words:

For when the One Great Scorer comes to mark against your name,
He writes — not that you've won or lost — but how you played the game.

Rice always tried to find the most favorable qualities in an athlete and seldom ever wrote about their failings. His columns would begin with a poem. A whimsical verse that painted an image of the times. Author John J. Ward proclaimed, "The amount of clever verse which he dashes off in the course of a year would stagger an epic poet of the old school."[26]

His off-the-cuff remarks were as remarkable as those set in type. Once in 1948 he quipped, "Cleveland didn't deserve to win the pennant. It had a weak infield — and no hotels."

While working for the *Atlanta Journal* in 1904, Rice began to receive telegrams and postcards hailing a dashing, young baseball star playing with an outlaw league team in Alabama. The correspondence, some of which was unsigned, urged him to write a piece on this 18-year-old hero of the diamond: one Ty Cobb.

Rice wrote a sparkling review and later went down to Alabama to see Cobb for himself. He agreed that the testimonials were accurate.

Forty years later Cobb admitted to Rice that he had been the author of those postcards. "I was in a hurry," Cobb replied when Rice demanded an explanation.[27]

Within six years of coming to New York to write, Rice was commanding the highest salary of any sportswriter in the country. In 1915 *Baseball Magazine* estimated his annual salary, "between $15–$20,000 per year." His 53-year career was legendary.

Damon Runyon of the *New York American* sported wire-rimmed glasses and wore his black hair slicked back to the style of the times. He was the sartorial dandy of the golden age. When Casey Stengel hit an inside-the-park home run in the 1922 World Series, Runyon took seven sentences to describe the run. His eloquence was unmatched.

He also began sketching short biographies of New York's nocturnal community. From this collection he eventually wrote *Guys and Dolls*.

Ford Frick wrote for the *New York Evening Journal* for nearly 15 years before he went to work at the National League offices in 1934. By 1951 he became the third commissioner of baseball.

For many years Frick was Babe Ruth's ghost writer.[8]

Paul Gallico of the *Daily News* was articulate and physically powerful. He abruptly quit journalism to write fiction. His two greatest works were *The Snow Geese* and *The Poseidon Adventure*.

Shirley Povich was 92 years old when he died and it took the intervention of angels to end his 75-year writing career.

Povich joined the *Washington Post* in 1924 as a copy boy and continued to write up until the day he died in June 1998. He was one of the few who crusaded for racial integration of all sports that he covered, including baseball.

In his later years he railed against the Washington football club for being so slow to sign black football players. In one classic article he wrote, "Jim Brown, born ineligible to play for the Redskins, integrated their end zone three times yesterday."

He has been eulogized as "The one clear voice that influenced Washington from Prohibition ... to Watergate."

To give some perspective to his career, imagine this. He interviewed the young Lou Gehrig during his first full season with the Yankees and was on hand to cover the 1995 contest in which Cal Ripken broke Gehrig's consecutive game record.

Ring Lardner did it all. He was a novelist, playwright, lyricist, humorist, and sportswriter. Lardner wrote a popular fictional series for the *Saturday Evening Post* about a young ballplayer trying to break into the majors, "You Know Me Al — A Busher's Letters." Eighty-three years after this collection of humorous and poignant letters was published it is still considered to be some of the finest baseball fiction ever written.

Other newspapermen during that time, who cannot be excluded, were Fred Lieb, Ed Sullivan, H. G. Salsinger, Fred Russell and Heywood Broun.

Even frontier legend Bat Masterson did occasional editorials on corruption in sports for the *New York Telegraph* until his death in October 1921.[61]

They were the best in the best of times.

When live radio broadcasts of ball games began in the early 1920s several writers took a turn at this novelty. Grantland Rice announced both the 1922 and 1923 World Series. Two of the games he was scheduled to cover were never aired because of trouble finding sponsors.[28]

Ring Lardner was not so impressed. Enduring one game in which he sat next to pioneer broadcaster Graham McNamee, he scrawled, "I don't know which game to write about — the one I saw today, or the one I heard Graham McNamee announce."[28]

One of the most popular sports magazines available during the 1920s was *Baseball Magazine*, which began publication in 1908. Selling for 20 cents an issue, it reached an audience of 500,000 fans by the time the Depression began. It featured articles authored by the great players of the day and boasted that it was "Brimful of live baseball dope."

Contrary to popular belief, there is only one sportswriter who has been inducted into the Hall of Fame. Henry Chadwick, a British born journalist, is credited with several innovations in baseball, including designing the system that we use for scoring. Since his induction in 1938, the great baseball writers of the twentieth century have been honored with the J. G. Taylor Spink Award. This honor is presented by the National Baseball Hall of Fame for meritorious contributions to baseball writing.

Being recognized with this award is not an induction to the Hall of Fame, but it is one of the highest awards a baseball writer can achieve. According to Cooperstown officials, "It's only technically correct to use the term Hall of Fame sportswriter. It should be clarified that the writer won the Spink Award." The J. G. Spink Award has been given to 49 men from 1962 to 1998. Included on that list are Runyon, Lardner, Rice, Salsinger, Broun, Lieb, and Povich.

WILL CLONEY
Born October 29, 1911

Will Cloney was destined to be a writer. After graduating from Boston Latin (Prep) School in 1929, he went directly to the copy desk of the Boston Globe. *His work on the paper put him through Harvard University and earned him a lifetime of awards, including the Boston Gridiron Club and the Harvard Varsity Club awards.*

After 70 years of writing and winning recognition from his colleagues he modestly jokes about the notoriety. "For twenty years I had my name in Who's Who in America *right next to Rosemary Clooney. After a 20-year run my name was removed. I guess I was too old for them," he quipped.*

Cloney still lives in the Boston area.

I was born and raised in Boston and I grew up as a fan of baseball, not just the Red Sox or the Braves. I was five or six when I started seeing the Red Sox and of course I saw Babe Ruth and Cobb. That was from the stands. I didn't see them up close until later when I interviewed them both.

I was not on the school newspaper but during high school in the 1920s I submitted a few things to little sports publications. It was a few paragraphs on sports. Just quips and oddities. That's where it began for me. I started at Harvard in 1929 and quickly went to work at the *Boston Herald*. That was the start of the Great Depression, but I didn't even know it, because I had a regular job.

I immediately started to learn how to become a copy editor. It was a pretty fortunate situation, because I was so young to do that. I corrected mistakes and turned ideas into readable English. Correcting the spelling and all that sort of stuff.

Our best sports writer at that time in the 1920s and 1930s was probably Stanley Woodward, who became the editor of the *Herald Tribune* and later became the first editor of *Sports Illustrated*. He was eccentric and colorful and he was so very versatile.

The sports room was not very raucous. It was fairly business, but not quite like it was portrayed in the old movies. There were no women in there at all, so it was more like a men's club than anything else. It was loose during the free time between the time you put the paper to bed and when the first copies came out. You waited to see if it came out the way you expected. That would be the time that you would send out for pints of ice cream or go across the street to a speakeasy for a short beer during prohibition. When things were dull we'd play hockey with rolled-up pieces of paper and sometimes

Will Cloney in the 1950s. Courtesy of Marc Okkonen.

we'd throw glue pots around with open tops. A few minor items like that.

When I first started a very good writer gave me a lecture and said, "Now just keep your nose clean and you'll be fine. Stay away from alcohol and that kind of stuff and you'll be fine." So three years later he was fired for drinking.

I wrote college sports primarily in the early days and I would do an occasional major league baseball game, but not a regular beat. In those days Ivy League sports was much more important than they are now. I got to know the baseball coach at Harvard, Fred Mitchell, pretty well. He played major league baseball after the turn of the century for Boston [*American and National League teams*] and Brooklyn. He was crusty, but pretty sharp. As a matter of fact he is still remembered with great admiration.

When I started covering the big leagues it was less difficult than it is today. The games were all played in the daytime and the farthest west was St. Louis, which made covering the games easy. You could finish a three o'clock game and get down to the locker room, talk to the players and the manager, and get back to the press box to have the story ready for deadline.

The method of transcription was completely different, because we had a Morse code telegrapher right at our elbow in the press box. We'd dictate to him and he would have a direct line to our office. Today you don't have that middle man at all because of computers.

In those days you covered *the game* and you didn't get into all the deep personal background stuff on the players that people are doing now. It was a much looser type of thing then than it is now. It's become a great deal more business than it was in those days. I'd go into the locker room and just talk to the players and listen and look. We could just go in and wander around before and after the game. Once in a while we were restricted from going into the medical room.

The manager's office was the focal point of the locker room, and it still is. We would congregate in the manager's office for a post-game conference. You could easily get a quote, but it would depend on the individual personality. They were, in general, not well schooled compared to the present-day ballplayer. Most ballplayers now have gone to college or graduated from high school. A lot of the players were pretty raw-boned back in those days. Their replies would be less informational.

They were like just any other group of men. You got some who were very voluble and some men who were silent. But they didn't seem to have the vendetta that baseball players have now. Some of them won't talk to writers at all and they've just taken a vow of silence. You had very, very little of that in those days. It was a long, long time ago, but one of the first interviews I had was with Billy Southworth, who was a great outfielder before he managed the Braves. He and I got to be pretty friendly.

In the old days there were relatively few sportswriters covering baseball. When the Red Sox play here [*today*], the *Boston Globe* may have five staff writers covering it. Sixty or seventy years ago we'd have one.

There was a complete difference in the way you'd cover the out-of-town games, because normally you might not travel with the team. When we had two teams in Boston — the Braves and the Red Sox — there was always a home game every day. So the beat writer or the sports editor would stay in Boston and cover whichever team happened to be in town. Then you'd get the details of the other game from the local sportswriter in the town that the other team was playing in. Later the teams provided transportation and room and board so most papers would staff the out-of-town games.

I never fraternized with the ballplayers and I never drank at all when I was a sportswriter. That is very unusual, because after Prohibition every baseball park had a free bar for reporters. They had what we called the "work and recreation room" up behind the press box at Fenway Park. They had a bar there and they served free hot dogs and hamburgers. A half of an hour before the game you'd have to leave the dugout and to fill the time you'd go up there and eat. That's all changed.

I remember distinctly that they didn't have air conditioning in the press boxes and so we would take off our shirts. We'd be dressed just in our undershirts. This was on very hot days. In the late 1940s they introduced women telegraphers and so we had to leave our shirts on. Up to that time there were no women sportswriters at all, so you could be free and easy in the press box.

Back then there was a fellow reporter who was notorious for being late. I won't tell you what his name was, but he used to come in about the fourth or fifth inning and say, "Well, what happened?" And we'd have to fill him in, and as he wrote he'd say, "Yehhhs, yehhhs." He wrote the story as if he was there all the time. All I can say is that he was with another Boston paper.

You took care of each other. We had great camaraderie.

When you traveled by train you got a chance to mingle with the players a lot more than today where you have a quick plane ride. I've got this one little train anecdote which is kind of silly, but I'll tell you.

"Birdie" Tebbetts of Detroit was a prankster. I remember one night we were sitting around the train and their shortstop, Johnny Pesky, said, "Gee, I wish I had some candy."

Tebbetts heard him and said, "Oh, I just threw some candy bars in my berth on lower number 17. Go help yourself." So Pesky went down and he didn't come back for about five minutes. And Tebbetts had a funny look on his face. When Pesky finally came back he was all red in the face. He looked at Tebbetts and said, "You dirty so and so. When I reached my hand into that lower berth there was an old lady in there. She was quite upset."

They loved to pull tricks on one another. It was a good way to really get to know them.

We had quite a few colorful writers too. There was one, whom I will not name, who existed on liquor and candy bars in the press box. He had a great affinity for Pittsburgh and he somehow got in a scrape with the law after one game. He went staggering out of Forbes Field toward his hotel when he was stopped. In the course of the interrogation on the street he said to the police officer, "I will have to tell Mr. Rooney about this inquisition."

The policeman took a deep breath and said, "You know the Pirates owner, Art Rooney?"

The writer stopped for a second and drew himself up and said, "No, I don't mean Art Rooney! I mean Francis X. Rooney. The bartender at Forbes Field."

I've never forgotten that incident. Right out of W. C. Fields.

I had written about Ty Cobb as a ballplayer and of course I saw him play a great many times. Later on he came to Boston for an operation when

I was a pretty young writer. Well, an interview was arranged through the paper and I went up to the hospital. I had heard about how tough he was so I went up there with the idea of spending maybe 15 minutes with him. I didn't know what I was getting myself into. I got in his room and I found him charming and gracious. I couldn't get out of there. I must have been there for three hours with a guy who was supposed to be so tough that he would spike his own mother to get into second base. But then, I'm a pretty soft person. I try to find the nice parts about a person rather than the bad parts.

And then there was Babe Ruth. I talked to Ruth six or eight times, but the events at the end of his life stand out for me most. He finished up his career with the old Boston Braves here and I remember covering his last press conference. It was in a hotel room and he could hardly speak, because his voice was practically gone.

It was his death that I'll never forget. I was in New York when he died. I was traveling with the Braves and the game was rained out the day of the services. I remember he was being waked in the rotunda of Yankee Stadium and I walked over from the Polo Grounds to Yankee Stadium with Arthur Dely, the columnist for the *New York Times*.

We did not have to get in line, but rather we stood right at his bier the entire time! As we stood there I felt it was the most moving sight I've ever seen. There were all these people walking by, sobbing, touching the casket. The flowers and baskets and all the top celebrities in the city. Thousands of people came through. That was a touching scene.

To attend his funeral the next day you had to have a pass to get in. William Bendix, the actor who had played Babe Ruth in the movie, was among the pallbearers and that was quite a moving experience, too. As I thought back to his life I realized Ruth was more spectacular striking out than a regular ballplayer was hitting a home run. There was just something charismatic about the guy. [*For more information on the funeral see the postscript.*]

Joe DiMaggio was another one we loved to talk to. We all loved Joe. He was friendly and open and natural. As you can imagine, there were a lot of writers who were hero-worshipers. But when you're exposed to these people so intimately over such extended periods, its almost like man to man rather than hero worship. Just a little hero worship remains, but it becomes business. I treated them all as a business proposition.

I've been doing this so long I don't remember the first interview I ever did. Someone asked me if I kept clippings of all my stories, and I said I'd need Madison Square Garden to put it all in. No, I don't have any of the old stuff at all.

The one I remember most affectionately was Casey Stengel. Casey was a shrewd, smart guy and he knew that I knew that he was putting on an act most of the time. Every once in a while he'd give a double-talk answer to somebody and then look over at me and kind of smirk as if to say, "Boy I'm putting this one over pretty good." But he was no dope; as a matter of fact he could speak English if he wanted to. But he did have some colorful phrases which were not contrived.

After managing the Dodgers, he came to Boston in 1938 to manage the Braves. He used to get in all kinds of trouble. Some of the Boston writers didn't take him too seriously and gave him a hard time. He once was in a taxicab accident in Kenmore Square and when Casey was laid up in the hospital they wanted to give the cab driver a medal for his good work.

I thought it was kind of bad, because he did a pretty fair job. He was open to writers and in fact it was as if he was onstage. He'd sit in that dugout and just talk. He could give you a good story without him even knowing he gave you one.

One can't talk about Boston baseball without discussing Ted Williams. I could tell you all kinds of hair-raising stories about some of these people like Williams, but I won't. I will say this. I used to do a lot of speaking at communion breakfasts and sports' nights in this area, and invariably someone would ask how I feel about the way Ted Williams treated sportswriters.

I had a stock answer. I would say, "Ted Williams is paid to hit the ball over the fence, not to be nice to sportswriters."

Ted Williams, now, is completely, absolutely, different from the way he was. That's all I'll say about his early days. Quite a few years ago I happened to be in Winterhaven, Florida, when the Red Sox were training and Ted was there as the batting instructor. I was visiting the camp and talking to some of the writers in the outfield when I noticed Ted was standing nearby, all alone.

So I said to the writers, "Watch this and see what happens."

So I walked over and when I got maybe ten feet away from him he said, "Willie, my old friend." And he held out his arms and he gave me a big hug.

I said, "Ted, it wasn't so long ago that we had those terrible fights."

And he stepped back and showed mock amazement and said, "Well, we never had any fights did we?" (We had a couple of beauts too.)

So there was a pause for a minute and he asked, in a joking way, "Well, I won, didn't I?"

Babe Ruth's funeral was attended by thousands of people from all over the United States. Two of the pallbearers were his old New

York teammates Joe Dugan and Waite Hoyt. After laboring under the weight of the casket Dugan remarked, "I'd give a hundred dollars for a cold beer." "So would the Babe," replied Hoyt.[7, 8]

As mentioned by Cloney, William Bendix was present at the funeral. Bendix portrayed Ruth in the 1948 Hollywood flop The Babe Ruth Story.

In 1949 a baseball writer named Bill Stern published the story that, as a young boy, Bendix was hired as a batboy for the Yankees. "The chunky little batboy" latched onto Ruth and spent his days shining the Bambino's shoes, running errands, and genuflecting in worship. According to Stern, Bendix was the delivery boy who brought Ruth the dozen hot dogs and dozen bottles of soda pop that led to the "Bellyache heard 'round the world."[12] Although this legend has entertainment value, it has never been proven.

FRED RUSSELL
Born August 27, 1906

Fred Russell has had many accolades in his lifetime, but he wears the mantle of "Dean of the Southern Sportswriters" best. With the death of Shirley Povich in 1998, Russell was believed to be the oldest living sportswriter in America at the time of these interviews.

After graduating from Vanderbilt University, he quickly abandoned his career as a lawyer in favor of a job on the Nashville Banner. *From June 1929 until the paper folded in February 1998 Russell was the loyal and trustworthy prophet of sports in the South.*

He was held in such high regard by his colleagues that they convinced him to write an autobiography. In 1957 his memoirs, Bury Me in an Old Press Box *was published by A. S. Barnes.*

Within the past several years Russell endured two terrible losses. His wife of over 70 years, Kaye Early Russell, died and the paper he labored at for 69 years closed its doors. Despite these losses, he remains a gracious Southern gentleman.

Russell continues to live in Nashville, where he is considered to be an icon among the journalists of that area.

People are surprised when they hear that I didn't write for my high school or college papers. And when I entered Vanderbilt I only wanted to study law and become an attorney. But after graduating it didn't take long to change my occupation. When I started on the *Nashville Banner* in late June 1929 I was a police reporter. And it's true, that was my first writing experience.

But I was extremely lucky because the sports editor, Ralph McGill, left to join the *Atlanta Constitution* and they didn't replace him immediately. So in September of that year the publisher, James G. Stahlman, assigned me to the sports department to cover Vanderbilt football. One year later he named me the sports editor. Had McGill not made that move, my life would have been entirely different.

When I started, the basic salary was $6 a week plus extra for what you wrote. They had a system where they took what you wrote and it was actually measured out. You were paid for that. After five or six weeks I was put on a regular salary of $15 a week.

In 1929 I filled in when the baseball writer couldn't cover a game for some reason. I covered the Nashville Vols, short for Volunteers, which was in the Southern Association League. This was the team that I grew up watching. Their history goes back to 1900 and during this time they have been an independently owned team which had supplied players to the Cincinnati Reds and New York Giants.

I covered mainly minor league clubs, but I also covered the Nashville Negro club, called the Nashville Elite, pronounced Ee-Light. My first big assignment came in December 1929 when I was sent to cover the minor league convention in Chattanooga, Tennessee. It was about 130 miles from Nashville and all the baseball people from the major leagues and minor leagues attended it every year. It lasted about five or six days. It was the first time I saw Connie Mack and John McGraw.

My first interview was with Ty Cobb. Actually it was my first byline and it happened in the fall of 1929. He was coming through Nashville and was spending the night with a friend of his who had lived in Detroit. I went directly to his friends' house and we conducted the interview in his living room. We knew of his reputation, but since the interview was at his friend's house I felt there was no chance for anything unpleasant to happen. The circumstances were favorable for that. I found him naturally pleasant and he couldn't have been more responsive.

We were an afternoon paper and we had probably four or five editions. Our first edition was around 11 o'clock and our last edition was designed to catch the street cars that were taking the workers home at 4:30.

Covering ball games really was a leisurely assignment. Games started weekdays at three o'clock. I would get there about one o'clock and go into the dressing rooms and dugouts and talk to the players. I'd take notes and get enough stuff before the game to get a column out of it. I'd write about these conversations in the press box during the game so afterward we would have only the game to write about. Sports writing was a more leisurely thing back then.

Since I was also a correspondent for the newspapers in the member cities in the Southern Association, I had to be conscious of deadlines and file Western Union from the press box two or three times a game. I remember the *New Orleans Times* and the *Atlanta Constitution* had early deadlines and you had to make those editions by the fifth or the seventh inning.

The Yankees came through Nashville each spring, in early April, for an exhibition game. They were on their way north from St. Petersburg one year in the early 1930s and a friend of Babe Ruth's said he would try to set up an interview for me. This friend knew Ruth when he lived in New York and only been in Nashville for a few months working in the library. He arranged the interview for that day when the Yankees arrived.

They had traveled by train and arrived in the morning and I met the train and tried to interview him. That didn't work so I went to their hotel and met up with Ruth there. I didn't take too much of his time in the lobby of the hotel for the interview, because he was in a hurry to get somewhere. I talked to him for a few minutes and I thanked him and told him good-bye. But he surprised me by inviting me up to the hotel room to sit in on a card game.

The interview wasn't important enough for him to miss the card game and I didn't expect him to. It seems he enjoyed playing a few hands of bridge before the afternoon game at two o'clock, to relax. I went into the room, but I was sitting as far away as I could get, not to get in the way. But I wanted to see everything.

There were a couple of newspapermen from New York in the game and Ruth had a string of bad cards. After several bad hands, Ruth picked up the entire deck and tore them in two! You know a deck of cards is hard to tear, but he did it. I was really impressed with his strength. I thought it was thoroughly unexpected, but the other men at the table acted as if that was a regular thing.

Well, they had another deck, but within a few minutes his luck had not improved. He continued to get exceptionally bad cards. The funny thing was that some sportswriter named Richards Vidmer of the *Herald Tribune* in New York, saw Ruth's bad hands for the next 30 minutes. He must have thought that they were going to lose another deck, because he quickly went up to the telephone and called the newsstand in the lobby of the hotel and demanded a new deck of cards.

I have one, and only one, baseball "discovery." That was Truett Sewell.

"Rip" Sewell they called him. He was a cousin of Joe and Luke Sewell and he had a great major league career.

Sewell went to Vanderbilt and was a football player there for one year. He was working at Dupont in Nashville since he'd been out of college. One day in 1932 he called me. He wanted to play pro ball and so I took him down to the Nashville Vols' office to introduce him around. They gave him a tryout and he signed with Nashville a few weeks later. After playing outfield occasionally he was farmed to the Piedmont League, and was sold to the Detroit Tigers in August after he led the Piedmont League in winning percentages as a pitcher. He also set the record for strikeouts.

His claim to fame was that he invented the blooper pitch. He would use it two or three times a game. It was an extremely high and slow pitch. Ted Williams hit a home run off that pitch in an All-Star game once.

For 40 odd years I went to Florida to write about spring training, covering mainly the Yankees and later the Cincinnati Reds. I would spend about a month down in Florida with them. I was covering the Yankees in 1936 and I remember Joe DiMaggio just joining the team for his first year. He was so well mannered and a true gentleman.

I knew Grantland Rice very well. He was born in Murfreesboro about 30 miles south of Nashville. He went to New York about 1911.

He was working on his memoirs, *The Tumult and the Shouting*, but he died before it was finished. Dave Camerer finished it for him. Not many people know that. He was the greatest gentlemen in the newspaper business and I admired him very much.

I had been on the *Nashville Banner* for 25 years when the publisher and owner, James Stahlman, decided to have a banquet for me at the Vanderbilt gymnasium. He picked out a date in the fall and he invited all the sportswriters from the South. Red Smith from the *New York Herald Tribune* and Bill Corum from the Hearst papers were there, among many other sportswriters I knew. Grantland Rice sent a poem. He was ill at the time and the illness prevented him from coming.

But I had a big surprise waiting for me. Mr. Stahlman had Bobby Jones come in from Atlanta. Jack Dempsey came in from New York. Red Grange also came in to be with me. It was wonderful evening for me. I'll never forget that night [*see photograph*].

Mr. Russell is modest about the close friendship that he enjoyed with one of the great sportswriters of the time, Grantland Rice. In the recent biography, Sportswriter — The Life and Times of Grantland Rice, *the author, Charles Fountain, refers to their relationship as "profound and as enduring as that of a son for his father."*

Fred Russell in 1953 at the anniversary banquet of his 25th year at the *Nashville Banner*, with the greatest names in sports from the 1920s. *Left to right:* Red Grange, Bobby Jones, Fred Russell, and Jack Dempsey. Courtesy of the Fred Russell family collection.

HAROLD ROSENTHAL
Born March 11, 1914

In the early 1920s Harold Rosenthal was just another kid growing up in the center of baseball heaven. One moment he was in the Bronx with a bat in his hand, dreaming about baseball. The next moment he was in Manhattan with a pen in his hand, writing about baseball.

His recollections of growing up in the heart of baseball land during the greatest era of the game are priceless. Rosenthal got his first newspaper job at the age of 17 and was still writing almost 70 years later.

Despite a stroke in early 1998, the tough Bronx kid fought his way back and resumed his nostalgia column for College and Pro-Football Weekly *magazine. A second stroke took his life in June 1999.*

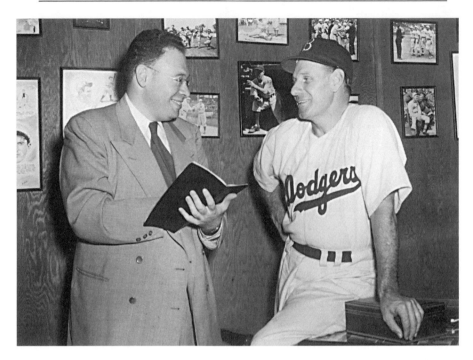

Harold Rosenthal in early 1941 with Leo Durocher. Courtesy of Harold Rosenthal.

Harold Rosenthal's contribution to this book was immense. Without his guidance and insight this chapter would never have been possible.

I still remember the lineup for the Yankees in the early 1920s. We'd memorize all that stuff when we were kids and you never forgot it. In New York we would polarize between Yankee rooters and Giant rooters. Of course, Brooklyn was 10,000 miles away and you didn't bother with Brooklyn at all. Yankees and Giants were the points of contention.

I grew up in four-story walkup tenement building, the kind where 10 to 25 families lived in four-room apartments. During Prohibition my Dad distilled whiskey on our stove top using corn or prunes. My mother's sheer terror was that the prune pits might get stuck in the still and blow the roof off the building. A lot of people in our neighborhood made their own. The Italians would have a barrel of wine down in the cellar. The Irish made home brew in the cellar. It seemed to satisfy the populace.

We played baseball between buildings on an unconstructed site. There would be very little playing in the parks, so we'd play in the rocks and broken glass with a paper sack for a base. That was our baseball.

Bronx was bisected by trolley lines that crisscrossed the borough. They were a five-cent ride and I'd take the trolley to Yankee Stadium and carry my lunch with me. It was standard stuff to sneak into the ballpark or the movies back in the 1920s. We were lucky though, because we didn't have to sneak into the Polo Grounds [*Home of the Giants*]. We went to the right field exit and stood there and waited until about two innings elapsed. Then a very gruff, but kindhearted superintendent would come out and say, "OK kids, go in." We couldn't go into the main area with the good seats, but we'd get into the bleachers. And oh, we would sit there and make a lot of noise. We'd do all that by cutting classes.

The first major leaguer that I had exposure to as a writer was a guy I knew about as a kid. In those days the kids didn't have the big money to spend on baseball cards. But we had a strip of laundry cardboard with baseball pictures printed on them in sequence. I was about ten years old, but I remember that there would be about a dozen pictures. You'd buy them for a penny and you'd cut out your favorite player.

The people who put these out didn't have much money I guess, because they never changed the pictures or the format. They were a muggy looking print on a rough cardboard and you could hardly make out the picture. We called them baseball tickets.

Well, the strip always started out with a picture of Hank Gowdy so I always had a lot of Gowdy pictures. Well, 20 some years later I came out of the army at the end of the Second World War and I'm covering the Giants for the paper. Hank Gowdy is now a coach for them and he was about 60.

So when I finally met him I started out the conversation by saying, "You know I used to collect you on those laundry board tickets." He stared at me. He didn't know what the hell I was talking about.

Pretty much everybody had nicknames back in the 1920s. If a kid had red hair they'd call him "Red." They called me "Skinny," because I was a fat kid. I remember that. Kids can be cruel. There was a kid who had a nervous twitch and instead of commiserating with the poor bastard they called him "Bugs." I haven't thought of that in a long time.

Very few people had radios back then, so all of your up-to-date information came from the papers. In those days there were maybe a half of a dozen afternoon papers. The *Sun*, the *Telegram*, the *Journal*. And they would make an effort to give you the late scores by 4:30 or 5 o'clock so you would know how the Yankees made out. You could get all your information without buying the paper because the afternoon papers would put the results on page one and they would lay them down, face up, on the newsstand. Afternoon papers were three cents and morning papers were two cents.

In those days, in New York, the big thing was to get a Jewish ballplayer, because there were so many Jews in New York. Rightfully, they thought that if they gave them somebody to root for they would come to the box office.

John McGraw discovered a kid named Andy Cohen who played second base in the Texas League and he brought him to New York to play for the Giants in 1926. They tried to have him appear to be the Jewish Babe Ruth. He had a hell of a spring in his first year but lasted in the major leagues only three seasons. He created more of a sensation than he was really worth. [*For more information on Andy Cohen, see the postscript.*]

People were more open in their prejudice back then than they are today. They're still prejudiced, but they conceal it. Back then when there was a Jewish player they would call him a name and think nothing of it. If there was an Italian player they'd call him a name and think nothing of it. If there had been any blacks in the major leagues God only knows what they would have said and done back then.

Hank Greenberg had to endure less than most because of his size. He was about 6 feet 4 inches and he was a tremendously powerful guy. He had a couple of fights to straighten some people out. I remember a fight with a Pittsburgh first baseman in particular. Once he started to hit home runs the way he did a lot of that prejudice started to fall away.

Hank came from the Bronx and he came from a middle-class, pretty good family. His father was in the dress or garment business downtown. When I was in high school, I remember, he was the star athlete for James Monroe High School and for some unknown reason they called him "Bruggy" Greenberg. He was only three years older than me. [*For more information on Hank Greenberg see the Bill Rogell interview.*]

I was pretty young when Babe Ruth started with the Yankees, but there is an interesting piece of information that most people don't know. The rookie right fielder for the Yankees in 1919 who was replaced by Ruth was George Halas. Halas, of course, went on to own the Chicago Bears and become a legend in the NFL. He didn't play very much for the Yankees because he injured himself sliding into base or something like that, but it makes for good information. [*For more information on Halas' baseball career see the postscript.*]

The method for getting into a professional writing job back then was to write for your high school paper. Then you'd hear someone say, "The *New York Post* needs a guy to call high school scores in." They'd give you 50 cents a score. Then the next school year the guy who did it for the *World Telegram*, for instance, would have graduated. In the end I was covering scores for five papers. I was busier than my father on some days.

I was 17 when I got my first job at the *Herald Tribune* in New York.

Getting a job was the be-all and end-all of everything. I did all kinds of jobs to stay on. I ran errands and brought coffee. The faint of heart fell back and the others managed to stay with it and qualify.

Everybody smoked in those days and every other day there would be a fire in the waste basket from somebody throwing a match in there after lighting a cigarette. It was endemic to the era.

You would make $35 a week and there wasn't a lot left over for whiskey or good food.

The greatest names in sportswriting were there in New York during the 1920s and 1930s. There was Damon Runyon and Heywood Broun. On my paper we had a fellow named Richards Vidmer, who oddly enough has a son who lives near us in Colorado.

Ed Sullivan also had been a sportswriter in New York. Most people don't know that he was a sportswriter on the old *Daily Graphic*. He didn't make what he thought was enough money so he went over to entertainment at the *News*. It paid well, because on the side you could get $50 or so for a mention in a column. That wrote his destiny. He became the top in entertainment.

Grantland Rice was a very good guy and he was interested in young writers. He had a trick of reading a story written by a young guy coming up, one with potential. Then he'd remember some particularly good line in the story and the next time he saw the young fellow he'd quote him that line.

He'd say, "I liked that story the other day. Particularly that line where you said such and such." Well, then he's got you forever. It was flattery. He did that to me a couple of times.

Damon Runyon was brought east from Colorado by Hearst. Hearst was the best payer of all the newspapers at this time. I met Runyon after he had lost his voice. He had cancer of the throat, so the only way we could communicate was for him to write something on a pad as an answer to my comments. It was the only way he could communicate. He pretty much dictated the way things ran in New York for a long, long time and he made big money doing it.

The owner of the *Washington Post* was Edward B. McLean, a powerful man in Washington. Every summer he would go up to Bar Harbor, Maine, and play a little golf. One day young Shirley Povich happened to caddie for him. He was just a kid then and he was trying to pick up a couple of bucks caddying. McLean was taken with Shirley, and he said, "Listen, if you ever want to go into the newspaper business look me up." Later Shirley went down to Washington and he did get a job on the *Post* where he stayed for the next 60 years.

I knew Shirley and his wife Ethel very well. He was a very fussy guy and everything had to be right. He dressed like the secretary of state. Very conservative, in banker's gray and a white shirt. Everybody liked him and he never gave you much of an argument, but he was full of knowledge.

Later in my career my paper, the *Herald Tribune*, went out of business [*in 1966*] and I went to work for the National Football League. As such, I had to help with the third Super Bowl in Miami. Part of my job was to be attentive to the housing needs of the visiting newspaper guys during the Super Bowl period.

We all liked Shirley a lot, but he was a little fussy and his room had to be perfect. No noise, perfect light, comfortable bed. Every time we had Shirley visit us he would check in and come down to our headquarters with a complaint. The room was too near the freight elevators or the air conditioning didn't work or there wasn't enough closet space. It got to be kind of comical. So just as we were preparing for the fourth Super Bowl festivities, I took a routine phone call from someone regarding minor business. Later my boss asked me, "Who was that on the phone?" And I jokingly said, "Oh, that was Shirley Povich. He's driving down from Washington and he's in Gadsten, Alabama. He just called up to complain about his room here."

We joked about him like that, but he was virtually perfect in my book.

There was very little idealism back then when I started and actually there is very little idealism on a sports desk today. Anything idealistic you want to write, concerning a 22-year-old kid making it in the major leagues, is canceled out by the fact that some agent just got him 11 million dollars to put his signature on a piece of paper.

During the 1920s the *Times* was not the great paper that it is today. There were a dozen papers in New York at that time. In fact, every major town had at least three or four papers. But New York was the focal point. Not that any of them made a great deal of money. The *Times* muddled along making a little money, but it held itself above the others. There was a line under a *New Yorker* cartoon back then that had a butler announcing visitors. "There are four newspaper men and a gentleman from the *Times*."

When I was just a kid, there was a Cuban guy named Alex Pompez who successfully promoted Negro baseball in New York. He would organize a doubleheader in the Polo Grounds on Sundays and he would draw 10–15,000 black people, which was one hell of a crowd. The other major league teams in New York would draw about 18,000 on many days. But they couldn't crack the New York papers. There was a tacit agreement among the papers that they wouldn't print anything on Negro baseball.

As an 18-year-old kid I'd be on the rewrite desk and some guy would call up and say, "I have the results of the Negro National League double-header at the Polo Grounds. We had 16,751 people." He knew it would be turned down, but he called faithfully every Sunday. I would have to tell him that I was sorry, but this paper didn't print the Negro National League. They were simply shut out.

Meanwhile, some papers would take some under-the-table bribes to print the scores of the white semipro teams like the Bushwicks and the Hoboken Reds. Fortunately today, there would be six Supreme Court cases on it.

I got to know quite a few of the players who were heroes during my boyhood in the 1920s. I got to know Frankie Frisch very well after he became a manager. He was a highly educated guy who went to Fordham University and unfortunately he was thrown in with the worst gang of rowdies ever, the Gashouse Gang.

Once, when he was the manager of the Cubs, he got into an argument with umpire Larry Goetz over a play at first base and they threw Frisch out of the game. That night we were doing a little drinking after the game and someone gave him a book to read, because they knew he was a great reader. So the next day there was a Saturday afternoon game and Frisch brought the book into the dugout with him. Before the game even started Frisch started to antagonize Goetz again about the previous night. Well, this got under Goetz's skin and he threw him out of the game again. Frisch was beside himself and he reached for the nearest thing to throw at Goetz and he grabbed the book and threw it. It's the first time I ever saw a book at home plate. So someone ran out to get the book and gave it back to Frisch.

At the end of the day I asked him about what happened and I asked him about that book he threw out. Someone looked at the book and laughingly said that the name of it was *Quiet Street* by Zelda Popkin. Quiet Street, yeah!

I knew Rogers Hornsby in his last year in baseball, because he worked for the Mets. Stengel gave him a job because Hornsby didn't have much money. Actually, he was broke and Stengel knew Hornsby from playing against him in the early days. He was a terrible better and he didn't know what he was doing. Instead of being contrite about it he was just the opposite. He argued with people.

"You can't tell me what to do!" he'd say. Commissioner Landis called Hornsby in one day and accused him of betting on the horses. That was a terrible thing in those days. You could be thrown out of baseball. He not only admitted to it, but he challenged the commissioner. He was hitting over .400, what could Landis do? He was a pretty tough guy.

In the end he was an old guy with a big belly, but he could still hit a ball. He would stand there in batting practice and just drill them out. The young players would just stand there with their tongues hanging out because he could hit the ball within three inches of where they were standing.

He died after that year with the 1962 Mets. He had an operation on his eyes, which was ironic, because he always tried to protect his eyes. He never read a book or went to a movie because he thought it would strain his eyes. They put him on the table for a simple cataract operation and he just died. That was the end of his adventure. [*Hornsby suffered a stroke followed by heart failure just after the eye operation was completed.*]

Hornsby came from a small town in Texas and had never met big city people. He came away from there with some bigotry. He thought everybody was after his money and all Jews had big noses and that kind of thing.

I kind of befriended him and I'd have breakfasts with him and lunches with him. During this brief period I considered myself an amateur psychiatrist, so I was working on him all the time. I just wanted to see how far I could get. I don't think he mellowed any. He went out thinking just the same way he was before.

So one day we're flying down from Milwaukee to Houston and I automatically sat next to him on the airplane. It was a terrible ride. Storms and everything else all the way down. When we got near Texas it was even worse.

It was about four in the morning and I said to him, "Rogers, I'm going to try to get some sleep so don't wake me. See?"

So I finally fell asleep and all of a sudden someone was shaking me and I said, "Are we there?"

And he says, "No, no, no. We're in Dallas. We couldn't get into Houston."

So I said, "Why the hell did you wake me?"

"Well," he said, "the American Airlines people are serving free breakfast in the airport. The airline is paying for it." Now here's a guy that made the present-day equivalent of millions of dollars and he gets excited over a free breakfast!

My experience with Cobb was brief, but interesting. In the 1950s Cobb was a Shriner so as a great stunt they made him a traveling companion to the leader of the Shriners. Now the leader of the Shriners was suddenly a very popular man, because he had Ty Cobb with him. And so newspaper men, who wouldn't normally come out to meet a traveling Shriner, were coming out to see Cobb. My bosses sent me to Newark to meet Cobb and this guy. They said, "This could be a good column for you."

So he came out to meet with us. Most people don't know this, but

Cobb was a tall man. He was well over six feet tall. There were a few of us around and soon the talk gravitated to baseball. Well, these were the years when the catchers ruled the American and National leagues. Yogi Berra was the most valuable player in his league three times and Roy Campanella was the most valuable player in the National League three times. I really liked "Campy" because he was a very decent guy.

So we got to talking baseball with Cobb and someone brought up Berra and I chimed in, "Well, what about 'Campy'? He's just as good." And Cobb turned on me and with his baleful yellow eyes stared at me and said, "Why the hell are you telling me that that n____ is just as good as Berra?"

He was terribly prejudiced. If we were alone in a room he probably would have challenged me to a fight over what I said. I believe his physical nature was just below the surface. You could always see it bubbling underneath.

Well, the story is that Cobb lived in Atherton, California, and in the 1930s he used to watch Joe DiMaggio play for the San Francisco Seals. He realized that this was a tremendous talent. Well, the Yankees came after him and poor Joe was a greenhorn. His only experience with commercialism was selling newspapers on the corner of Market Street when he was in high school. So Cobb interceded for him. Cobb told him what to write when he corresponded with Ed Barrow, the owner of the Yankees. You see, Cobb was secretly dictating to him.

So Barrow sends him the standard contract for a certain amount and DiMaggio sends it back saying, "Mr. Barrow, this is not enough."

So Barrow sends him another one. DiMaggio shows it to Cobb again and Cobb says, "What is this? Tell him it's not enough. Send it back."

Finally here comes another contract from Barrow and it says, "I am enclosing a contract for $8,000. This is our final offer. No matter what Ty Cobb says."

The only time I met Grover Cleveland Alexander was after the 1947 World Series. He came to the party after the Yankees beat Brooklyn. He was a very tall man and he stood straight. But the booze had pretty well wiped him out. He came from a small town and he learned to drink early and he liked it. When I saw him he had developed a cancerous growth on his ear and they had patched him up with some adhesive tape and gauze. He was a grotesque and very sad-looking guy. But, he was one of the greatest pitchers at one time. He had pitched something like 90 shutouts in his career. [*For more information on Grover Cleveland Alexander's last years see the postscript.*]

I'll tell you my favorite Casey Stengel story.

There was a shortstop who came up in the early 1950s named Billy

Hunter. He was a college kid. He was a fairly good player and he could hit a little. He went from the Browns to Baltimore and somehow he was dealt to the Yankees, because Phil Rizzuto was getting old.

Billy Hunter plays a half of a season and looks pretty good, but he breaks his ankle and it takes him out for the season. Over the [*off-*] season he rehabilitates and he comes to spring training, but the ankle is stiff and he isn't moving so well on it.

When the season starts Billy isn't the starting shortstop. The general manager, Weiss, gets a bad medical report on him and figures he would fob him off on the Chicago White Sox. The franchise was run by a young Chuck Comiskey, who they thought could be taken in a deal if the press published favorable reports on Hunter.

So Stengel had the visiting Chicago writers sitting in the dugout watching the pregame workout in which Hunter is taking infield practice. And Stengel is trying to point out all the good things about Billy, because Stengel and Weiss are convinced they can get $50,000 or more for him.

He arbitrarily throws flattering comments into the conversation with these veteran Chicago writers. Phrases like, "Hey, look at that Hunter go! He's pretty good! You know that busted ankle never hurt him one bit. He's better than ever!"

And I'm sitting there listening to this and I can't take it anymore.

Finally I say, "Casey, he isn't any better today than he was in spring training."

Stengel quickly turns around at me in front of all those writers and says, "You know you're full of shit and someday I'll tell you why."

I said to him, "I don't want to hear why." I was so mad at him I didn't speak to him for two weeks.

Stengel was the most important sports personality I ever met. He told me to always keep my eye on the ball. It was so obvious, but important. If you want to follow the progress of the game don't let your attention be diverted. If you follow the ball you'll be able to stay on top of the game.

The George Halas story is one of the all-time great bits of baseball lore. Halas was signed by the Yankees after his junior year at the University of Illinois and played in 12 games during the 1919 season. After a minor hip injury and a threatened salary reduction for the 1920 season, Halas quit.

He retired from major league baseball with a batting average of .091, after legging out only two singles. Ty Cobb became his lifelong friend, despite nearly coming to blows with Halas after a game in Detroit outside the locker room.

Soon after he left the Yankees, Halas purchased the Decatur (Illinois) Staleys football club and by 1922 had moved the franchise to Chicago and eventually changed their name to the Bears.[45]

When Rosenthal saw Grover Cleveland Alexander in October 1947 the effects of alcohol and epilepsy had reduced him to a pathetic shell. In the 150-year history of baseball only two men — Cy Young and Walter Johnson — have won more games than Alexander. His 20-year career ended in 1930 with an astonishing ERA of 2.56 and 373 victories. Historians can only guess what Alexander would have achieved if he had stayed sober.

Former Yankee great George Pipgras told about meeting Alexander in a pre-game ceremony in the second game of the 1928 World Series. "I put out my hand for him to shake and he reached for it and I swear he missed it by a foot. He was so drunk; either that or he had a wicked hangover. He just waved his hand around in the air until we made contact."[38]

Alexander was pulled in the fourth inning of that game after the Yankees had blasted him for seven runs.

After his retirement from the game his downward spiral was only briefly interrupted by jobs as an airplane hangar guard, a café floor manager, and a pool-hall janitor.

In 1939, the year he was formally inducted into the Baseball Hall of Fame, Alexander was employed as a sideshow attraction in a flea circus on Forty-Second Street in New York.

He died alone and penniless in a one-room apartment in St. Paul, Nebraska, in 1950, at the age of 63.[1, 6] In a Hollywood tribute, Ronald Reagan portrayed Alexander in the half-baked film biography The Winning Team in 1952.

Rosenthal had numerous childhood recollections of the Jewish Babe Ruth, Andy Cohen. McGraw brought Cohen to the Giants in 1928 as the infield replacement for Rogers Hornsby. He left major league baseball after three years with a batting average of .281.

In an earlier attempt to draw the Jewish community to the Giants' games, McGraw promoted a local kid named Moses Solomon in 1923. After clubbing 49 home runs in the Southwestern League, the Giants hyped Solomon as "the Rabbi of Swat." Their questionable attempts at promotion failed after only two games. The 22-year-old outfielder soon vanished into obscurity after it was discovered he had *trouble catching fly balls.[7] Solomon found that it was easier to catch a football and eventually landed a career on the gridiron.*

CARL LUNDQUIST
Born October 24, 1913

Carl Lundquist started writing for the Kansas City Star *as a teenager covering the sheep market and editing baseball game highlights. As he approaches the age of 86, Lundquist shows no signs of slowing down.*

He interrupted several deadline stories he was attempting to finish when he granted these interviews. Articulate and precise, Lundquist went directly to the stories that he felt were most important. He was able to offer a rare look at minor league baseball in the 1920s, from the perspective of a young boy, and a sad look at Babe Ruth in his final years.

One story he modestly neglected to tell during the first interview was about a newsman he befriended in 1938. He later revealed: "We were working for United Press in the old Kansas City Journal *building when this young reporter joined us from our Dallas office. We were all journeymen and we went out on the beat together. With the other reporters in the office we became five swinging bachelors for about one and one half years. Walter Cronkite and I still correspond with each other. It became a permanent friendship."*

I grew up in Kansas City and I really loved to play baseball. Unfortunately I was born with a deformity. I had two left feet. So I became a great fan of our local club, the Kansas City Blues.

In 1924 I joined the Kansas City Blues Knot Hole Gang Club and I still have the celluloid pin with my club number on it. With this pin we were admitted to the park, twice a week, free. We would sit in the grandstand, not the bleachers, because they couldn't fill a ballpark, no matter what.

In 1923 they played in old Association Park, which was a bandbox park with fences that were somewhere between 275 and 300 at the foul line. This made for pretty easy home runs. They won the pennant that year and were in the Little World Series and knocked off Baltimore.

One of our big, civic-minded people, a guy named George Muehlbach,

Carl Lundquist in 1972. Courtesy of the Carl
Lundquist family collection.

who was a brewer prior to Prohibition, stepped in. He was well-to-do, so he built this brand new ballpark and called it Muehlbach Field. It was a gigantic pasture without cattle. These little 280 foot fly balls would have gone over the fence in Association Park, but in Muehlbach Field they were pop-ups. The Blues ended up dead last in 1924 because they couldn't cope with the new park.

The guy who designed the park didn't know too much about ballpark architecture. In right field there was a embankment with a terrace at a steep angle, so the right fielder could go up a few strides and could take away a home run from someone.

Our local hero was Joe Hauser who was an authentic slugger. He played for the Philadelphia Athletics and later he became the home run king of the minor leagues. He hit 60 home runs a couple of times in Minneapolis.

In his first or second year with Kansas City, on a Saturday afternoon, he hit one over this concrete wall which sat atop the right field embankment. There was a streetcar line and a sign board across the street which guys would climb on top to watch the game. When his home run landed across the street near the sign board, fans began passing hats around for collections. The next morning the *Kansas City Times* reported that they had collected $100 for Hauser.

Sunday he hit another one which was even farther. As soon as the game was over the team grabbed some cabs and cars and went to Union Station for a road trip. They left the stadium in their uniforms and went out. Ernie Mel, who was the sports editor of the *Kansas City Star* had helped to gather up all of the money that they collected for this second home run. It was way over 100 bucks. He barely made it to the station in time and went into the dining car of the train and presented the money to him.

Hauser was stunned. It was unheard of that something so spontaneous would happen. "Gosh I got another hundred bucks," was all Hauser could say.

The people around our area loved him because he was the Babe Ruth of the minor leagues. He was a hero. There is a lot of background on Joe Hauser and very few people ever heard of him [*see the postscript*].

My first major league stories were about the 1931 and 1932 World Series. Unfortunately, our sports desk could only take the play by play until the seventh or eighth inning, because of the deadline. From the newspaper I went over to the United Press in 1937 and transferred to the St. Louis office in 1942. The United Press office in St. Louis, I remember, was very exciting. St. Louis was a major league city.

However, in the office, the smoke was so thick that the teletype operators complained that they couldn't see the clock.

I then transferred to New York and had a chance to develop a relationship with two giants of the golden age, Babe Ruth and Grantland Rice.

It was a tremendous privilege for me that while I was at United Press, I was assigned to sit next to Grantland Rice in the press box in Brooklyn or at Yankee Stadium or wherever we covered. It was about 1947 and Rice wrote for the North American Newspaper Alliance. By happy happenstance his seat was next to mine.

He was beginning to have eyesight problems and he wasn't seeing too well when little things came up. He would ask me questions about this player or that incident down on the field and I couldn't help but feel honored that I could work with such a man. He would sit there and muse and suddenly come off with a delightful line and you knew it would appear in the *New York Sun* the next day. It was prose and the man spoke so eloquently. There was a great deal of reverence involved. He was a real untouchable in the positive sense. It was about 1947.

I'll never forget one dramatic experience in particular. It was at Yankee Stadium and the year was 1946. I was down on the field taking it all in. The war was over and it was opening day. It was a happy new year in baseball, because there were no losers yet. The flowers were in bloom and hopes were high and everybody turned out. The Yankees had nearly a capacity crowd. They had Guy Lombardo's band on the field and all that phoof-er-all. So I'm leaving the field and walking up to the mezzanine press box when I spotted a little gathering of a few people. I thought maybe somebody had fainted and I walked up quickly. And there, sitting all by himself, in his big tan polo coat and his traditional cap was the Babe. This was a chilly spring day but he had said to himself, "What the heck, I'll go to the ball game." Nobody sent him a ticket and the new regime at the Yankees didn't even send him an invitation.

When I got up there, Babe spotted me. He couldn't remember my name, but he did recognize me.

He said, "I've got to tell you something. At the last minute I just decided to come."

And he said, "I'll probably get a tough letter from the management saying that I interfered with their opening day ceremonies."

The pathos of the moment was stunning. How could they overlook the guy? My God, he should have been down on the field. He came in by himself and he found a seat in the *unreserved* grandstand seats far behind home plate. There wasn't any talk about memory lane, but he was scoffing at [*the fact*] that nobody had asked him to come.

That story just hit me. How could anybody so brazenly overlook the fact that he built this ballpark. It was the house that Ruth built. [*For more information on this story see the postscript.*]

During the summer of 1948 Babe was on his deathbed. Every newspaper in the country was prepared to cover what was happening at that New York hospital. However, the baseball writers in New York and Brooklyn had planned their annual trip to Bear Mountain for a day of fun. It was scheduled for mid–August and they chose this date since there were no important games scheduled. The writers always had a ball game with a keg of beer at third base and we'd have great fun. And after the game we'd have a marvelous dinner and then come home.

Everyone felt comfortable in leaving town because Babe had been up and around on Sunday. He was walking and telling people he was improving. A girlfriend of one of our writers was an experienced senior nurse specializing in cancer cases. Well, she called our writer and said, "I understand you guys are headed for Bear Mountain. But if you want to keep your jobs you better stay in town, because it's worse than you think." She said that there could be a fatal relapse at any time. So instead of going to Bear Mountain and drinking our bellies full of beer we worked. Since our sports editor was taking a much-needed vacation, I was in charge. I would have been fired if something had gone wrong. The pressure was enormous.

Milton Richmond went immediately to the hospital. He knew how to get things done. John Griffin, who later became sports editor of United Press, was with me in the office and at one minute past eight we got the terrible call from Milt. The Babe had died.

As he spoke to me over the phone I dictated, because it was the fastest way of getting a story on the wire. Our best teletype operator was there and was ready to move instantly. We went into the story extemporaneously between what Milt was telling me and the background material we had. We had no time to waste. John Griffin was there to edit and correct my mistakes. Grantland Rice came in and added a couple of things.

We beat the Associated Press by two minutes, which is the equivalent

to two hours on a breaking story like this. The papers bought breaking stories from whoever came first. We got the play everywhere and we won an
award for it. But through it all, I could not write this article without being
emotional.

> Lundquist's local baseball hero, Joe Hauser, was truly a great
> home run hitter who could never seem to get the big breaks in the
> major leagues. Joseph John Hauser hit more than 60 home runs
> in two minor league seasons with the Minneapolis Millers. His best
> season was in 1933 when he hit 69 homers, drove in 182 RBIs, and
> batted .322. Prior to that phenomenal feat he hit 63 round-trippers in
> 1930.
>
> Bob Poser (AL pitcher, 1932 and 1935), remembers Hauser from
> their days playing in the minor leagues. "He was one of the first
> power hitters I had ever seen who used a lightweight bat," he said.
> "Joe used a 31 oz. bat, which was unusual back then. Just as a refer-
> ence, Babe Ruth used a 52 oz. bat before August then switched to a 49
> oz. bat late in the season."[65]
>
> Hauser played first base for the Philadelphia A's and Cleveland
> Indians from 1922 to 1929 and retired from the major leagues with a
> batting average of .284. Long after he retired Hauser was still consid-
> ered a baseball legend in the communities surrounding his birthplace
> in north and central Wisconsin. When he died at age 98 in July 1997,
> a large funeral was planned in Sheboygan as a final tribute. As the
> pallbearers started to bring his casket out of the church, the organist
> broke into a somber rendition of "Take Me Out to the Ball Game."[9]
>
> Larry MacPhail was the head executive with the Yankees when,
> according to Lundquist, Babe Ruth was snubbed at opening day.
> There is no supporting evidence to prove that MacPhail personally
> conspired to alienate Ruth.
>
> MacPhail was an executive with the Brooklyn Dodgers when he
> hired Babe as a coach in 1938. Ruth had expected an eventual promo-
> tion to team manager, but the offer never materialized. Many believe
> he had been hired simply as a box-office draw. By the time MacPhail
> had joined the Yankees just after World War II, he had been credited
> with introducing night baseball to the majors and revitalizing the
> Reds and the Dodgers into pennant winners.
>
> One night, after a long drinking session, Red Sox owner Tom
> Yawkey and MacPhail hatched an idea to trade the Yankee Joe
> DiMaggio for Ted Williams of the Red Sox. When sober heads pre-
> vailed the next day, the historic offer was withdrawn.[7]

WILL GRIMSLEY
Born January 14, 1914

Although Will Grimsley is not the oldest sportswriter alive today, there are few who have covered as many major events. He started writing for the Nashville Tennessean *at the age of 18 and retired 52 years later from the Associated Press. In addition to baseball, Grimsley covered 15 Wimbledons, eight Summer Olympics, and six Winter Olympics.*

"I guess I did a lot of talking and writing in my life," he modestly admitted.

When I graduated from high school in Nashville it was during the height of the Depression. Since I had no way of going to college, I started writing for the *Tennessean,* which was a bankrupt paper at the time. I started out covering high school games and they paid me nothing for one year. Then I was paid $10 per week and then raised to $15 per week. When they gradually raised me to $34 per week it seemed like I was a millionaire. I was there until just before 1960.

During my career I met a lot of famous players and I've got many of their pictures on my wall. I got to know Satchel Paige and many of the black ballplayers very well because they played nearby at Sulphur Dell.

Shirley Povich was a very good friend of mine after I came to New York to write. He had the foresight to write about subjects that people would eventually be talking about.

Jim Thorpe died just after I came to New York, but I did have a chance to meet him and write about him. I had only a brief relationship with Thorpe, but it was compelling. Although he was a very nice person I had this feeling that he was angry. He felt he was forgotten. He was still resentful over the way he was treated. [*For more information on Thorpe see the postscript.*]

My greatest baseball memory is the no-hit, no-run World Series game that Don Larson pitched. I kept score of the game and I still have the scorecard chart and notes that newspapermen used to cover the game. Later I had Don Larson sign that scorecard.

When I started my professional career in 1932 I covered high school sports and Southern Association League baseball and Vanderbilt sports. For baseball I covered the Nashville Vols and the Birmingham Barons and the Atlanta Crackers and Memphis. But, I wasn't an expert on baseball at all when I started. All the major league teams trained in the South and they would play exhibition games in our area as they moved north. The ball

Will Grimsley in a 1972 Olympics promotional photograph. Courtesy of Barbara Lockert, National Sportscasters and Sportswriters Association.

clubs played in a place called Sulphur Dell and it was so bad the right fielder had to stand on a hill to play the position.

While I was still a cub reporter the Yankees came to town and I was sent out to try to interview Babe Ruth. Well, Nashville had only four hotels and he was staying in none of them, but was registered in all of them.

I set out to try to find Ruth and I couldn't locate him in town so I went out to the ballpark. I told somebody of my frustration and this man said, "Why don't you go over and talk to that man over there. He's famous."

And I said, "Who is that?"

"Why, that's Lou Gehrig," he replied.

I had sort of heard of him, but I wasn't quite sure. So I went over to ask him where Ruth was, but he was talking to somebody.

He said to me, "Listen son, I'm kind of busy, I'm sorry I can't talk to you." So I went to the entrance of the park and waited.

Finally a cab crept up to the gate and Babe Ruth got out. He came in carrying his spike shoes in his hand. I'll never forget that. The baseball field was subterranean so when you entered the stadium you'd be on the second floor looking down at the field. Well he stopped just before he was going down and I said, "Mr. Ruth, may I talk to you?"

Surprisingly he said, "Sure son, what do you want to know?"

So I had all of these questions written out like who's your favorite movie star, and what's your favorite play, and what's your favorite movie. And he just stood there and answered all of them right down the line. I've still got the copy of those questions.

Meanwhile, the Yankees took the field and they were starting to play and they were yelling for him to come on down and take his position. So he yelled on down to them to forget it. He just stayed there and talked to me and delayed the game about ten or fifteen minutes. He was very kind.

At the end of the interview he just looked at me and said, "You don't know too much about sports do you?"

I said, "Not much."

That's how I got started.

Jim Thorpe was not only recognized as one of the greatest athletes of the twentieth century, but he was the first American Indian to achieve superstar status. Unfortunately baseball was the source of many painful experiences for him.

After he stunned the world by winning two gold medals in the 1912 Olympic Games, it was revealed that he had played professional baseball in the minor leagues three years earlier. Because of a ruling that prohibited professional athletes from participating in the Olympics, he was unfairly stripped of his medals.

He eventually returned to baseball when John McGraw offered him a $5,000 contract to play for the Giants. During his stay in the big leagues he was continuously roasted in the press for his inability to hit a curveball.

Baseball scribe W. R. Hoefer mused, "Thorpe is the fastest runner in baseball but when he swings at a curve Jim ain't got anything to run for."[63]

Baseball Magazine *sarcastically remarked that Thorpe was showing signs of consistency. "He can't hit a curveball from either side of the plate."*

After completing six mediocre seasons with three major league teams, Thorpe found the minor leagues more inviting. In 1920 he played an entire season with Akron in the International League where he hit .360.[64] *Each fall, however, Thorpe instinctively returned to the sport he truly loved: football.*

Epilogue:
The Financial Reality
of the Golden Age Player

"There ought to be some well-established system for deal-
ing justly with unfortunate ball players ... something that
will insure a fund for deserving cases. A fund to which any
ballplayer can apply without feeling that he is dependent on
charity. Baseball should look after its own."

Ty Cobb, 1923[52]

For many of the surviving ballplayers from the 1920s through the
1940s there is very little gold in their golden years. Their careers in professional and semipro baseball offered modest compensation and nothing
for retirement. The era of mammoth salaries and slick agents was over 50
years away when the men interviewed for this book first drew a paycheck.

In 1999 the absolute minimum that a major league ballplayer could
make was $170,000. The average salary was $1.3 million. In 1929 the three
highest paid players were Babe Ruth ($70,000), Rogers Hornsby ($40,000),
and Dazzy Vance ($25,000).[29]

In terms of today's dollars, Ruth's salary falls short of the average by
over $300,000. Vance's salary falls short by nearly $1 million. The typical
salary for a young ballplayer at that time was between $400 and $600 per
month. Why is this information relevant?

Today there are several dozen men still alive who played during the
1920s and 1930s, and even more who played in the 1940s. There is very little published about the financial plight that many of these former heroes face.

The current Major League Baseball Players Pension Plan was launched in 1947. Although it was hailed as baseball's first safety net, it excluded any man who finished his career prior to 1946.[50]

Given the current major league salaries it is difficult to believe that any Hall of Fame ballplayer could be living in poverty. However, Grover Alexander, Jimmie Foxx, Honus Wagner, Joe Tinker, Willie Keeler, and Hack Wilson are just a few of the well-known ballplayers who suffered economic hardships after their careers were over.

One of the few resources available to the old-time players today is a privately funded organization called BAT (Baseball Assistance Team). This group offers financial aid to over 300 former major league and Negro League players, scouts, umpires, and their surviving family members. Jim Martin, the executive director of BAT, explains the dilemma facing many older retired players.

> The biggest problem facing the fellows that are in their eighties and nineties concerns medical and health. The majority of them don't have health benefits. Their medication bills could be in excess of $500 per month. Couple that with the rent increases and other things, it's a major problem. I would suspect that in their day some of them made a good salary compared to the average worker. But their disposable income wasn't as great back then as it is today. Because of their name a lot of guys were talked into investing in businesses that weren't going anywhere, like bowling alleys, used car dealerships, and whatever. That's where a lot of their money was unfortunately misdirected. In those days a lot of those guys came right off the farm or right from home. Today's kids are coming out of colleges and they are more sophisticated when it comes to investing.
>
> Back then a ballplayer didn't say to himself, "Well, when I turn 29 or 33 I'll have to retire from baseball and here's what I'm going to do." In truth, one morning they get up and they can't throw any longer. Their skills are worn down by age. They can't compete with the 19-year-old kid coming in. I don't think most athletes were prepared to move on to something else when it happened.

Some of these men are the trusting targets of con artists and thieves within the souvenir market. Referring to the sudden increase in value of Negro League memorabilia, Wilmer Fields, the director of the Negro Leagues Players' Association, stated that he has had numerous reports of retired players being robbed. One of the most famous incidents was that of Hall of Fame inductee James "Cool Papa" Bell, who was robbed of his mementos in 1989 by two men posing as autograph seekers. Three weeks later Bell suffered a stroke.

Cashing in on the lucrative memorabilia craze, some former players are being exploited for their autographs, personal photos, and even equipment, receiving little or no compensation. Several men who were interviewed for this book either have been a victim or knew someone who was a victim of this scam.

No matter how obscure their careers were, or how long ago they may have played, they still receive requests for autographs and pictures. In the course of writing this book I found that very few of the men demanded compensation for their autographs, despite their financial needs. Many of them depleted their personal photo collections to satisfy the requests of collectors.

Elden Auker, a pitcher for the Detroit Tigers in the 1930s, is one of many former superstars who have been targeted. He confirmed that it is not unusual for him to receive a single parcel of mail, requesting that he sign ten or more balls or photos at one time without compensation. "It's obvious that it's from a collector who will resell this for a profit. I will refuse to sign for them," he said.

Cowan "Bubber" Hyde, who played his first Negro League game with the Birmingham Black Barons in 1930, told the author that he regularly receives letters from autograph seekers in which there are multiple photos enclosed. He said, "I answer their letters and tell them what I expect. Some of them even have copies of photos that I thought only belonged to me."

Officials at BAT and the Negro League Museum are aware of the rip-offs that these retired ballplayers are exposed to, but there is little that can be done except to warn them.

For more information write to:
Baseball Assistance Team
245 Park Avenue
31st Floor
New York, NY 10167

Negro Leagues Baseball Museum
1616 East 18th Street
Kansas City, MO 64141

Bibliography

1. *Baseball Legends and Lore*, David Cataneo. Barnes and Noble.
2. Professional Football Hall of Fame archives.
3. Interview with author Bob Carroll.
4. *Ultimate Baseball Book*, Daniel Okrent and Harris Lewine. Houghton Mifflin.
5. *The Soaring Twenties*, Thomas Gilbert. Franklin Watts.
6. *Ol' Pete*, Jack Kavanagh. Diamond Communications.
7. *The Ballplayers*, Mike Shatzkin. Arbor House: William Morrow.
8. *Baseball Babylon*, Dan Gutman. Penguin.
9. *Sheboygan Press*, sports editor, Michael Knuth.
10. *Moe Berg: Athlete, Scholar ... Spy*, Louis Kaufman. Little, Brown.
11. *Baseball Hall of Shame*, Bruce Nash and Allan Zullo. Wallaby.
12. *Bill Stern's Favorite Baseball Stories*, Bill Stern. Pocket Books.
13. *Biographical Encyclopedia of Negro Leagues*, James A. Riley. Carroll and Graf.
14. *Who, What, When, Where and Why of Baseball*, Jim Charlton. Barnes and Noble.
15. *Blackball Stars*, John B. Holway. Meckler.
16. *Viva Baseball*, Samuel O. Regalado. University of Illinois Press.
17. *Only the Ball Was White*, Robert Peterson, Oxford University Press.
18. *Beisbol, Latin Americans and the Grand Old Game*, Michael and Mary Adams Oleksak. Masters.
19. *John McGraw*, Charles C. Alexander. Penguin.
20. *Sports Illustrated*, March 21, 1960: "The Private World of the Negro Ballplayer," Robert Boyle.
21. *Family Spirits: The Bacardi Saga*, Peter Foster. MacFarlane Walter and Ross.
22. Interview with Myron Hayworth, former American League catcher, November 1998.
23. *Latinos in Beisbol*, James D. Cockcroft. Franklin Watts: Division of Grolier.
24. *Ted "Double Duty" Radcliffe*, Kyle P. McNary. McNary Publishing.
25. Interview with Don Motley, director, Negro Leagues Baseball Museum.
26. *Baseball Magazine*, June 1917.
27. *Ty Cobb, His Tumultuous Life and Times*, Richard Bak. Taylor Publishing.

28. *Voices of the Game*, Curt Smith. Diamond Communications.
29. *Baseball Magazine*, July 1929.
30. *Maybe I'll Pitch Forever*, Leroy Satchel Paige. Grove.
31. *Baseball Magazine*, August 1915.
32. Thomas Gilbert interview, December 18, 1998.
33. *Baseball Magazine*, April 1920.
34. *Bill James Historical Abstract*, Bill James. Villard Books.
35. *Baseball as I Have Known It*, Fred Lieb. University of Nebraska Press.
36. *Sports Illustrated*, December 28, 1998.
37. *My Life in Baseball — The True Record*, Ty Cobb with Al Stump. Doubleday.
38. *Baseball, When the Grass Was Green*, Donald Honig. Coward, McCann and Geoghegan.
39. *Baseball with a Latin Beat*, Peter Bjarkman. McFarland.
40. *Walter Johnson: Baseball's Big Train*, Henry W. Thomas. Phenom Press.
41. Interview with author David Pietrusza, biographer of Kenesaw Mountain Landis.
42. Interview Peter Bjarkman, January 10, 1999.
43. *Le Leyenda del Béisbol Cubano*, Angel Torres. Angel Torres, publisher.
44. Interview Angel Torres, February 5, 1999.
45. *Halas by Halas*, George Halas with Gwen Morgan and Arthur Veysey. McGraw-Hill.
46. *Baseball's Golden Age*, Neal and Constantine McCabe. Harry Abrams.
47. *Baseball Magazine*, November 1917.
48. *Baseball's Hall of Fame — Cooperstown — Where Legends Live Forever*, Lowell Reidenbaugh. Crescent.
49. Major League Baseball, Inc.
50. Interview with Angie Rowan, Major League Baseball Player's Pension Plan, William M. Mercer. February 28, 1999.
51. *USA Baseball Weekly*, John B. Holway author, November 1–7, 1995.
52. *Baseball Magazine*, February 1923.
53. Letter from Rodolfo Fernandez, March 14, 1999.
54. Letter from Rodolfo Fernandez, December 28, 1998.
55. Excerpt from editorial by Cuban sportswriter Marino Martinez, June 27, 1998.
56. *Baseball Magazine*, August 1926.
57. Interview with Frank Haraway, April 16, 1999.
58. Interviews with Ray Kelly and Peter Sgroi, April 14, 1999.
59. *Baseball Magazine*, June 1921.
60. *The Negro Leagues Book*, Dick Clark and Larry Lester. SABR.
61. *Bat Masterson — The Man and the Legend*, Robert K. DeArment. University of Oklahoma Press.
62. *Baseball Magazine*, July 1913.
63. *Baseball Magazine*, July 1917.
64. *The International League*, Bill O'Neal. Eakin.
65. Interview with Bob Poser, June 30, 1999.
66. Interview with Bill Werber, July 9, 1999.
67. *Baseballs Greatest Quotes*, Kevin Nelson. Simon and Schuster.
68. Interview with Lester Rodney, July 10, 1999.

In addition, the following items also were used for research:

Baseball Between the Lies, Bob Carroll. Perigee.
Baseball Chronicles, Mike Blake. Betterway.
Baseball: An Illustrated History, Geoffrey C. Ward and Ken Burns. Alfred A. Knopf.
Black Diamonds, John B. Holway. Meckler.
Elden Auker interview, April 24, 1999.
El Tiante, The Luis Tiant Story, Luis Tiant and Joe Fitzgerald. Doubleday.
Felipe Alou ... My Life and Baseball, Felipe Alou with Herm Weiskopf. World Books.
Honus Wagner: A Biography, Dennis and Jeanne Burke DeValeria. Henry Holt.
Murderers' Row: The 1927 New York Yankees, G. H. Fleming. William Morrow.
No Cheering in the Press Box, Jerome Holtzman. Henry Holt.
100 Greatest Pitchers, Brent P. Kelley. Barnes and Noble.
Rogers Hornsby: A Biography, Charles C. Alexander. Henry Holt.
Saturday Evening Post, The Best from, edited by Harry Paxton. Thomas Nelson and Sons.
Sportswriter, the Life and Times of Grantland Rice, Charles Fountain. Oxford University Press.
Stengel: His Life and Times, Robert W. Creamer. Simon and Schuster.
Voices from Cooperstown. Anthony J. Connor. Collier.
Voices from the Great Black Baseball Leagues, John Holway. Dodd, Mead.
Was Baseball Really Invented in Maine? Will Anderson. Will Anderson, publisher.

Index